Organizational Change and Change Management

Dag Ingvar Jacobsen

Organizational Change and Change Management

FAGBOKFORLAGET

First Edition / Printing 1

ISBN: 978-82-450-2458-6

Graphic production: John Grieg, Bergen
Coverphoto: © Shutterstock/Dmitriy Rybin

Enquiries about this text can be directed to:
Fagbokforlaget
Kanalveien 51
5068 Bergen
Tel.: 55 38 88 00
Fax: 55 38 88 01
email: fagbokforlaget@fagbokforlaget.no
www.fagbokforlaget.no

Introduction

This is a translated version of a book I first wrote in 2004. To be honest, I never thought that the book was going to be revised, not to mention that it would end up being translated into English. But after only a few years on the market the book became quite popular, and was translated into both Swedish and Danish. In recent years I have received more and more requests for an English translation. The first and most obvious reason for this is the internationalization process taking place in Scandinavian higher education. Incoming students from other countries attend courses where there is a mix of Norwegian and foreign students. In many cases these students use different books, although they attend the same course, a situation fuelling some frustration among both groups of students.

The second reason for a translation is a wish to convey what could probably be termed a "Scandinavian perspective" on planned organizational change. Most of the international literature on planned change is characterized by pure instrumentalism. By this I mean that the main focus is on "how to succeed" with organizational change, and there is a fondness for checklists on "how to proceed". This is an approach that is not very well received within the Scandinavian stream of organizational research and theorizing. The Scandinavian approach, if such a thing exists, is more critical and reflective in nature, building on institutional approaches without abandoning the possibility of agency. This book is clearly placed within such an approach.

A book like this, having reached adolescence, is of course formed by the variety of feedback that has been received over the years. Previous editions have benefitted greatly from constructive comments from Inger Stensaker, Gro Ladegård, Haldor Byrkjeflot and Erik Døving. Then there are the comments from students, both my "ordinary" students at Agder University and a great variety of participants at lectures all over Norway. The book would not have been possible without support from my editor, Knut Ebeltoft, and the publisher, Fagbokforlaget.

It may be a manifestation of hubris, but I decided to translate the book myself in parallel with revising the 3rd edition of the Norwegian book. This was an intense learning process, often deeply frustrating when my limited knowledge of the English language became evident.

Without the assistance from Shari Nilsen in "cleaning up" the manuscript, the final product would have been of a much lesser quality. All inaccuracies and faults are, of course, my responsibility.

Kristiansand, June 2018
Dag Ingvar Jacobsen

Contents

Part I

Organizational change

Chapter 1

Change and stability

We live in a time of highly visible change. Change is most obvious for us in the field of technology, where an ever-expanding internet, artificial intelligence and "big data" give rise to totally new organizations while eradicating traditional ones. Businesses like Uber, Spotify, Facebook, and Airbnb, and phenomena like virtual currency and block-chain technology, represent enormous challenges for traditional businesses like taxis, hotels, banks, insurance companies, newspapers and media houses. At the same time, the world is ever more interwoven economically, politically and culturally. Movements on the stock market in Shanghai immediately affect stock markets all over the world, political turbulence in one country unleashes streams of refugees crossing borders, news about sexual harassment in Hollywood is – in hours – transformed into a global campaign affecting companies and public organizations all over the world, and a change in a country's tax laws directly influences decisions made by a local entrepreneur on where to localize production. Traditional airline companies struggle continuously to meet the competition from low-fare companies like Ryan Air and easyJet.

The public sector is not shielded from change and reform. On the contrary. In most European countries there is strong pressure towards amalgamation of municipalities and regional political-administrative units like counties and districts. Massive numbers of public employees will be assigned new tasks, new places to work, and new colleagues. The health sector is struggling to keep pace with the technological opportunities, and to treat an increasingly older population. Schools are experiencing the same pressure, both for fusions to create larger and more economically efficient units, and to implement new technologies into pedagogical practices.

The traditional nation-state is also experiencing profound changes. Traditional political structures have been shaken to their foundations by the rise of both right-wing and left-wing populism, and by the election of presidents without a base in the traditional party structure in important countries like USA and France. Well-established supra-national structures like the EU are challenged by the UK leaving the union, as well as by tendencies for newer member states to move in a non-democratic direction. International agreements, on both trade and climate change, are threatened by a more isolationist USA.

Even rich and stable nations like Norway are also deeply affected by global change. In the summer of 2014, the price of a barrel of North Sea oil reached 115 dollars. A year later, the price was less than half that. Many of the large oil companies had to implement programmes for large lay-offs, and smaller companies went bankrupt or were swallowed by bigger and financially stronger competitors. The National Statistical Bureau estimated the loss of jobs to be at least 25,000, a substantial number in a small country. In our daily life, we see the direct impact of new technology as an increasing number of shops introduce self-service and self-payment, while washing and cleaning are taken over more and more by robots.

This increasing pace of change is also reflected in the evolution of organization theory and research. From a focus on stability – either on bureaucratic structures to standardize behaviour or to shield the operative core from external disturbances – the focus has shifted to dynamics and change. How does change happen? Why do organizations change in so many different ways? How should we proceed to obtain change? Change has become so central to organization theory that the editors of the 1996 version of the *Sage Handbook of Organization Studies* explicitly decided not to include an separate chapter on change. Change was, according to the editors, integrated into the other chapters.[1]

Concurrently there is a strong increase in research on organizational change: a title search for "organization" and "change" in the Web of Science database for the period 1980 until 2017 yielded 2354 hits, and a topic search revealed more than 94,000 articles. The result is displayed in figure 1.1.

As the figure shows, there has been a nearly explosive increase in the research on organizational change from the beginning of the 1990s until today.[2]

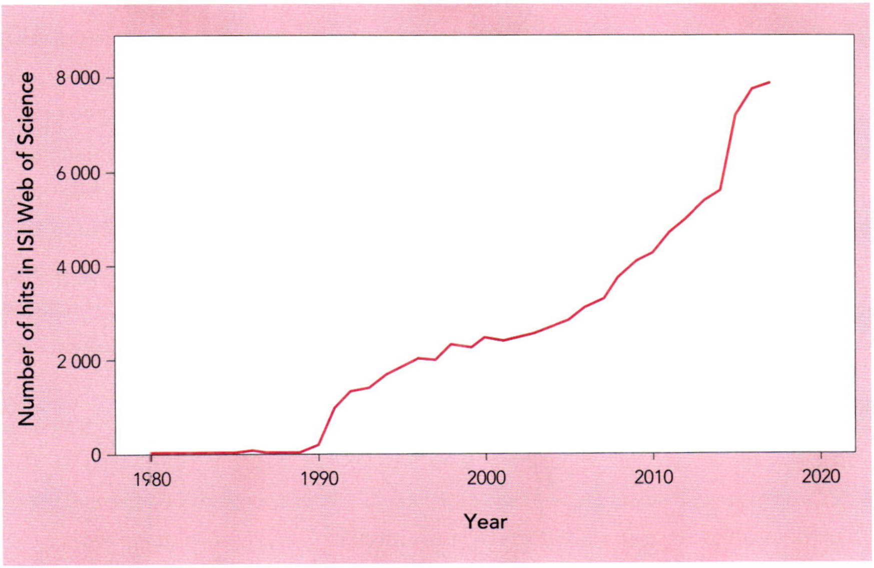

FIGURE 1.1: Topic search for "change*" and "organization*" publications in the Web of Science database from 1980 to 2017 (search conducted April 2018). Vertical axis = yearly number of hits.

However, not everything is change.[3] This book is founded on the assumption that stability is still the "normal" situation. Most of us go to work or school with the assurance that today is going to be quite similar to previous days. We go to our office or school, we meet colleagues and fellow students that we know, and we eat lunch at approximately the same time. Things are *predictable*. Change is something that disrupts this predictability. This is not same as organizations being static or inert. No organization – or other social system – will ever stand completely still. Where there are people, there will be action and reaction, dynamism, and a certain "flow". You will get to know your colleague or fellow student a little better, you will discover a better way to use your PC, and you will choose to use the stairs instead of the elevator. None of these changes challenges your feeling of predictability. Small, incremental changes will only increase your experience of stability. Being able to make small changes increases your sense of mastering a specific job or educational programme; you refine what you already know. Actions that have proven favourable over the years tend to be replicated with only minor changes.[4] Such adjustments do not, in this book, qualify as change. Change is defined as something that interrupts previous patterns of behavior, something that creates a sense of unpredictability. This book is not about everyday dynamics or processes.

That is not the same as refuting the prevalence and importance of such processes; they are just not the main focus.

Moreover, this book will be about one perspective on change, more specifically planned or intentional change. Much of the everyday change will be emergent, continuous, and not necessarily planned or intended. Things just happen. This book is based on the assumption that we, as humans, are able to intentionally improve our lives, and thus our organizations. That we intend to make things better does not mean that we succeed in doing so. Having an intention is not the same as realizing it. The following quotation sums up this line of reasoning nicely:[5]

> Why can't we change our organizations? Year after year, the list of companies that no longer exist because they were unable to evolve continues to grow. (…) After six decades of study, untold investment, and the best efforts of scholars, executives, and consultants, most organizational change efforts still underperform, fail, or make things worse.

In a global survey of more than 3000 executives, more than two-thirds of the respondents answered that implemented change efforts had not produced expected results.[6] In more general terms it is usually assumed that as many as 70% of planned change efforts fail.[7] This picture is probably (hopefully?) overtly pessimistic, but it points to something important: there are many people trying to change their organizations for the better, but they do not always reach this objective. This book's ambition is to provide some knowledge on organizational change that may increase the probability of succeeding with intentional change. It provides no guarantee or recipe for successful change. Rather, it is a collection of insights from theory and research on organizational change that may be helpful in planning and implementing change.

The intentions of this book are twofold. First, it is to provide an analytical approach to the phenomenon of organizational change. "Change" is a word used in daily language in a way that gives the impression of one single, unambiguous phenomenon. Thus it becomes so abstract as to become void of empirical content.[8] This book emphasizes that change represents many different phenomena, takes on multiple forms, can have a multitude of causes, and can proceed in an wide array of ways. An analytical approach is essential to understanding whether, and under what contingencies, planned change will be feasible. The second intention is to make a contribution to a constructive theory on planned change in that it indicates how knowledge of organizational change can be used to improve the probability of succeeding with a planned change. However, do not expect any "set menu" over techniques and models. The hope is that the book will provide some guidelines for actions, and under what circumstances one action will probably be better than another. After having read the book, you might have more questions than answers. But your questions may be more knowledgeable.

Unpacking planned change

There are a multitude of definitions of change, but most of them contain something about altered or different states. In this book, I will use the following definition of change: an organization has changed when it displays different characteristics at (at least) two different points in time. Even more precise is the following definition: "Change (...) is an empirical observation of difference in form, quality or state over time in an organizational entity."[9] Change is thus something referring to a difference in, for instance, formal structure or collaborative behaviour in an organization at points T1 and T2 in time.

This definition draws our attention to two central elements in change. The first one is *time.*[10] It is not possible to understand change without including the time dimension. Detecting change is based on a comparison of different states at different points in time. The other element in the definition is that change must be connected to some sort of *object, phenomenon* or *state*. In this book the object or

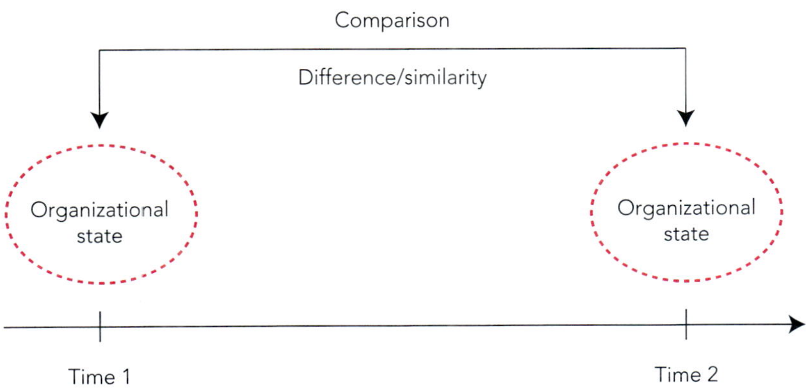

FIGURE 1.2: Change as difference in state between two points in time

phenomenon is organization. It might sound strange, but acknowledging that change is connected to an object is also acknowledging that change presupposes stability. We need to be able to describe a stable object or phenomenon to be able to see whether or not it has changed. Only with comparison over time will it be possible to establish change as an empirical fact. Figure 1.2 illustrates the above argument.

As discussed initially, the assumption of organizational stability is not unproblematic. Organizations are social systems, not (only) physical objects, and will thus be in some kind of permanent flux.[11] It is not possible to claim that a group of people – the basic building block of any organization – is exactly similar at two points in time. An extreme interpretation of this situation is that everything is constantly changing, or "everything flows". Such a world view is ascribed to the Greek philosopher Heraclitus, as exemplified in the statement "No man ever steps in the same river twice."[12] Water, continuously flowing, makes it impossible for the river to be the same at two different points in time. Socrates made an elegant counterargument, claiming that the world was both stable and fluid, but that human recognition presupposes a minimum of stability.[13] One cannot know what isn't. This book holds a view that is closer to that of Socrates than to that of Heraclitus. Newer interpretations of Heraclitus describe him more as a philosopher of contradictions, and as maintaining that change and stability are two sides of the same coin. Even if the water changes all the time, one can easily claim that the river is the same. In fact, Heraclitus can also be interpreted as pointing to the fact that change is necessary for stability. If the water were not running all the time, even the river would take on another form, and thus become something different from a river.[14]

Even if we accept the notion of organizations as stable entities, there are plenty of other problems that arise. One of these is to delimit when an organization has changed. How great must the difference in state be between the two points in time to define it as change? On the other hand, it may be problematic to draw a line between change and total transformation, i.e. an organization changing into something completely different. Traditional newspapers are withering under the pressure of the internet and social media, and the ones surviving are going through radical changes. Newspapers have transmuted into "media houses" working more with moving pictures, films, live shows and commentaries, podcasts, and Facebook updates than paper. Is an old newspaper comparable to the new "media house"? Answering these questions is probably impossible, and beyond the scope of this book. Still, such questions will pop up throughout the book.

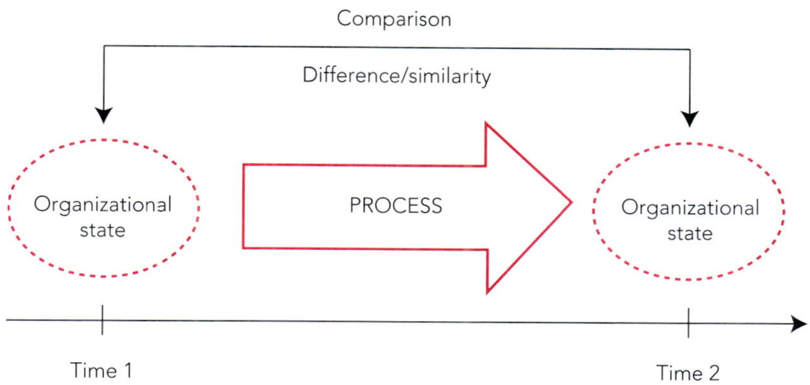

FIGURE 1.3: Change as the outcome of a process

To most people it is obvious that change cannot be defined only as a difference in state. Change must imply some kind of movement over time. Change must thus also be a *process*, a stream of actions and events that bring the organization from one state to another.[15] Figure 1.3 extends the previous discussion with the change process.

Defining change as a process accentuates the importance of time. In figure 1.2, time only indicated a period between two points. In figure 1.3, time becomes a central *explanans*, or a central cause of the outcome of change processes. As we are going to delve into more deeply later in the book, events happening after each other in time may be ordered as causes and effects, events happening simultaneously may have an impact on each other, and the subjective feeling of having much or little time may heavily influence human behaviour.

Combining two different perspectives of change – organizations as entities and processes – forces us to decide when a change process starts (from one stable state) and when it ends (to another stable state). Establishing unequivocally when a process starts and when it ends is clearly difficult. However, this book uses one specific perspective on change – planned or intentional change – that makes this problem less pressing. Planned change implies that it is initiated by someone, a person or a group of people. The starting point of a planned change process will thus start with someone taking an initiative. This does not necessarily imply that such change processes will have a clear ending point in time. Some initiated change processes may have an "eternity perspective", for instance continuous

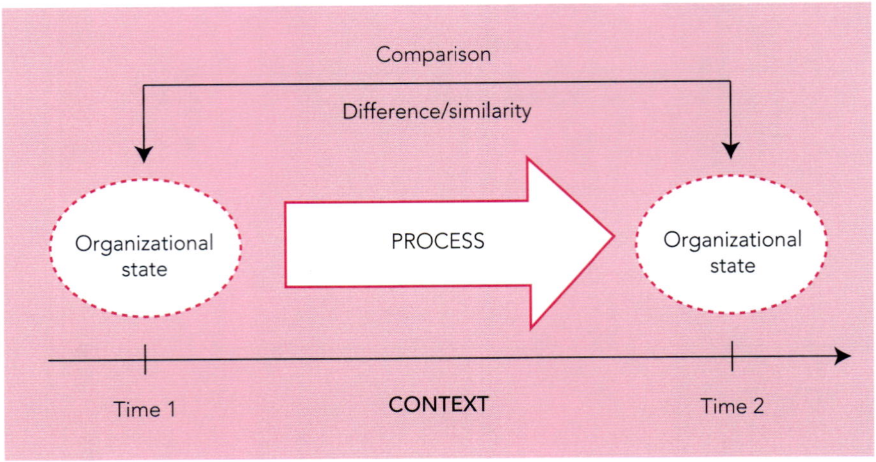

FIGURE 1.4: Change taking place in a specific context

improvement. An example of such initiated change is to be found in the literature on quality management, where quality improvement is regarded as a continuous process rather than a project that is going to be terminated.[16] This challenge will be discussed in more detail later in the book.

Thus far, change has been described in generic terms. The models displayed in figures 1.2 and 1.3 are applicable to all organizations, in all possible situations. Such generic models are, of course, too simple. All change is unique in the sense that each change has specific characteristics that we will not see in other settings. Such variation can only be detected through contextualizing change. By contextualizing, we mean seeing change as something that happens in a specific context, i.e. a specific organization in a specific environment at a specific time. Changing a business organization in the US is clearly not the same as changing a similar business organization in Norway. And changing a hospital is clearly not the same as changing a manufacturing plant. These two previous sentences hint at contextual differences concerning country / nation (Norway and USA) and function / task (hospital / plant). Contextualizing change is illustrated in figure 1.4.

Contextualizing is necessary in order to give a realistic picture of organizational change. In its extreme form, change can be regarded as a generic phenomenon, decoupled from any specific context. Adhering to such a view implies a perspective where general theories of change are assumed to be valid across both space and time. On the other hand, there are those who believe that change is something local and unique, and that generalizing from one change to another is a fallacy.[17]

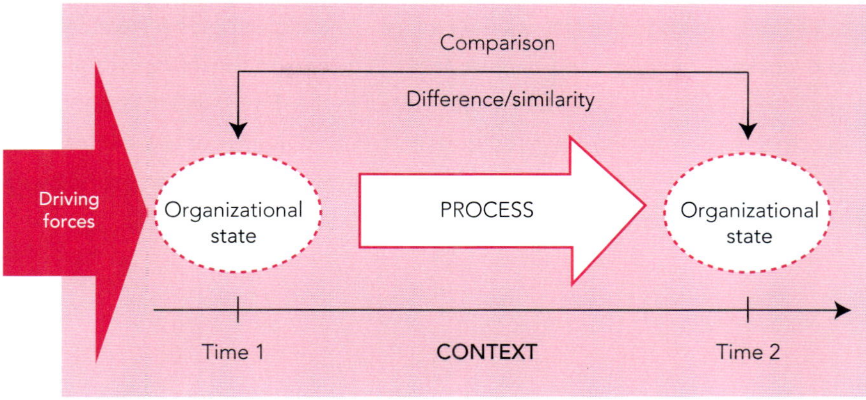

FIGURE 1.5: Driving forces initiating change

In this book, I try to carve out a middle position, refuting both the argument for theories being valid across all contexts and the argument for change being purely contextual. Organizational change, I argue, has some common denominators for all organizations, most obviously that we are studying human behaviour and change in such behaviour. Although humans differ, they also have commonalities. On the other hand, no theory or research findings can be "automatically" transferred from one context to another. To be applicable, research findings from one context and theories derived from these must be adapted or "translated" from this context to another.[18]

As noted previously, this book is based on the notion that planned change has a starting point and – although not as clearly – an ending point. Such a notion implies that stability is the norm, and that change is a deviation from the norm. Classic organization theory is based on the idea that organizations seek predictability and stability.[19] Under stable and predictable conditions, organizations can refine their production and increase their efficiency.[20] In this perspective, change will be a "nuisance", something threatening operative efficiency. If this is the case, why do organizations start change processes at all? What are the driving forces initiating change? The driving forces are included in the model in figure 1.5.

There is a long tradition of making a distinction between internal and external driving forces, referring to internal forces as forces within the organization and external forces as forces in the organization's environment. Making this distinction is difficult, and in many instances also impossible, as the demarcation between organization and environment in many instances is quite fuzzy. In the perspective of this book – planned or intentional change – the distinction between internal and external is also regarded as quite futile. The reason for this is that planned change will always be initiated by some actor. Driving forces will thus not be any "objective" forces, but the interpretations and understandings of these actors. The driving forces will be some *change agents*, i.e. some individuals or groups with a perception that change is necessary or will be beneficial.

Towards a conceptual model of planned change

As mentioned several times above, traditional organization theory has been mostly concerned with stability,[21] The focus has been placed on structural arrangements that make people repeat specific behaviours and thus replicate and reinforce existing structures, following rules and routines, complying with incentives, or organizational culture as a means of creating security and a sense of community, and reducing anxiety. Some go to the extreme of claiming that organization is stability, and that organizational change is an oxymoron.[22] Thus, the first element in a theory of planned change should be about understanding why organizations break with stability and predictability, and engage in processes that by nature are open-ended and insecure. In our model, this element will be denoted as the *driving forces of change*.

As discussed in depth in the introduction to this chapter, we need stability to be able to empirically study change. Change is moving from one relatively stable state to another relatively stable state. Thus we must be able to define and describe what these changes are, and the scope or radicality of the change. We must be able to define and describe the *content of change.*[23] Organizational change can differ greatly with regard to the content and scope of change. Some changes may affect the whole organization, while other changes may be more delimited to changing some structures, some routines, and some cultural elements. By forcing ourselves to define the content of change, we also link the study of organizational change to traditional concepts like structure, power, culture, and strategy in organization theory. Change has been a central element in most theories about organizations, from Weber's essay on bureaucracy to neo-institutional theory, but in most cases the phenomenon of change – or instability – has only been loosely coupled to more traditional organization theory. This has been pointed out by James March, who claims that "in its fundamental structure a theory of organizational change should not be remarkably different from a theory of ordinary action".[24] In other words, theories of change and theories of stability should be approximately the same. Change and stability should not be regarded as opposites demanding specific theories to be understood, but rather as two interdependent phenomena that are possible to describe and understand using the same set of concepts.

Closely connected to the content of change we find the scope or magnitude of change.[25] We all know that changes are experienced as different in terms of radicality. Some changes we make are almost routine, involving only small adjustments to what we have done before. Other changes are perceived as more dramatic or "larger", for instance when we have to learn something completely new or a basic conception of ours is challenged. Such large changes will be perceived as more difficult, demanding and sometimes downright painful than more routine adjustments.

As mentioned, change should be contextualized. Organizations are clearly embedded in a context, but they also represent a context for people working in the organization. Context is important because it both impedes and enables action. Thus, context draws our attention toward the complex interplay between agency and context, individual and structure, and organization and environment.[26] To analyse context, it is helpful to distinguish between the inner and the outer context:

> Outer context includes the economic, social, political, and sectoral environment in which the firm is located. Inner context refers to features of the structural, cultural, and political environment through which ideas for change proceed.[27]

Distinguishing between inner and outer context also makes us aware of the need to analyse change at different levels of analysis. Two levels are of particular interest in the context of this book: the relation between the individual and the inner context (organization), and the relation between the organization and its environment (outer context).

Finally, planned change must be analysed as a process or a set of actions and events evolving over time and moving the organization from one state to another.[28] Focusing on processes forces us to concentrate on identifiable actors, and how these actors affect the progression or path of change.[29] In planned change, change does not merely emerge out of thin air. Change is something that is driven by someone, individuals or groups of people, both in conflict and in collaboration with others. Planned change is intentional, and intention is only a characteristic of a thinking actor.

Bringing in actors is also bringing in human characteristics. Change processes will affect individuals, and will activate their perspectives on the world, their interests, and their emotions. Change is thus something involving a complex interplay between individuals. An attempt to change an organization in a certain direction – an action – will always create reactions from "others". The complex pattern of action and reaction will create processes that will never or very seldom be linear; rather, they will be impossible to predict perfectly. All attempts at organizational change will create "unintended consequences" .[30] Stated somewhat differently: planned organizational change can never be predicted perfectly. Intended change is to obtain something in the future, and the future will always be uncertain. Consequently, there will always be the possibility of intended change processes moving in unintended directions. To understand why the final result deviates from the intention it is necessary to understand the process of change.

We can conclude this discussion by identifying four basic elements necessary to outline a theory of planned change:

1. The driving forces of change. This addresses the question of "why?" We assume that organizations are seeking stability and predictability. We must understand why they engage in a process of change that is inherently ambiguous and uncertain.
2. The content and scope of change. This addresses the "what?" question. To be able to assess whether change has taken place at all, and how dramatic it is, we have to be able to specify the content of change. The description of this content should use similar concepts to those used to understand and explain organizational stability.
3. The context of change, addressing the question of "where?" the change takes place. A theory of planned change should be able to specify the context of change, both at the organizational and at the environmental levels. Dimensions of the organization, its domain or field, and its national characteristics must be defined, and it must be specified how these dimensions affect planned change processes.
4. The process of change. This element addresses the "how?" question. A theory of planned change should be able to define the process of change, the actions and events "producing" (or not) change, and the actors involved. The theory should take into account the fact that intentions and final results do not always coincide.

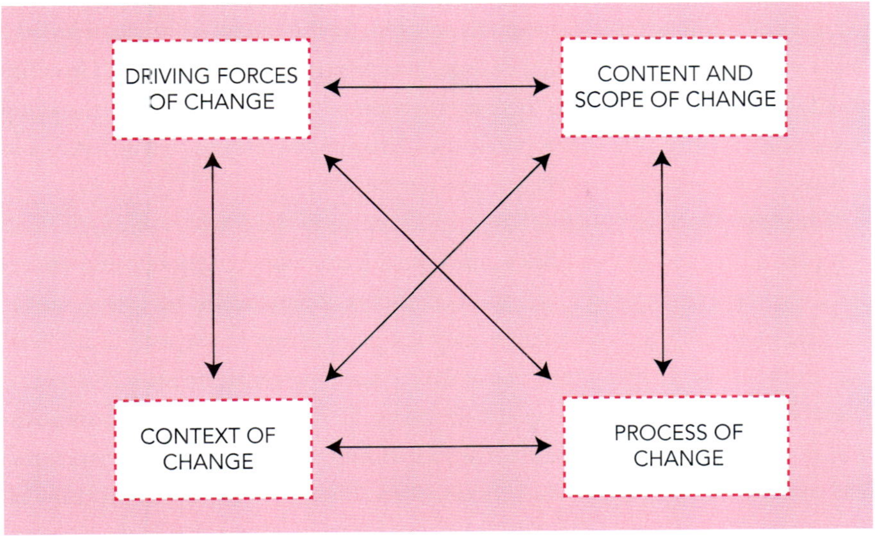

FIGURE 1.6: The central elements in a theory of planned change

The relationship between the four elements is illustrated in figure 1.6.

Some comments on the model in figure 1.6 are necessary. First, this model is not empirical, but conceptual. Thus, it is not a model to be empirically "tested". Rather, it should be understood as a kind of pedagogical tool, a way to structure information. If this model is to be used as a starting point for empirical studies, it has to be specified much more clearly in terms of variables or phenomena and relations between them. Examples could be a study of whether there is a relationship between the content of change (structure versus culture) and the time it takes to change, or whether it is more difficult to change professional bureaucracies than machine bureaucracies. Second, although this book will be using word "change" an enormous number of times, the model is meant to illustrate that "change" is not a unitary or one-dimensional phenomenon. Changes will vary across several dimensions. Some may be structural, while others may focus more on the cultural side of organizations. Some will occur quickly, while others might take years to complete. Some may be characterized by conflict and resistance, others by harmony and collaboration. Potential variation is great. Third, through the arrows, the model is intended to illustrate the complexity of change. The different dimensions are not independent of each other. On the contrary, they affect each other causally. For instance, it is highly probable that characteristics of the driving forces will have consequences for the change process, or that the context of change will influence the scope of change. Finally, the model combines a process and a variance view on planned change, and this tries to integrate both stability and dynamics.[31] The elements focusing on content/scope and context are mainly based on a variance perspective, while the elements concerning driving forces and process are mainly based on the process perspective.

The structure of the book follows the elements in the conceptual model. The first part of the book establishes a conceptual framework to describe and understand the complexity of change, and how different dimensions of change correlate and interact. It is thus a purely analytical perspective. In the second and final part of the book, insights from the analytical part are transferred to constructive knowledge on how to conduct planned change. In this part, we will discuss possibilities of conducting planned change by focusing on different change strategies and change management. Those looking for a "how-to" manual will probably be disappointed. It is hoped that this book will function as an antidote to oversimplified techniques and recipes for successful organizational change.[32] Such recipes are often highly normative, often taking a universal approach in the sense that the same change strategy and management will be successful in all contexts, although they lack solid empirical evidence.[33] Thus, they are in sharp contrast to "normal" aspirations in modern organization research emphasizing empirical descriptions of how change happens, and how context limits possibilities of generalizing findings.[34] Concerning the constructive part of this book, the ambition is to describe several ways organizations can be changed and to show that most of them have ended up as both successes and failures. Rather than selling one change strategy or one type of change management, the basic message of the book is that a good change strategy will depend on characteristics of the driving forces, the content and scope of change, the context of change, and the process of change. A competent change manager – or change agent – should be able to analyse these elements, and choose change strategy and management style accordingly.

Part II

Organizational change – driving forces, content and scope, context, and process

Chapter 2: Why change? The driving forces of change

Chapter 3: What changes? The content and scope of change

Chapter 4: Where is change taking place? The change context

Chapter 5: How does change happen? The change process

Chapter 2

Why change? The driving forces of change

Why and how social systems change – move from one state to another – has always been one of the basic questions in the social sciences.[35] A multitude of perspectives on change has resulted in a proliferation of theories of what drives change, and how change happens. Van de Ven and Poole (1995) conducted a much cited meta-study on perspectives on organizational change with the aim of constructing a synthesis of the research. On the basis of more than 200 articles, they identified 20 different perspective on organizational change that could further be narrowed down to four main categories. Each of these four categories represents "fundamentally different event sequences and generative mechanisms – we will call the motors – to explain how and why changes unfold".[36]

The concept of "motor" will in this book be equated with driving forces, as the four perspectives represent deeply different views on why change happens.[37] In this chapter, the four main perspectives will be described in more detail, and will be complemented by a fifth perspective. One of the main points of this discussion is to highlight the great differences attributed to human agency in each of the perspectives. Contrary to the basic principle in planned change as something being driven forward by intentional actors, the other perspectives tone down the role of intentional actors in organizational change. Thus, the discussion will clarify the prerequisites on which the idea of planned change is founded.

Perspective 1: Planned change – intentions as driving force

This perspective is based on a teleological view of change, or a type of change which takes place because some actors want to solve some problems and thus change their organization to do so. Organizations are viewed as tools used to obtain goals. We will call this perspective planned change. The are several assumptions connected to this perspective, and the most central one is the idea of intentions.[38] In short, such a perspective implies that an actor – a person or a group of people – has analysed the situation, concluded that it is unsatisfactory or could be even better, elaborated some actions to better the situation, and finally implemented some changes. Once changes are implemented, the effects of these changes are measured to see if they are in line with expectations. It is an analytical and rational process,[39] where the main driving forces are intentional actors or *change agents*.[40] Figure 2.1 illustrates the logic behind the planned change perspective.[41]

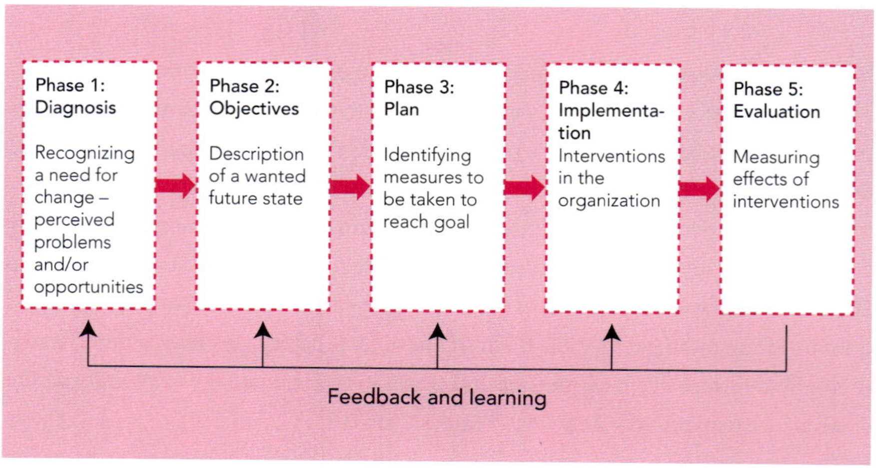

FIGURE 2.1: Phases in a planned change process

In the first phase, someone perceives the situation as sub-optimal. This could be in the form of the organization experiencing a decrease in sales, low customer loyalty, or high turnover among central staff. This situation is then analysed, in an effort to define the problem and to determine its causes. A typical activity in this phase will be gathering data through surveys or focus groups, sometimes with the assistance of external consultants or researchers. Equally common is that the need for change is detected through some type of strategic analysis, for instance a SWOT analysis: strength and weaknesses (internal factors), opportunities and threats (external factors).[42] Such analyses may lead to a recognition of a need for change, as well as a commitment to change by devoting resources to this analysis.

Phase 2 is the development of goals. Here, the change agents set up images of the wanted future state through techniques ranging from vague visions to specific milestones. In phase 3, a plan to reach the goals is elaborated: how to meet the threats, compensate for weaknesses, utilize strengths, and seize opportunities. A plan usually consists of specific actions, often with a deadline, and with specified responsibilities for the actions to be taken. Implementation – phase 4 – is the concretization of the plan into specific actions, for instance sending people off to training, reshuffling tasks, or changing the incentive schemes. The final phase consists of evaluation of the effects of the specific changes that have been made, to see whether the expectations have been met, for instance that income stopped declining, customer loyalty increased, or employee turnover decreased. If the change is regarded as successful, the next step is to stabilize or institutionalize the changes, that is to make people in the organization comply with and reinforce the changes.[43] If changes are evaluated as not having met expectations, measures are taken to learn to be able to correct the course. Thus, the organization engages in a learning cycle where feedback is used to engage in new analyses, sett new goals, elaborate new plans, and implement new measures.

This way of thinking – that we are able to analyse the situation, set goals, find solutions, and implement them – is an essential part of Western culture. Humans are masters of their lives, and not only have the possibility, but also the moral duty, to improve it. But even if rationality is the dominating narrative in our culture, it is not the same as to say that all organizational changes are rational. A basic characteristic of organizations is that they are social systems, and as so they are indeterministic.[44] Indeterminism implies that it is impossible to predict with absolute certainty how social entities like organizations will react to an impulse or stimulus. Planned change, being such an impulse, may fail. Intentions proved to be too ambitious, measures intended to have an effect did not have the wanted effect, a project just made the situation worse, or the proposed deadline was impossible to meet.

As mentioned at the beginning of this book, change agents in a wide array of organizations express great frustration with their ability to implement changes. At the same time, organizations change, although not in an orderly, planned way. Some organizations try their best to change, but no matter how hard they try, they still "die".[45] This cries out for alternative perspectives on organizational change.

Perspective 2: Life-cycle change – growth as driving force

One such alternative perspective is the life-cycle model of organizational change. This perspective leaves some room for intention and human choice, but it builds on an assumption that organizations change in a predestined way. Changes follow a pattern of evolution determined by an "underlying form, logic, program or code that regulates the process of change and moves the entity from a given point of departure toward a subsequent end that is prefigured in the present state".[46] All organizations thus follow a predestined set of phases in their lifetime.

Such a perspective is partly found in the highly influential writings of Henry Mintzberg (1979), indicating that organizations move from one configuration to another as they grow. When organizations are established for the first time – or "born" – they will be small and have weakly elaborated structures, administrative systems, rules, and routines. Coordination, usually among only a few people, happens informally, through direct contact and communication. Division of labour is rather vague, while the position of leader is very clear as the entrepreneur is both the owner and the leader. As the organization grows, more people will have to coordinate activities, giving rise to more formalized systems of coordination and control, and thus to a more formalized hierarchy. Increasing size also opens up for more specialization, as well as for routinization and standardization. To elaborate and control systems, professional staffs are established. It becomes more difficult for the leader to have an overview, resulting in more impersonal systems for control and supervision. The organization moves into the bureaucracy form.

Increasing size, however, also results in greater complexity, both horizontally and vertically. Coordination, supervision, and control become more intricate, demanding ever more resources, again resulting in increasing staff and expanding hierarchy. This again slows down decision making and fragments responsibilities. To solve this, organizations are split up into several smaller units, and the organization moves from an integrated bureaucracy to a divisionalized firm. Control and coordination move from routines and behaviour to the control of outputs and outcomes. In every divisionalized firm there will be strong centrifugal forces threatening to rip the organization apart. Thus, in their final phase, steps are taken to integrate organizations through a multitude of horizontal connections, ending up with a more organic or matrix-type of organization where much of the actual production or work is performed through projects.

What Mintzberg is sketching out is a pattern of phases in an organization's life forced forward by growth in the number of employees. This view of change is explained even more clearly in Larry Greiner's work (1972/1988). He claims that organizations move through five definite stages, where there is always a possibility that the organization will not make it through to the next stage. Every stage or phase of relative stability is punctuated by a crisis that has to be tackled for the organization to be able to move on to the next, more "mature", phase.

Greiner calls the first phase "creativity". In this phase, the organization consists of a few entrepreneurs with a clear sense of ownership of the core idea of the organization. It is small, dominated by informal communication and coordination. As the organization grows, it encounters a crisis of leadership. The original entrepreneurs are more interested in production than in leading other people or devising well-functioning administrative systems. To be able to progress, the organization needs competent leadership. So the organization moves into the next phase of "direction". The formal structure of the organization is elaborated, systems for work, marketing, and sales are developed, and decision making is centralized. As growth continues, the weaknesses of central direction become clear as decisions take too long and employees feel excluded from decisions they should have been involved in. A crisis connected to a need for more autonomy emerges, and moves the organization into the phase of "delegation". In this phase, decisional powers are delegated to lower echelons of the organization, and top management gets less involved in everyday activities in the organization. The stronger autonomy will in turn, according to Greiner, lead to fragmentation and thus to a crisis of control. This leads to the next phase, that of "coordination". The coordination phase is characterized by increasingly sophisticated measures to obtain horizontal coordination, including a stronger top management and staff focusing on control of departments and divisions to avoid sub-optimization. However, in this phase, an increasing divide between top management and the rest of the organization emerges. Divisions experience lack of autonomy and an excess of control systems, routines, and procedures, leading to a "red tape crisis". The final phase in this perspective is "collaboration", including the abolishment of rules and routines, and a focus on more flexible structure through the use of teams, projects, and matrix structures.

The evolution can be shown as in figure 2.2.

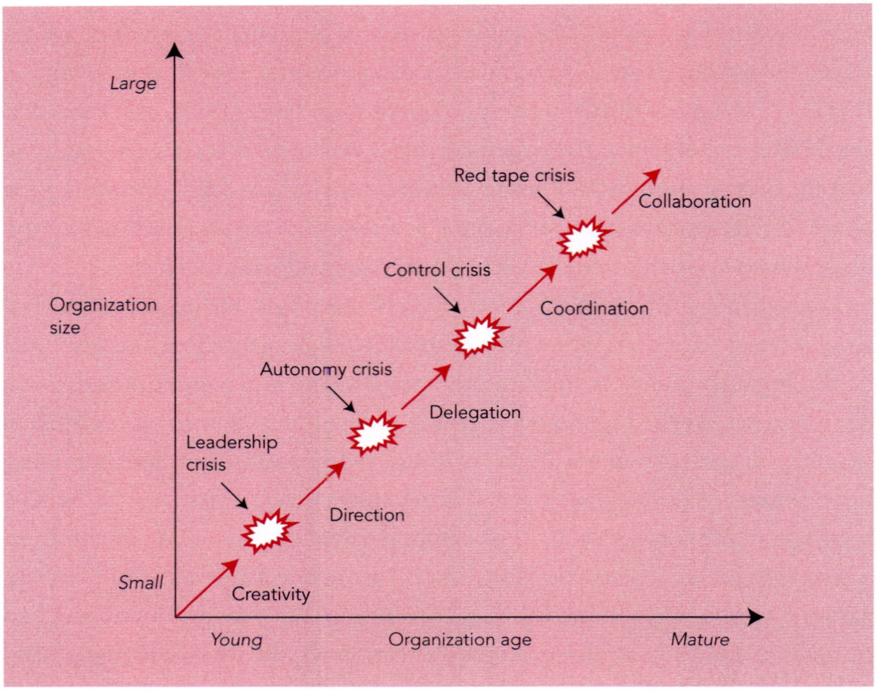

FIGURE 2.2: Greiner's phases of organizational growth

This perspective still leaves room for human agency, in the sense that not all organizations will succeed in moving from one phase to another. They will "die" if they are not capable of handling the transition – i.e. a crisis – between phases. Still, the number of choice alternatives is highly limited. When an organization grows out of the creativity phase, the only possible choice for the change agent is to centralize and professionalize leadership. With continuing growth, the only choice to grow further is to decentralize, etc. It is possible to regard this perspective as a variant of planned change, only with extremely limited opportunities for choice. A change agent will only be important insofar as he or she makes the "right" decision when a crisis emerges.[47]

This perspective is easy to criticize for being overtly deterministic, i.e. the only way for an organization to survive is through the predestined phases.[48] Empirical research is also questioning whether these phases are all necessary. Many of today's largest organizations are, for instance, highly bureaucratized,[49] while other organizations grow without taking on more bureaucratic or divisionalized forms.[50] Changes may also follow quite different paths than the one described by Greiner, usually by "skipping" some phases or moving "backwards" to an old form.[51] So, there is still a need for complementing perspective on change.

Perspective 3: Change as natural selection – competition for scarce resources as driving force

This perspective is clearly inspired by the work of Charles Darwin on the origin of species. The starting point for Darwin was the inertia of the single individual, be it human, animal or plant. A giraffe does not develop a long neck by stretching for food at the top of the trees. No matter how much a specific giraffe stretches its neck, the neck does not get significantly longer. Thus, change does not take place at the level of the individual, but at the level of the species. The giraffes with the longest necks survive, and get the possibility to spread their genes. Over time, short-necked giraffes will become extinct in favour of those with long necks. This is the basic mechanism behind the idea of the survival of the fittest, that is to say the species that is best fitted to acquire resources from the environment. Changes in the species will be a reflection of changes in the environment or the availability of resources.

Transferred to organization theory, the environment can be equated with what is often called an organizational field. A field is a market or a domain where organizations compete for the same limited resources. This could apply to banks and insurance companies competing for the same customers, or universities competing for students. In addition, this perspective is based on an idea of organizations being characterized by individual inertia.[52] Strong inertial forces are found both inside most organizations and outside them, in their environments. These inertial forces make it difficult, sometimes impossible, to change, especially to succeed with more discontinuous changes like moving into a totally new market or completely abandoning an old way of doing things.

The natural selection perspective contains three central concepts: variation, selection, and retention.[53] The relation between them is illustrated in figure 2.3.

Within the borders of a field there will always be some variation in organizational forms, indicating that organizations competing for the same scarce resources display somewhat different characteristics. Insurance companies do the same task and compete for the same resources (customers), but they vary somewhat in the way they do it. Within most fields, there is a tendency for a higher number of organizations to exist than can be kept alive by the existing amount of resources

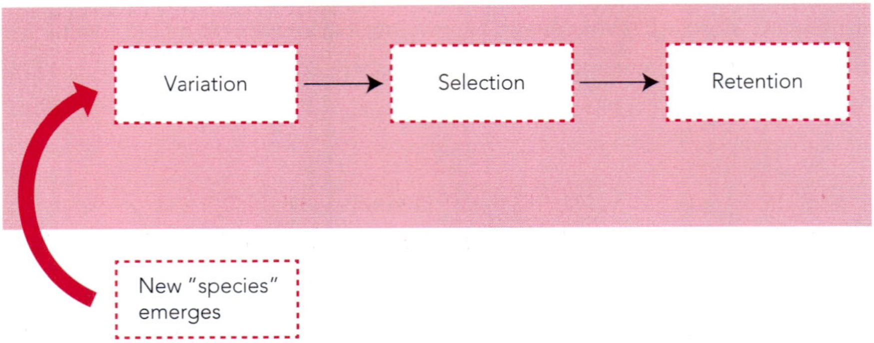

FIGURE 2.3: Basic concepts in the process of natural selection

in the field. The least efficient organizations, i.e. those least capable of acquiring necessary resources to survive, will try to change by imitating those that do well.[54]

However, as most organizations according to this perspective are characterized by inertia, most of the attempts to change will fail. As a consequence, they will go bankrupt, be shut down and "die". A recent, and ongoing, example is the strong decline in the number of shopping malls in the US.[55] The reason for this is mainly the increasing tendency for customers to shop on the internet, for instance through major actors like Amazon. Even though the threat from internet-based shopping had been evident for more than a decade, many malls and other physical shops more or less denied the need for a radical change. Most shops set up web pages to promote internet shopping, but the physical shop was still the focus. Other arguments for the need for physical shops were activated, like "people want to see and try before they buy", "you don't meet people on the net", or "how about a virtual cup of coffee with a friend?" As unfit organizations "die", some room may open up in the field for new organizations like shops operating exclusively on the net, or shops with a wider variety of products and services that are hard to distribute virtually. One example of this is how many book shops have survived by offering live readings by authors combined with concerts and the serving of wine, beer, and light meals. This way the structure of the field changes, not by changes being made in the individual organization, but rather by new organizational forms invading the field.

Still, it is not necessarily the most efficient organizations that survive, and the least efficient that "die". Within every field one finds strong ideals concerning what a legitimate organization should look like. Specific values are associated with specific organizations, making them strong institutions, not only tools that can be easily discarded if they are not good enough.[56] Consider the following thought experiment: it would probably be possible, quite easily, to train nurses to conduct more trivial and routine surgery without their having to fulfil a full, formal medical education. If this were possible, one could establish something called "semi-hospitals" specializing in simple surgical operations, but without licensed doctors. This might be highly efficient, as nurses usually cost less than doctors, and doctors could be relieved from more routine operations and could focus more on the most complex surgery. Such an arrangement is not very likely to emerge, partly because it would stand in strong contrast to established norms in the field of health services. The medical profession would most likely protest vehemently, as would public authorities, and most probably the market (patients) would also oppose this idea. All these internal and external forces will see to that the old organizational form is upheld, even though the new form might be much more efficient.

As illustrated by the previous example, change is driven not only by the competition for resources, but also by the quest for legitimacy.[57] Within a field, there will always be a dominating set of ideas of what constitutes an "appropriate" organization. Organizations that are able to produce symbols signalling that they are "modern" and "efficient" will also be the ones to mobilize the strongest support. Thus, there will always be pressure towards isomorphy, i.e. organizations will tend to become more similar in form and function over time to comply with the dominating norms in the field. Minor change will thus take the form of imitating the organizations that are viewed as the best within the field.

In the perspective of natural selection, changes at the field level will "trickle down" to the single organization. Change at the individual level will thus not be planned, but a reflection of small changes in the environment. Good examples of such changes are hospitals. It is very hard to change the way professional medical personnel work through centralized decisions and coercion.[58] Change is most likely to happen when the professional field develops new knowledge. New medical insights, or new techniques of efficient nursing, are developed through research and development at the institutions training the professional staff. The main change takes place outside the hospital, in universities, medical firms, and research institutions. Changes in the organization then "mirror" changes initiated outside the organization. The same process or mechanism occurs when the knowledge produced in schools changes, or the demography and thus the working force changes.[59] Change is, in this perspective, regarded as a rather passive, incremental, and non-intentional adaptation to changes in the environment, and thus something that is outside organizational control.[60]

At the macrolevel, the natural selection perspective has a certain flavour of development optimism in the sense that natural selection represents a form of progression towards a better state.[61] The best or most fit survive. The perspective is not necessarily the opposite of the perspective of planned change. Natural selection can also, in part, be a form of active adaptation to create a fit between demands from the field and organizational characteristics.[62] However, the main contribution from this perspective is the highlighting of organizational inertia and barriers to planned change, and thus to explain why change is so difficult and so many attempts at organizational change seem to fail.[63]

Perspective 4: Dialectic change – conflict of interest as driving force

This perspective on change is inspired by the Hegelian assumption that society changes as a consequence of constant confrontations between groups, interests, and ideas. Change is a struggle for power and dominance as a "thesis" (the dominating group or idea at a moment in time) meets an "anti-thesis" (a challenging idea or group), ending up in a "synthesis". This is illustrated in figure 2.4.

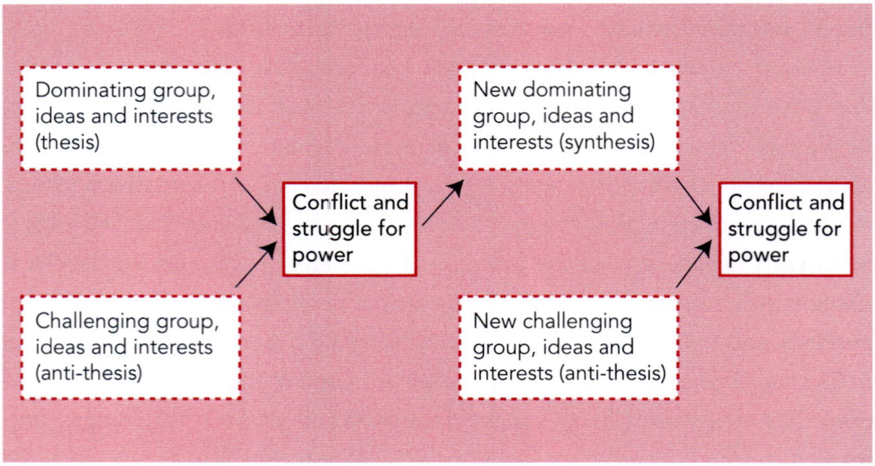

FIGURE 2.4: Change as a dialectical process

This process can be applied to both the societal and the organizational levels. At the organizational level change is a product of a struggle for power or the possibility to dominate the organization and design it to benefit the dominating group.[64] Change is thus a conflictual process. At a given point in time, there will always, according to this perspective, be a dominating group or coalition deciding on the organizational design. This situation will be relatively stable. But, as organizations – and societies – consist of different groups with different interests, there will always exist a potential for protest, uprising, and revolt.

In periods with a strong dominating coalition or group, this group will be free to design the organization according to its interests. But it is only able to do this as long as its power base is maintained. Changes, both inside and outside the organization, may alter these power bases. A well-known example is how the power relation between employers and employees is affected by the situation on the labour market.[65] In periods when the supply of labour is plentiful, the power of the employer becomes strong. The employer can choose freely among many job applicants, and it will be hard for employees to find a new job if they loses the one they have. In periods with a shortage of labour, the power relation will be reversed. This becomes clearly visible with regard to the evolution of wages in organizations. In periods of plentiful labour, wages fall as the employees lose their power to negotiate. Changes are in favour of the employers. In periods of shortage of labour, wages rise as the negotiating power of employees is strengthened.

In many organizations, power will be rather evenly distributed, and in such situations many decisions will be characterized by negotiation.[66] The outcome of negotiations will usually take on the form of compromise. Change is thus not dominated by one part only, but by several parts having partial success in getting their interests through. A compromise might, in fact, be a solution leaving all the involved parties dissatisfied. In some situations, due to lack of information about the initial positions and interests of the involved parties, the outcome might even be worse for all parts than what they could have obtained through cooperation. Given such circumstances, if several actors act rationally on their own behalf, irrational solutions might result.[67]

The same process can be detected at a higher level of analysis, the organizational field. Organizations within the same field will be competing for the same scarce resources. In a natural selection perspective, the organization with the best fit between design and environment will survive. The dialectical perspective contains a less optimistic view of change. The most fit might not win; rather, it might be the strongest that survives. An example of this is when financially strong organizations take over weaker competitors to get rid of competition. The weaker organization might have a better fit with the environment, at least at the current point in time, but it still dies because it loses the struggle for power and dominance within the field. This is a case that has received a lot of attention in studies of so-called horizontal integration, market leadership, and the rise of cartels and monopolies.[68] Change happens, but not always for the better.

Perspective 5: Change as anarchy – coincidences as driving forces

Instead of regarding change as driven by intentional actors, specific life-cycles, natural selection or struggle for power and dominance, change could also be a result of *coincidences*.[69] James March once wrote: "Organizations are continually changing, routinely, easily, and responsively, but change within them cannot ordinarily be arbitrarily controlled."[70]

Behind this statement lies an assumption that organizations are complex entities where many things happen simultaneously, and where no single actor can have total oversight and control. The situation is characterized by uncertainty and ambiguity.[71] In general terms, this perspective assumes organizational change to be a product of temporal concurrence of organizational "streams". The basic point is that in organizations, humans (actors) meet at different arenas (choice opportunities). These actors carry with them some energy and ideas consisting of problems they want to solve, and solutions for the problems. Who meets whom, where, and at what time, will decide the coupling of problems and solutions. The best solution will not necessarily be chosen; rather, one will choose the solution available at the actual point in time. This process of change is illustrated in figure 2.5.

The main point in this model is that the outcome, in this context change, is produced by the coupling of actors. The coupling of actors will in many instances be highly regulated and predictable, for instance when the structure defines who should participate where, for example that someone must be at a meeting because it is part of his/her job. It is also common that the topics that can legitimately be discussed in a specific forum are defined. Still, what is decided will depend heavily on who is participating. People are carriers of interests; they bring with them perceptions of the problem to be discussed and how it could be solved. Sometime, people will bring a preference for a certain solution, with almost no regard to what the problem is.

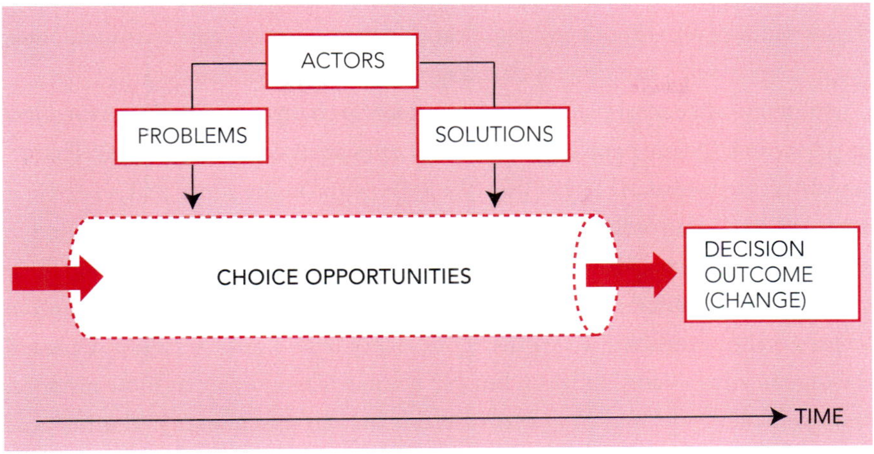

FIGURE 2.5: Basic elements in an anarchic perspective on organizational change

But who is participating is only partly determined by specifications in the formal structure. In most organizations, we find highly ambiguous structure.[72] One thing that can never be planned in advance is who will have the energy, time, and opportunity to participate, for instance, in a meeting. A person may be occupied with something else, for instance by having double-booked a meeting or having to stay at home because of sick children, and will thus not be able to attend the meeting. Thus, that person's perceptions of problems and solutions will not be taken into consideration, and the final result may be quite different than it would have been if that specific person had been present. On other occasions, people simply meet, find out that they share a common problem, and thus decide there and then to do something. Change can in such situations be rather spontaneous, not necessarily as a response to a problem defined by the organization. The end result may be that the organization changes at many levels simultaneously, but without any common plan. Kjell Arne Røvik has pointed to the fact that organizations often take on the form of "multi-standard organizations", indicating that one organization adopts different changes at different points in time.[73] Change happens, but is incoherent and unplanned.

Changes also happen through the ordinary daily activities of the organization. Somebody finds out that a routine is not working optimally for him or her, and chooses to adjust it somewhat. A conflict between two people is solved by ensuring that they no longer work together, thus separating them both formally and physically. Both changes described above are rational. The point is that they are implemented at the individual level, without any organizational plan. Change happens continuously, but is not planned. Over time, such changes might be substantial.[74]

Another source of unplanned and coincidental change is found in the turnover of personnel.[75] Some people quit, and new ones are recruited. One basic characteristic of organizations is that they are impersonal in the sense that a person is assumed to comply with the demands of the job, not vice versa. Still, research shows that this assumption of impersonality is not quite realistic.[76] In any job there will be room for discretion so that newly recruited people may adjust the job to fit personal interests and strengths. Thus, every time a new person is recruited the organization changes slightly, but still not in a planned way. In some instance, change of personnel may have dramatic, unplanned consequences. This happens when whole cohorts of personnel change, changing the demographic composition of the organization.[77] In some periods organizations recruit many people at the same time. It could be because of an increase in demand, a new political strategy, or the retirement of a cohort of older employees. This could lead to a situation where a large group of people within a specific age group, educational type, or gender is recruited. The abrupt change in organizational demography may, in turn, skew the power relations between groups, again resulting in organizational changes in favour of the new groups. Such changes are seldom planned, and they are seldom chosen as a conscious step to solve a specific problem.

This perspective does not necessarily contradict the idea of human agency. Much of what is described above could easily be classified as rational choices made at the individual level. People starting in a new job adapt the job to themselves, and people participating in a decision arena fight for their perceptions and ideas. The main point, however, is that rational decisions at the individual level do not necessarily amount to rational decisions at the organizational level. On the contrary, this perspective illustrates a situation where individual choices and actions are difficult or impossible to control and steer. Organizations still change, but without any unitary plan.

Driving forces – objective and subjective

In most of the literature on planned change, driving forces are treated as though they were objective and impersonal, almost physical, forces. This is found in its clearest form in the body of work on organizational strategy where SWOT analyses remain powerful tools for rationally adopting and responding to challenges. In these analyses, focus is set on external elements such as technological development, changes in the market structure, competition, labour market, and political changes, as well as internal elements such as conflicts, production flow, sickness absence, turnover, and a host of other problems.

Presented this way, driving forces acquire objective attributes, which can be perceived in the same way by everyone involved if they examine them attentively. Such forces are, of course, also objective phenomena, and will in many instances nearly force an organization to change. Still, from this point of view, driving forces will create change, but it will only to a small extent be planned change. Planned change is rooted in the idea that someone intentionally takes the initiative to change an organization, a situation that presupposes that the driving force has been identified, and that a decision has been made to act on the driving force. Thus, in planned change, the driving force will always be a *change agent*, a human agent. According to this way of thinking, planned change will always be driven by perceptions of driving forces, not by the driving forces themselves. Such a view of change has deep and radical consequences for how we theorize about change.

DRIVING FORCES – SUBJECTIVE PERCEPTIONS, NOT OBJECTIVE "MOTORS"

As has been stated previously, the main characteristic of planned change is the pivotal role of human agency or change agents. It will always be actors who drive planned change. These actors must then perceive a need for change and transform this need into change processes. Or, to put it another way:[78]

> It is important to emphasize that an impulse in itself is not the change, or not even necessarily connected to the change. There are several possible reactions to an impulse, and an impulse can also wither away without leaving any traces (…) Impulses are always carried by actors. Somebody creates an idea; somebody transmits the scope for action.

The driving forces are not faceless and objective, but conveyed by humans. Let me illustrate this point by comparing organizational change to climate change. Climate change, as in global warming, is clearly driven by physical forces. Most researchers on the topic agree that this is partly generated by human activity and the emission of CO_2. CO_2 is a physical driving force in climate change, whether or not we humans register it. Even if CO_2 emissions and climate change are clearly of direct importance for many organizations – just think about energy firms, insurance companies and public authorities – they are not objective driving forces for organizational change. For climate change to trigger organizational change, the change in climate has to be identified, somebody must define it as a threat or opportunity for the organization, and then a decision must be made as to what steps to take to meet the threat or grasp the opportunity.[79] Objective driving forces must be registered and transformed into actionable ideas before becoming driving forces in a planned change process. The driving forces are ideas, not "things" or objective "forces". Figure 2.6 illustrates this line of reasoning.

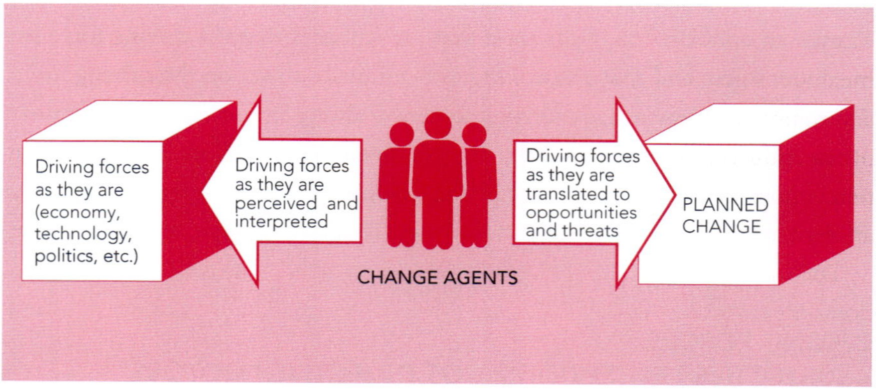

FIGURE 2.6: Driving forces, change agents, and change processes

The figure illustrates an important Kantian notion, that of the distinction between things as they are ("das Ding an sich") and things as they are perceived ("das Ding für mich"). In a planned change perspective, no driving forces are "objective motors" that only will have one interpretation with one single consequence. Many driving forces will, on the contrary, appear as complex, multifaceted, and ambiguous, giving several change impulses to the organization.[80] Growth can be rather easily measured by counting the number of employees or the size of the budget. Translating this into actionable knowledge is, however, much more complex. Do we need to change now, or should we wait until we reach a level of 30 employees? Or maybe 40? Finding the correct answers to such questions is not an easy task.

Even a driving force like technological change – that many will perceive as very clear and objective – is difficult to translate into "What does it mean for us?" Everybody can imagine that social media, artificial intelligence, and "big data" will change the way we live, and thus how organizations function. But registering these changes is not the same as predicting the specific impact on a specific organization. Technological changes do not give clear and unambiguous guidelines to organizations, with correspondingly clear and unambiguous answers as to what to do. Technological changes seem rather to open up a "space of opportunity".[81] Organizations can choose whether they will respond to technological changes or not, and they can choose different responses to the same impulse. This does automatically imply that those not reacting to an impulse will "die". A prominent example is the Swiss clock industry that, for a wide array of reasons, did not respond to the emergence of digital watch technology.[82] They, or at least the high end of the production, continued making clocks with mechanical clockwork. Today, these types of watches are highly sought after, and many producers make higher profits than before. At the same time, parts of the industry were able to exploit the new possibilities opened up by digital technology by starting to produce Swatch watches: cheap digital watches with an eye-catching design.

The message in this short discussion is that in order for driving forces to function as driving forces in a planned change process, they must be interpreted. Somebody must perceive and register the driving forces, and somebody has to translate these into consequences for the organization. The cue is the pronoun "somebody". In every organization, there will be diverging interpretations of driving forces, a situation grounded in to basic conditions:

1. REALITY PRESENTS ITSELF IN DIFFERENT WAYS FOR DIFFERENT PEOPLE [83]

This insight, stemming from phenomenology, implies that even if humans exist in the same world, we are exposed to different aspects of it. In a school, teachers will be exposed to a different reality than the principal. There will be a systematic bias in their exposure to impulses from the environment. Whereas the teachers will obtain impulses from pupils, colleagues, and parents, the principals will more often meet other principals, their own staff, and administrative staff in the municipality. Their organizational positions put them in situations that create different realities, even if they share the same organization, the school.

2. REALITY IS VIEWED DIFFERENTLY BY DIFFERENT PEOPLE [84]

This insight, stemming from cognitive psychology, is based on the notion that during their lifetimes, people elaborate cognitive schemes or maps. These schemes make it possible for us to arrange information, to store information, and to decide which information is worth our attention and which is not. These cognitive schemes create a systematic bias in how we see reality, as we have a tendency to see and store only information that fits with our schemes. Thus, an economist will probably view the same reality differently from a social worker. They will see and emphasize different aspects of the same reality.

The final result is that people in the same organization will probably perceive, register, and interpret different impulses for change. Different people construct different realities depending on their organizational role or position, and cognitive schemes. Leaders will construct a different reality from workers on the production floor, and a person working with marketing will probably see reality differently from a person working with production flows. Thus, there will not necessarily be unanimity on the perceived need for change, or on proposals for how to solve a problem or grasp an opportunity.

The driving forces in planned change are thus the change agent's perceptions of a need for change (driving forces), and an interpretation of what to do (solutions). Change initiatives from change agents should thus be treated as ideas or interpretations, not truths.[85] They are ideas based on the *perceptions* of the need for change, what they *perceive* to be the goal to achieve, what possibilities they *believe* they have, and how they *assume* that problems can be solved. Planned change is then based in somebody's ideas about driving forces and solutions. Again, we should emphasize "somebody", as opposed to "all". If the change agents are not "all", then there should be an awareness that people might have different ideas.

Now we are at the heart of the problem of planned change: the fact that somebody has an idea that change is needed does not necessarily imply that all members or stakeholders in the organization share this idea. There may be different ideas about driving forces, and about the solutions that are proposed. Or, formulated in another fashion:[86]

> (…) Various organizational stakeholders will view concrete reality differently. (…) In seeking fit, managers pursue their own definition of it, based on their own interests, but to survive, they must also often recognize and accommodate the constructed environments of other powerful organizational stakeholders.

This quotation makes it clear that the more ambiguous and open to interpretation the driving forces are, the more different interpretations one should expect. Ambiguity and openness of driving forces will, in turn, increase the scope for political activity.[87] For instance, somebody will benefit from defining a situation as a crisis, while others will not. While somebody will reap benefits from claiming that a new data system should be bought and implemented, others will have to bear the costs. As long as driving forces are not crystal clear and accepted by all, change agents should expect to meet resistance towards any proposed change.

DRIVING FORCES – CLARITY AND STRENGTH

The main message conveyed in the previous section is that driving forces – understood as forces starting planned or intentional change processes – are not objective forces. Driving forces must be interpreted and communicated to have any organizational impact. Extending this line of thought, driving forces should be treated as ideas with different degrees of *clarity*.[88] Some ideas may be equivocal, and leave substantial scope for different interpretations. Examples could be general ideas such as "digitalization", "globalization", or "coordination problems". These ideas or concepts are themselves equivocal, and it is not always clear what types of problems they are, or what problems they address.[89] In other situations, the driving forces may be very clear, restricting the scope for different interpretations. Reporting economic deficits of several hundred million kroner in consecutive years, as did the airline SAS in the 1980s and early 2000s, is a very clear signal that change is needed.[90] The same could be said for a newspaper experiencing a loss of 5% of its subscribers in a year, or a university seeing a sharp decline in student applications.

Clarity should not be confounded with truth. The correct phrase is intersubjectivity, i.e. many or all members of an organization perceive a situation in the same way.[91] The more people there are who perceive the driving force in the same fashion, the stronger the clarity will be. Clarity will in turn depend on how, and by whom, it is presented. Some ways of presenting driving forces are more readily accepted as "objective" than others. Few will question an economic report from an external accountant when it comes to understanding the financial situation of an organization, in the same way as few will question a decrease in the number of student applications from last year. A report on the psychosocial climate of an organization, based on a survey, will probably constitute a source with less clarity. It may be questioned how phenomena were measured, how they were analysed, how to interpret results, etc. A memo from an "ordinary employee" claiming to have been sexually harassed will also score low on clarity.

The strength of the driving force is clearly linked to its clarity, but it entails an additional component: What consequences does it have for the organization?[92] It is possible to agree on a driving force, but to disagree on its consequences. When the airline SAS was met with fierce competition from Norwegian Airlines, a perception spread within SAS that bankruptcy was a reality. This gave enormous strength to the driving force for change as it became a question of life and death for the organization. But there are also several examples of rather weak driving forces, where the consequences if the organization does not change is unclear. Many oil companies in Norway were highly aware of the oil fracking activities in the US, but they were not able to see what consequences this might have for global oil prices. They did not acknowledge the problem before prices plummeted, and changes had to be made. The phenomenon of fracking was too far away, and the consequences it represented were too vague to be taken seriously as a driving force for change. In general terms we can claim that if there is a shared perception that the existence of the organization is threatened, the driving force will be very strong. The less the driving force is viewed to represent a threat, the weaker it becomes.

The strength and clarity of driving forces will thus vary as illustrated in figure 2.7:

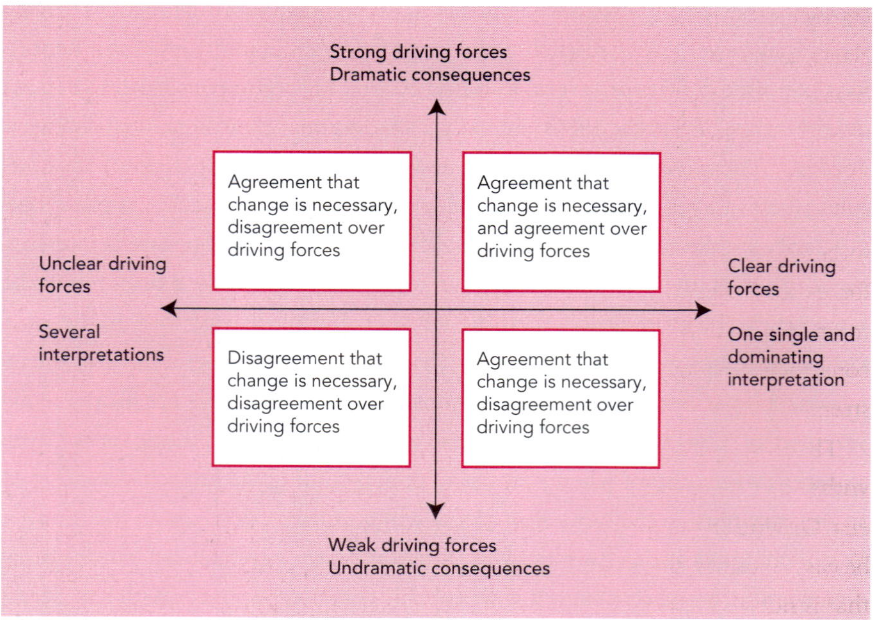

FIGURE 2.7: Driving forces – combining clarity and strength

As we will discuss in more depth below, the clarity and strength of the driving forces will have profound consequences for change leadership. The clarity and strength of the driving forces will influence the process of change, especially the amount of disagreement and political behaviour one should expect. How change leaders interpret and present the driving forces is essential in understanding the support of and resistance to any change process.

The figure indicates that different organizations will find themselves in situations where the driving forces will vary along the dimensions of clarity and strength. One persistent difference, in market feedback, is found between public and private organizations.[93] Private organizations dependent on selling their products or services to a market will receiveconstant feedback on how well they are doing through their continuous income. It may be difficult to determine why sales go down, but at least plummeting sales and income give a rather clear picture that "something" is wrong. Public organizations mostly lack this feedback mechanism, and will thus not receive such signals that something is wrong and that change is needed. Many public sector reforms have focused on introducing market-like mechanisms or quasi-markets.[94] Such reforms vary from introducing pay-per-patient in the hospital sector, via the pricing of internal services, to conducting systematic user surveys. Even if the objective of these reforms is to increase and clarify the feedback from the "market", these mechanisms will not have the same clarity as real market feedback.[95] Public organizations will also probably face less dramatic consequences of not changing, as they cannot go bankrupt in the same way that private firms do. Shutting down a public organization is a political process, working in a totally different way than what we find in the private sector.

Finally, one should be very aware that the clarity and strength of the driving forces say little about the solutions or measures to be taken. Even if the driving forces are clear and strong, there is plenty of scope in the choice of solutions. The main idea behind the previous discussion is to emphasize that driving forces are constructs, and that different ways of generating them will affect their clarity and strength.

That driving forces in planned change are constructs and ideas does not equate with their being totally decoupled from reality, and being only subjective phenomena. Driving forces are interpretations of a reality "out there", and this reality may be easy or difficult to interpret. On some occasions, reality presents itself in a way that is not very open to a variety of interpretations. On other occasions, reality is vague, equivocal, and ambiguous. On a final note we should emphasize that no matter how clear and strong driving forces are perceived to be, they are rarely capable of indicating clearly how to meet the challenges they pose. Solutions and measures will imply speculations about the future: what will work tomorrow to solve the problems we experience today. And, as we will come back to repeatedly in later chapters, if one thing is certain, it is that the future is uncertain.

Chapter 3

What changes? The content and scope of change

Change is a generic phenomenon taking place on all levels of society. When discussing organizational change, the phenomenon is delimited to a specific object: organization. As discussed initially, studying planned change requires a comparison of the same object – here: an organization – at a minimum of two different points in time. Thus we need a conceptual tool to describe this object. This tool is, within the framework of this book, organization theory. In modern organization theory it has become quite standard procedure to treat organization as systems.[96] A system perspective entails two basic assumptions. The first is that any organization can be split into smaller elements, and that these elements are interdependent and in sum constitute a whole that is greater than the sum of the parts. One of the first to propose such a perspective was Harold Leavitt (1965), who claimed that organizations could be split into four basic parts: 1) tasks, 2) people, 3) technology, and 4) structure.

The first three elements constitute the *operative core* of any organization. All organizations are constructed to perform some task. Prisons try to rehabilitate prisoners, and protect the general society from criminals; an IT firm works with the set-up of websites; and a school instils knowledge and values in young people. To accomplish these tasks, they employ people. Schools need teachers, IT firms need engineers, and prisons need prison officers. These people make use of certain technologies or tools to perform their tasks. These technologies include machines like cameras, books, and computers, but just as important is the knowledge each individual holds. The factual knowledge and pedagogical skills of teachers, the design knowledge of IT engineers, and the social competence of a prison officer are equally important as machines, perhaps more so.

The three basic elements in the operative core are the lowest level of analysis for detecting organizational change. We can study changes taking place in the tasks, the technology, and the people. It is possible to identify new machinery, new ways of carrying out tasks, or new behaviour among employees. Furthermore, the productive core is embedded in a wider *organizational context*. What Leavitt identifies as "structure" is a part of this context. Structure indicates who does what, how it is expected to be done, and how an employee or leader is expected to behave. In addition to structure, more recent organizational theory usually includes the following elements: 1) goals and strategies, 2) formal structure, 3) organizational culture, and 4) power relations.

The organizational context affects the production processes, that is, how people employ technology to carry out tasks. Goals can be defined as the ambitions laid down by the organization, while strategy is the plan for how to reach those goals.[97] Formal structure refers to the general architecture of the organization, that is, how tasks and responsibilities are distributed, and what systems the organization uses for coordination and control.[98] Organizational culture is the shared basic assumptions, values, and norms we find among people in an organization.[99] In addition, we must be aware that all organizations consist of a set of power relations where someone is able to make others do what they don't necessarily want to do voluntarily.[100] Such power relations are partly an element of the formal structure of the form of hierarchy, but organizations also consist of more informal power relations based on knowledge, personal charisma, and access to information.

Moreover, we assume that these elements are linked to some extent.[101] Change in one element will usually have a spillover effect on other elements.[102] A much used illustration is how information technology leads to changes in structure, tasks, and competences. Electronic communication devices work as a pressure to change communication channels in organizations, and at the same time they demand new competencies among employees so that they are able to use the new systems.

The second basic assumption implied in a system perspective is that organizations are embedded in a larger context often called the environment.[103] All organizations depend on resources from the environment, whether these are physical resources like income, people, and raw materials or immaterial goods like legitimacy and support. Very few, if any, organizations are self-contained with the necessary resources. Thus, a dependency relation exists between the organization and its environment. For organizations operating in a market, it is essential to sell enough goods or services to generate necessary incomes. The same organization is deeply dependent on the labour market for a supply of skilled employees, and on suppliers for a flow of raw materials. All organizations must also deliver something that is perceived by external actors as good or beneficial.

On an even higher level of analysis, organizations are also embedded in a geographical, cultural, political, and economic area, and thus must – at least to some extent – comply with general norms in this area.[104] In any society there will, at a given point in time, be a perception of what constitutes a good and beneficial organization. It is expected that organizations care for employees and their health, and do not expose them to unnecessary risks. It is expected that employees have the possibility of being assigned interesting work, of experiencing good working relationships with colleagues, and of participating in decision-making processes affecting their own working situation. Organizations not complying with these expectations can easily be perceived as "old fashioned" or "unfit", and might lose support and legitimacy among central actors in the environment. Environments thus represent a constant pressure on organizations, either by restricting their access to resources or by not providing support.

A system perspective is, as should have become clear through the previous discussion, thus a multilevel perspective. Organizations, and organizational change, must be analysed at different levels of analysis: operative core with a focus on production and behaviour, organizational context with a focus on formal and informal elements, and environmental level as an interplay between the organization and its environment. Such a multilevel system perspective is illustrated in figure 3.1.[105]

This is, of course, a simplified model aimed at providing a larger perspective, not the details. Still, this model is essential in enabling us to define more clearly what the content and scope of change are.

The content of change

Planned change is always, as emphasized in the previous chapter of this book, driven by one or more change agents. Planned change will always be based on

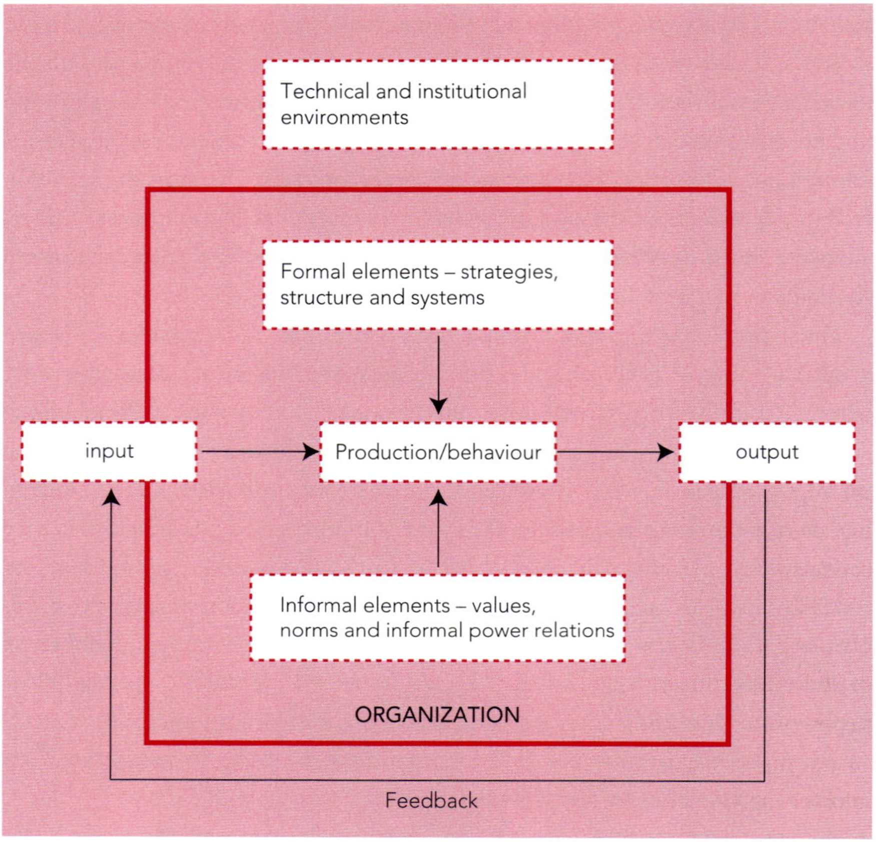

FIGURE 3.1: Jacobsen and Thorsvik's model of central elements in an organization

a wish to make things better, whether it is to exploit an opportunity, counter a threat, develop a strong side, or remedy a weakness. As an integral part of planned change, change agents will always encounter surprises (non-intentional consequences) and some degree of resistance.

In much of the research on the success or failure of planned change, the outcome of change is placed on a one-dimensional scale ranging from success to failure. This is clearly stated in the following:

> Over the past decade, I have watched more than 100 companies try to remake themselves into significantly better competitors. (...) A few of these corporate change efforts have been very successful. A few have been utter failures. Most fall somewhere in between, with a distinct tilt toward the lower end of the scale.[106]

Even if such statements are intuitively reasonable, they also tend to obscure the possibility that change may take place along several dimensions, and that a change may be a success on one of these dimensions, but not on others. What is defined as success or failure will depend on how change is measured. Thus we need concepts enabling us to measure change along several dimensions.

It seems to be most common to measure success or failure based on changes in the organization's *results* – output or outcome – following the organizational change. Examples of this could be changes in sales volumes, customer satisfaction, market share, or ability to attract skilled personnel. Or the measurement of change could concentrate on the *production or transformation process*, or the productive core of the organization, that is how people work and cooperate to produce results. Examples of such measures could be the number of production errors, the amount of sickness leave taken, or how good employees are at following safety routines. Focus will thus be placed on the behaviour, both individual and collective, of people in the organization.

Change can also be defined as observed changes in the organizational context. On one hand, one can measure *structural changes* or changes in the formal elements of the organization. Examples of such changes could be reorganizing of tasks, fusion of departments, changes in incentive systems, or changes in the meetings structure. On the other hand, one can focus on *cultural changes*, or changes in the informal organizational context. More specifically, cultural change refers to changes in the shared values, norms and basic assumptions of people working in the organization. Examples would include changed attitudes towards sexual harassment, views on innovation and experimenting, or norms concerning absenteeism.

It is easily assumed that changes in results are caused by changes in the production process and thus by changes in the behaviour of employees, for instance by getting better at collaborating or exploiting new technologies.[107] Changes in behaviour are, in turn, assumed to be caused by changes in the organizational context (structure and/or culture). Planned change is thus based on an assumption that elements in change are causally connected as illustrated in figure 3.2.

Change initiatives are rarely defined narrowly to changes in structure and/or culture. Usually such changes are – often implicitly – connected to changes in production and results. Some have even claimed that change has not occurred until one can observe changes in results,[108] and many of the examples of change failures mentioned in the introduction of this book are based on disappointments over lack of better results.

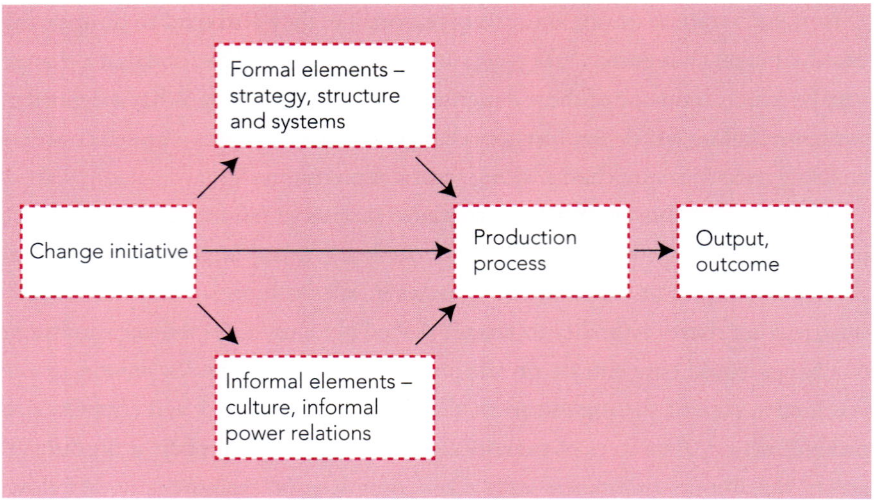

FIGURE 3.2: Assumed causal connections in planned change

In this book, organizational change is treated as an attempt to improve results. An attempt is not something that will always succeed, which will be discussed in detail in the next section. Change is thus, within the context of this book, treated as changes in the operative core or production process, or in the organizational context. However, these elements need further elaboration.

CHANGE CONTENT: THE PRODUCTION PROCESS

An obvious change, in the sense that it is highly visible, is one in the *physical production technology*. Examples include home care nurses using portable computers to register activities and communicate with others involved in the care process, doctors using advanced telecom devices to diagnose patients physically located miles away, or power plants installing new turbines. Increasing efficiency through automation is a process that has gone on for centuries, and has clearly accelerated in the last couple of decades.[109] One example of such change is the software called ERP, or Enterprise Resource Planning. This software is constructed to handle integrated production, that is, all aspects of the process from paying salaries and registering work hours, to logistics and sales.[110] The idea is to integrate all activities in the production process to streamline it, and thus to eradicate bottlenecks or other elements incurring unnecessary time and cost.

Several studies show, however, that changes in physical production technology only rarely produce the benefits promised by the sellers. Referring to the previouly mentioned ERP systems, research indicates that total benefits from implementing such systems are rather modest.[111] Explanations given for this can be roughly divided into two streams. The first is that the *human technology*, i.e. knowledge and skills, needed to utilize the physical technology is underdeveloped. Thus, changes must be measured by mapping to what degree employees have acquired new knowledge, new insight into how things work, and new skills to perform tasks. Such changes could also be implemented by recruiting new groups of employees with new educational backgrounds. Still, changes in knowledge are not always a guarantee that people will use this knowledge. Use of knowledge implies a change of *behaviour*. To produce better and cheaper products not only requires better machines, it also requires people who know how to use them, and who are able and willing to use them in the best way. Change is thus defined as how people act, how they cooperate and communicate, how much they discuss innovative ideas, or how much conflict they experience with co-workers. Behavioural change is seen by many as the key element in planned change, because it is the main link between improvement in the final results of the organization, or as has been pointed out: "[B]ehavior is the crucial link between intention as defined by strategy and desired outcomes as defined by profits, return on equity, market share, and customer satisfaction."[112]

But how do you get people to change their behaviour? Organization theory is founded on the assumption that behaviour can be altered by changing the organizational context, that is, either the formal elements of structure and strategies, or the informal elements of culture and power.

CHANGE CONTENT: FORMAL ELEMENTS (STRUCTURE)

A basic structural change is a change in the task portfolio of the organization. Such changes are usually labelled as strategic, as they often cause the organization to internalize or externalize tasks. A much studied change of this type is the decision to outsource tasks to other organizations.[113] Currently many, if not most, large organizations have outsourced responsibility for running the companies' IT systems. We see the same trend in tasks like Human Resource Management (HRM), cleaning and maintenance, and security control. But tasks are not just outsourced, they are also in many instances "offshored", that is to say that they are outsourced to external providers in other countries. The main point in doing this is to benefit from wage differences, and thus production costs. Sometimes tasks are offshored but remain in the "mother organization", while in other instances tasks are both outsourced and offshored. Examples of such changes are telecom companies outsourcing and offshoring their call centres and IT services to India or the Baltic states, where salaries are much lower than in the US and most European countries. Changes in the task portfolio are closely linked to the size and composition of the staff, and therefor directly to costs. Within the field of organizational strategy, this is reflected in a great interest in downsizing, on the one hand, and mergers and acquisitions, on the other.[114] Downsizing is often connected to outsourcing of tasks, while mergers and acquisitions are signs of tasks being internalized and thus connected to organizational growth.

Outsourcing and mergers and acquisitions are structural changes that will affect the organization's results without necessarily implying change in the behaviour of employees and managers in the organization. Still, most structural changes are adjustments in the already existing structure. Such changes can be defined along three dimensions.[115] The first is the *individual position*, that is, the job each employee occupies. A position or "job" can be changed according to the degree of specialization (the number of, and variation in, tasks), standardization (the number of rules and procedures applying to the position), and competency requirements (knowledge and skills). Second, the structure can be changed by *grouping*, or how tasks are clustered together in formal units like departments and divisions. Finally, structural changes can be made in the *decision-making system*, or the specification of who can decide what. This is closely related to centralization or decentralization, and the relation between staff and line organization.

These three structural dimensions can also be combined to form a set of structural configurations or organizational types. First, there is the simple structure, usually a small organization led by the founder in a rather autocratic way. The organization is specialized around one product or service, so division of labour is low, and there is usually a tight coupling of people as they see each other continually. Second, we have the machine bureaucracy, usually a large and old organization producing standardized products and/or services. The structure displays great degree of specialization at the individual position, a functional grouping, and a rather tight coupling between people and tasks caused by highly specified rules, procedures, and routines that must be followed. The reliance on procedures and rules places significant decision-making power with those who make the rules, the technostructure. Third, there is the professional bureaucracy, also a large and old organization driven by rules and procedures. What distinguishes this structural form from the machine bureaucracy is that the rules and procedures are determined by professional bodies, and implemented by highly educated and skilled personnel. Grouping is made on the base of profession or skill, and coupling between groups may be rather weak. In addition, this model is characterized by much decision-making power placed in the hands of the professionals themselves, so the formal influence of hierarchical leaders and staff is usually rather weak. The fourth model is called the divisionalized structure, or the M-form.[116] These are large organizations, producing a great variety of products and services for a great variety of markets. Every division is a more or less self-contained unit, and decision-making power is delegated to the divisions. However, tight control is maintained by the corporate management through specification of output and revenues. Coupling is weak between divisions, but may be strong within them. The final configuration is labelled adhocracy. This type is characterized by a fluid structure and ambiguous specification of both jobs and groups, and thus has substantial overlap between people and groups. Work is mostly performed in time-limited projects, resulting in a type of matrix organization. Tasks are complex, so highly skilled personnel are required, which in turn results in decentralization of decision-making power and limited influence on the part of top managers. It is a flat structure. Coupling between individuals and groups varies from very strong within projects to rather weak between projects.

Each of these configurations usually also pursues different strategies.[117] The simple structure usually follows a niche strategy, while the machine bureaucracy is coupled with a strategy of "milking" a market by producing standardized products and services of good quality at a low price. The divisionalized structure is usually used to follow a diversification strategy, while the professional bureaucracy is linked to optimization of the core competencies in the organization. Finally, the adhocracy is closely linked to an innovation strategy.

Structural changes are thus possible both as adjustments along the three dimensions (individual positions, grouping, and decision-making system), and at the organizational level as change between configurations. We will return to this discussion in more detail later in the chapter.

TABLE 3.1: Main characteristics of the five configurations along the three structural dimensions

	INDIVIDUAL POSITION	GROUPING	DECISION-MAKING SYSTEM
SIMPLE STRUCTURE	Small degree of specialization and formalization	Little degree of formal grouping	Centralized to leader (often founder), no or very small staff
MACHINE BUREAUCRACY	Strong degree of specialization and formalization	Highly formalized groups, often based on function	Centralized, much decision making power in the technostructure making and monitoring rules
PROFESSIONAL BUREAUCRACY	Strong degree of specialization and formalization, formal education required	Highly formalized groups, often based on skill	Decentralized, considerable decision-making power in the hands of professional staff
DIVISIONALIZED STRUCTURE	(Depends on what configuration one finds with each division)	Divisions grouped according to product/service or market	Decentralized on daily matters, centralized on control of results/revenue
ADHOCRACY	Small degree of specialization and formalization	Little degree of formal grouping	Decentralized, decisions are made for the individual project

CHANGE CONTENT: INFORMAL ELEMENTS (CULTURE)

Organizational culture is commonly regarded as a multi-level phenomenon.[118] The core, or basic, level is a set of basic assumptions. This is about how we see the world, and how things and events are connected. Such assumptions are deeply embedded in us as a result of a life-long socialization process. Basic assumptions are connected to the next cultural level, that of values and norms. Values are evaluations of what is good or bad, and thus what we should strive for in life. Norms are unwritten rules about what is acceptable behaviour in different situations one may encounter. Basic assumptions, values, and norms are intra-psychological phenomena, and thus not directly visible for us. Thus, cultures are made visible through artefacts, or talk, action, and physical symbols.

Usually, following a long tradition of separating thought (mind) and action (body), the three first levels of culture – assumptions, values, and norms – are treated separately from the artefacts.[119] In this book we define culture as assumptions, values, and norms being shared by members of an organization. Even if there are fewer attempts to make cultural configurations, it is still possible to define the basic elements needed to describe the content of organizational culture.[120]

The first dimension is *basic assumptions* about the characteristics of the organization, what its *raison d'être is*, and in what domain or field it belongs. This is about the basic assumptions of the organizational culture. When writing this book, a discussion has emerged concerning Norway's biggest bank, DNB.[121] The discussion revolves around the question of whether DNB is a classic bank or whether it is a technology firm. As a backdrop for the discussion, we find a situation where banks are not competing against other banks any more, but rather against credit card companies, specialized financial startups, or even shops selling cars and furniture offering financial services earlier reserved for banks. To meet this type of competition, traditional banks must utilize the possibilities opened up by new technology.

Another example is found in a narrative on Canadian sport organizations.[122] The researchers found a cultural divide between sport organizations focusing on "sport for the masses", with a vision closely connected to contributing to society in general, and "elite organizations", with a more narrow focus on athletes with the potential to win competitions. The first group of organizations shared the assumption that sport was an integral aspect of a well-functioning society in creating health for a large group of the population and for encouraging voluntary work and increasing social capital. The elite organizations focused on the selection of a few, were geared towards competition, and did not have much interest in their social function. Although the organizations performed the same function, they diverged dramatically in their basic assumption of what they were.

The second dimension is connected to perceptions of "how we do things around here", or how one should act and behave in an organization. This represents the *values* of the organization. One very central part of organizational values is defining who one accepts as making decisions, or the legitimacy of decision makers.[123] In the previously mentioned study of Canadian sport organizations, the researcher found substantial differences between the elite and the social organizations. In the group of social sport organizations, there was a common perception of being a voluntary organization where equality was a basic value. Thus, all members participating were also viewed as legitimate decision makers, resulting in decisions often being delegated to the person in charge of a certain group of athletes. In the elite type of organization, decisions were expected to be taken by the formal leaders, as they were viewed as the most competent in making decisions strengthening the strategy.

The third cultural dimension is about criteria for evaluating what is acceptable or appropriate behaviour, and thus about the unwritten *norms* in the organization. One central question here is how the organization regards innovative behaviour.[124] Innovation will require a type of behaviour based on trying things out, experimenting, and perhaps failing. This stands in sharp contrast to organizations emphasizing predictability and reliability, which do not accept much deviation from what is pre-determined through rules and procedures. This tension can also be detected in the discussion of who should evaluate academic staff at universities.[125] Academics have traditionally used systems of peer review, not hierarchical control. Through an increased use of measuring the "production" of candidates through their number of publications, one may detect a shift where hierarchical control of academic work has become more legitimate.

As can be seen, culture is closely connected with the informal power structure of an organization. Culture is, to a large degree, about who decides what is good or bad, what is appropriate or not, and consequently who will be rewarded or punished. Culture also influences the basic premises for making decisions, and how premises should be balanced. And, in the end, it is culture that determines who is regarded as a legitimate decision maker. In the same way as formal elements are expected to correlate, one should also expect cultural dimensions to correlate with power structures. Universities all over the Western world can illustrate this point. Universities are organizations that have gone through quite dramatic changes in the past few decades, many of these affecting cultural dimensions.[126] First of all, there is a basic discussion of what a university should be: an arena for free and critical thought, independent of powerful actors like state and business, or a responsive institution focusing on the wishes and needs of external actors. Second, this is directly connected to the question of who the legitimate decision makers are. Are they academics themselves through some kind of peer review, or should they also be under hierarchical control? Should one accept more professionalized leaders although they might lack qualifications in specific fields? And, finally, how should academics be rewarded – on the basis of quality, or on more narrow criteria of output and production? Discussions of this type can be found in most organizations.

LINKAGES BETWEEN FORMAL AND INFORMAL ELEMENTS – INSTITUTIONS AND ARCHETYPES

By separating formal and informal elements, it becomes quite clear that the content of change may very greatly from one organizational change to another. A change in how tasks are distributed among departments is quite different from changing concepts of "how we do it around here". At the same time it is of great importance to acknowledge organizations as systems, implying that elements are connected. The linkage between organizational elements is one of the main theoretical contributions of the so-called "new institutionalism".[127] Formal and informal elements constitute wholes, by some called archetypes, defined as:[128]

> (...) an underlying interpretive scheme, or set of beliefs and values, that is embodied in an organization's structures and systems. An archetype is thus a set of structures and systems that consistently embodies a single interpretive scheme. (...) Structures and systems, from our perspective, are not neutral instruments but embody – wittingly or otherwise – intentions, aspirations, and purposes.

Figure 3.3 illustrates the above argument.

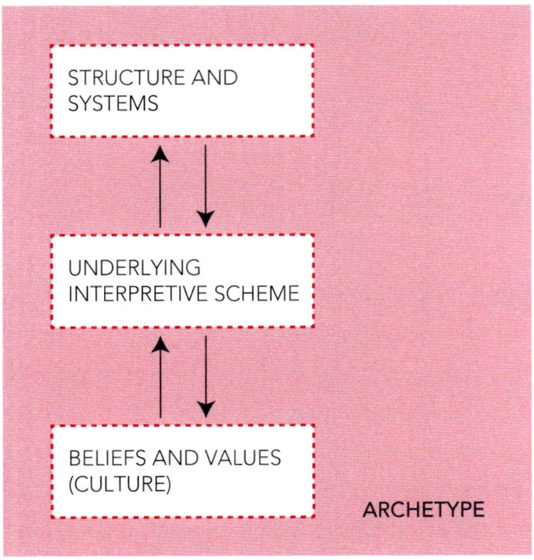

FIGURE 3.3: Organizations as archetypes

The notion of archetypes can be connected to the discussion in the previous paragraph on structural configurations. Each structural configuration may be connected to a specific type of culture, as table 3.2 displays.

TABLE 3.2: Cultural characteristics of structural configurations

STRUCTURAL CONFIGURATION	CULTURAL CHARACTERISTICS
THE SIMPLE STRUCTURE	Focus on the basic product/service. Organization founded on some kind of protest against dominating actors in the field. Strong focus on the founder/owner, sometimes verging on idolatry. Less focus on markets or customers.[129]
MACHINE BUREACRACY	Making production processes work optimally. A strong focus on process, application of rules and routines, and the improvement of processes. Streamlining production processes, strong focus on efficiency. Acceptance of hierarchical power. Less focus on markets or customers.[130]
PROFESSIONAL BUREAUCRACY	Professional standards and skills are the most important factors. A strong focus on professional and scientific production of knowledge. Peer review, and autonomy from hierarchy. An attitude, verging on paternalism, that one knows better than the customer what the customer needs.[131]
THE DIVISIONALIZED STRUCTURE	(Varies according to the type of configuration one finds within each division.) Common for all: strong focus on results and revenue, combined with an emphasis on autonomy from the mother company.[132]
ADHOCRACY	Creativity and flexibility most important values. Employees living as much for the job as from the job, vague distinctions between working life and private life. An emphasis on "fun". Customer needs often second to creativity.[133]

Treating organizations as archetypes has consequences for how we view organizations, and thus how we see organizational change. As a first step, it makes us aware of the possibility that change in one part of the organization may affect other elements. Changing the content of a job or a routine – both structural changes – can affect the basic beliefs and values the organization is grounded on. Change in one element can cause a chain reaction of changes in other elements. This insight is not very different from the insights provided by regarding organizations as systems. More important is the insight that the coupling of formal and informal elements may vary.[134] Put another way: not all elements are equally connected to each other. Some formal elements may be tightly linked cultural elements as they constitute important symbols (artefacts) of important cultural elements. Change in these formal elements will thus activate interests and emotions connected to central beliefs and values.[135] Attempts to centralize decision-making power in a hospital or a university may be viewed as an "attack" on professional freedom, a central value for professionals. Decentralization of decision-making power in a machine bureaucracy will be regarded as a violation of the values of stability and predictability, while the introduction of a new leader in the simple structure may be seen as "a murdering of the founder's lifework".

Real and symbolic change

Planned change is grounded on assumptions about causality, that changes in one element will cause changes in other elements. This was illustrated in figure 3.2 (p. 56). As an example, a change in structure will produce a change in behaviour, and a change in behaviour will produce a change in results. This, however, is only the ideal. In most real cases, the causal linkages may be loose or non-existent as there are several factors that may disconnect assumed causes and effects.

First of all, there is usually a highly ambiguous connection between changes in an organization's production and the results that they generate.[136] Many reasons can be given for this, for instance that the change in production or behaviour is not sufficiently great to affect the results. It could also be a case where competitors have changed concurrently, thus nullifying the effect of change. And it could be that the change in production simply was not the correct solution to the problem encountered. It will not help much for an organization's results to change the service level of the front personnel, if that is not what the customer wanted. Finally, the causal links between production and results are for many organizations complex and difficult to understand. This is often the case for organizations involved in complex service production. For such tasks it is difficult, sometimes impossible, to establish the causal link between an organization's activity and the results produced.[137] Police work may serve as an example of this. The police may change their way of working, but it will always be difficult to establish any clear link between such changes and changes in police results such as the incidence of crime or the number of cases resolved. Other, external factors may influence the results more than the organizational change, for instance changes in the general economy.

Second, changes in organizational culture do not automatically produce results in the production processes and behaviour. One explanation for this disruption is that intentions and attitudes are only loosely coupled with action.[138] We do not necessarily do what we believe is the right thing to do! A supplementary explanation is that structural elements do not "allow" changes in behaviour. If the organization punishes us for doing what we think is right, many will refrain from doing it. Such situations may occur when cultural change is not followed by a change in incentive systems. A final explanation is that cultural change is limited to "espoused theories", and that "theories in use" – those that guide action – have not been changed.[139] People in the organization have only learned to talk correctly about the new values, not to enact them.

Third, it is also possible that structural change is unconnected with production processes. One of the most studied phenomena in organization science is how loose the coupling between formal structure and behaviour is in many instances.[140] Changes in the formal elements of the organization – structure, systems, and strategies – risk ending up as "empty changes" or changes in structure without changes in behaviour.[141] An important stream within the new institutionalist studies on organizations is that behaviour and formal elements are often very loosely coupled.[142]

Loose coupling is a central concept in the previous discussion, and refers to a situation where change in one element is only weakly connected with any effects.[143] Special attention has been devoted to the missing link between formal elements and what some writers term the *praxis* of the organization.[144] Several studies indicate that people simply do not act as is expected by the formal structure, systems, and strategies. Change is not transformed into action; it remains "just talk". In such instances, the concept of *symbolic change* emerges.[145] Formal elements, machines, and strategies are changed, but the actual behaviour of people in the organization remains the same. New computers are bought, but employees continue using the old ones. New strategies are defined, but people keep one working according to the old strategy. And new rules for meetings can be proposed, but people still conduct meetings as they have always done.

Initially, symbolic change has a negative flavour, of something that did not work. But we must also be open to the possibility that not all changes, especially in formal elements, are intended to have any effect on behaviour. Formal elements like strategies and structures are highly visible, making them visible also for external stakeholders.[146] Change in this element may thus function as a signal to external groups, signalling for instance compliance with societal demands or with the desire to appear to be a modern organization. This, in turn, may increase legitimacy and support. Legitimacy is, of course, heavily dependent on how efficient and effective an organization is, but it is also based on appearance. What it looks like (symbols such as structures and strategies) and how it sounds are important for how it appears to external parties. Producing the right symbols is important in gaining legitimacy.[147]

Symbolic change may thus be an intentional change. Visible elements are changed to convey certain signals to external actors, not necessarily to create effects on production processes and behaviour. This is a strategy that is labelled by some as intended hypocrisy.[148] You say something, and do something else. The main point here is that organizations are expected to have a certain appearance. Such expectations are not always possible to combine with internal demands for productivity. One prominent and actual example is the increasing use of "certificates", or arrangements thatindicate some kind of approval as being certified. Organizations are certified as "green", "energy savers", "respecting diversity", "fighting child labour", and many other things.[149] Such certificates can be regarded as a part of the organization's formal structure, and are often loosely coupled to the praxis in the organization. Still, a considerable amount of time, money, and energy are invested in processes to obtain certification.

The scope of change – incremental or radical

Organizations, like humans, go through changes of varying scope and radicality. Some changes are dramatic, and represent ruptures with the past, while other changes are more incremental and represent a development of what one already knows and does. If you think back on your life, you will surely be able to detect the more dramatic shifts, because they were necessary steps in becoming what you are today.[150] Such ruptures with the past could be awareness of one's sexuality, the first boyfriend, moving away from home, having children, or getting divorced. Life consists of periods when we develop within a rather stable and well-known framework. We work with perfecting what we have already learned, and we continue to learn from our successes and failures. Thus, we continuously get better adapted to a specific context, be it a job, a family situation, orfriendships. But we change jobs, families are dissolved, and friends move out of town. Such changes are episodic and represent something unknown, and will in many instances be perceived as stressful and difficult to handle. The situation is new, so we do not have a suitable repertoire to meet it.

Groups, organizations, and societies seem to go through the same phases of relative stability and ruptures or crises.[151] Such a view of change is often called a "punctuated equilibrium perspective", a perspective we discussed under the heading of life-cycle perspective in chapter 2.[152] In this perspective, organizations are assumed to develop rather slowly for lengthy periods. During these periods, an organization constantly improves the fit between the different elements of the organization (goals, strategies, structures, culture, and power relations), and the fit between the organization and its environment. The organization is moving towards a point or equilibrium where all elements are in balance. Those organizations that master this developmental process most effectively will be best suited to winning the competition and to producing the best services and products.

But suddenly, organizations face new challenges, events that were impossible to foresee. These might be abrupt political turnarounds, a natural disaster, the emergence of a "competence breaking" technology, terrorism, sudden economic shifts, or corruption and fraud.[153] Such examples can be found everywhere. The traditional watch industry all over the world had not predicted the emergence of digital clocks, shipowners with a fleet of sailing ships did not foresee the revolution represented by steam engines, the music industry was not prepared for the transition from CDs to digital streaming, and many organizations struggle to understand how 3D printing is going to affect their business.[154] Public organizations have experienced shocks like an explosion of refugees after the so-called Arab Spring and the war in Syria, the rise of a strong political right wing, an American president threatening to severely limit world trade, and the UK leaving the EU. Such events are not possible to plan for; they are per definition surprises. Still, organizations have to address these surprises or shocks to survive.

In this book, these two types of change will be labelled as development versus rupture. These two concepts have several similarities to other concepts used to describe more or less the same phenomenon. Some distinguish between exploitation and exploration,[155] some between incremental (stepwise) and strategic change,[156] while others have called them continuous versus episodic change,[157] evolution versus revolution,[158] transition versus transformation,[159] convergence versus divergence or reorientation,[160] or first- and second-order change.[161] A pet child has many names. However, to define empirically what constitutes development versus rupture, it is necessary to link it to the content of change.

SCOPE OF CHANGE – PRODUCT/SERVICE AND MARKET

Change may take place because an organization has developed a new product or service they want to offer or sell to the market. On the other hand, organizations may want to penetrate new markets with products and services already well known to them. Such changes are, in literature on organizational strategy, often termed strategic changes.[162] Changes in products/services and markets are usually illustrated in a fourfold table.

		MARKET	
		EXISTING	NEW
PRODUCT	EXISTING	No strategic change	Introduction of an existing product in a new market
	NEW	Introduction of a new product in an existing market	Introduction of a new product in a new market

FIGURE 3.4: The product-market matrix

A well-known example of a new product in an existing market was the introduction of Apple's iPad. The product was at first aimed at customers who already owned Apple products, like computers and iPhones, but still it represented something totally new. In another example, the Norwegian firm Scanrope has based its 200 years of existence on the production of rope and wires for boats. With the emergence of the Norwegian oil industry, the focus of the firm shifted from boats to oil rigs and other oil installations at sea. The market was new, but the products remained mostly the same.[163] Amazon has built its enormous success on a never-ending introduction of new products in its portfolio, and has moved from being a bookseller to being a distributor of everything from antiques to cars, via dogfood and back to books.[164]

In general terms, the scope of change increases as one moves from the upper left to the lower right of figure 3.4. The most dramatic strategy change is to introduce new products in new markets, and this will represent a reorientation or a rupture with the past.[165] Moving into new markets or introducing new products will also represent dramatic changes, as this will require new competencies, new technologies, new distribution channels, and new cooperating partners. Remaining in the upper left square of figure 3.4 is not the same as inertia. Rather, it represents a situation where the organization changes continuously to improve what it already knows and does, and is thus a less dramatic change.

THE SCOPE OF CHANGE – TECHNOLOGY AND PRODUCTION

Much of what has been written about change as rupture has been linked to technological innovations.[166] Technology is not only hardware or machines, but also entails knowledge and the general process of production. However, technological innovations clearly represent different degrees of "newness". A common way to classify technological innovations is according to the degree to which they are "competence destroying" or "competence enhancing".[167]

Competence-destroying technology represents a rupture in the way an organization has previously produced its product or services. Such technological innovations will press for dramatic decisions in the organization.[168] First, the organization must decide what to do with the old machine technology, or hardware. Should we try to use it a bit longer, or do we need to make an investment now to keep up? These are important economic decisions that will challenge the finances of the organization. One example of this is how newspapers all over the world had invested large sums in printing technology, only to wake up one morning to find that physical printing had been made obsolete by computers and desktop printing, and later that printing on paper had been made obsolete by online editions. Digital technology thus erased the value of the whole machine capital of the media organizations. Arguably even more challenging is how innovations rupture the basic knowledge and competence that the organization is founded on. Remaining with the media example, the shift from physical to digital production and distribution also made many people's competencies obsolete. The old knowledge was just not applicable any more, demanding either a shift in personnel or a radical new training of existing staff.

Still, technological changes do not always represent ruptures. Up to now, the steady increase in information processing and storing capacity of computers does not represent a rupture. It resembles a kind of evolution more than a revolution.

At some point in time, the stepwise change may add up to a radical change. Some claim that we have reached that point today, and that computers have reached a level of information handling capacity where they can "think for themselves". "Artificial intelligence" is not the product of a totally new technology. Rather, it is a product of existing technology having reached a level of maturity that opens the door to totally new areas of use.[169] Even at such an incremental pace, many existing organizations struggle to keep up. Technological development has, for instance, made it possible to run retail stores without personnel. Amazon was, again, the first to take advantage of this development.[170] Through image detection, computers register what customers take with them from the shelves. These goods are then registered in an application on the customer's smart phone, and the payment is made digitally via a credit card or another digital solution. Amazon, which was never in the retail business before, may succeed with such a concept rather easily. It is more difficult for the traditional retail stores, because they have to obliterate the technology they have perfected over dozens and dozens of years. So even a stepwise, incremental change may be so radical as to threaten the existence of many organizations.

In the same way, automation is not necessarily a radical change for an organization. It represents a process innovation, a new way to produce a product or a service. As pointed out by preachers of the Business Process Reengineering (BPR) gospel, there is a danger that automation will make futile processes more efficient. Thus the slogan "Don't automate, obliterate!"[171] In this sense, process innovations may be radical in the sense that they produce totally new production lines, where some production processes become obsolete while new ones are introduced. However, changes in production processes are not only technological changes. To function in an efficient way, the organizations need to build systems and structures, as well as cultures, supporting the new processes.

THE SCOPE OF CHANGE – CHANGE OF CONFIGURATION OR ARCHETYPE

A basic notion in a configurational perspective on organizations is that, to obtain efficiency, there must be a fit between the organizational elements, and that in periods of relative stability there will be a move towards convergence among the elements.[172] Incremental change will, in this context, contain actions geared towards obtaining a fit between the different structural elements within the boundaries of a configuration. Within the framework of a professional bureaucracy one may experiment with delegation and centralization to obtain an optimal division of responsibility between professional and administrative staff. Still, such changes occur only within what the configuration "allows". Centralizing too much to the administrative staff may constitute a rupture with a basic element of the professional bureaucracy: professional autonomy.

A radical change in a configurational perspective thus takes place when an organization moves from one configuration to another. One example might be a professional bureaucracy changing into a machine bureaucracy, or a bureaucracy changing into an adhocracy. The latter change has taken place in many manufacturing organizations over the last few decades as production has become increasingly automated, leaving an organization devoid of blue collar workers, where the only employees are highly skilled personnel running the organization with "joy sticks".[173]

Cultural changes can both be radical and incremental. First of all, not all values and norms are equally essential.[174] Most organizational cultures contain some core values, while other values are more peripheral. In some cases, what are called values are just "ways of doing things" that have become routine. Reflect on the following values from a university: 1) students' learning should be based on their own activities, and 2) knowledge is best disseminated through lectures. In most universities, the first value will probably be closer to a core value than the second, indicating that changing the first value is a more radical step than changing the second. The activity expected by students is essential to the idea of what an university really is, while how knowledge is disseminated is probably more a question of what is the most efficient way of doing things. If new knowledge shows other techniques to be more efficient, then lectures can be abandoned.

Second, the radicality of cultural change can also be defined as to what degree new values and norms are perceived as different from the existing ones. Culture is per definition something we learn, and must be acquired through a learning process. Cultural change thus implies some sort of retraining.[175] Cognitive psychology tells us that learning takes at different degrees of complexity.[176] One type of learning is to expand what one already knows, which in the context of organizational culture will imply a strengthening of existing values. This is an incremental change. Basic values and norms remain the same, and are only marginally changed. Cultural change is somewhat more radical if new values and norms are added to the existing ones. This could be the introduction of a value concerning an aspect of the organization that has not been given much attention before. One example could be norms on customer handling in an organization traditionally most focused on production. The focus on customer handling is not a threat to the existing values and norms, but comes as an extra. Even more radical will the change be if existing values and norms are combined in new ways, for instance changing the priority of norms and values. In many organizations there will be values and norms connected to both production, professional quality, and processes, on the one hand, and to markets and customers, on the other. Still, such values and norms may have different priorities, indicating that one will be prioritized in situations where there is a conflict. Taking good care of the customer may be time consuming, and thus take time and energy away from the production process. In an organization where production values dominate, this value will be prioritized in meetings with the customer. For the customer, this might result in a situation where he or she feels ignored. Changing priorities of values and norms may be a rather radical change. The most radical change is when an organization makes a break with existing values, usually on the grounds that the existing values are dysfunctional for the organization. In such a case, people in the organization not only have to acquire new values and norms, but also unlearn the existing ones. Such changes represent a "cultural recreation".[177]

The main idea behind treating organizations as archetypes, as we discussed earlier, is to see them as an interwoven whole of both cultural and structural elements constituting what can be called the organization's "deep structure".[178] The deep structure consists of a set of basic assumptions about the organization, how things should be executed, and who are legitimate evaluators of what is done. Such structures are stable because they usually have a long history, and because there seems to be an tendency in all organizations to strengthen existing assumptions.

In such a perspective, radical change will take place when an organization shifts between archetypes. Such change is radical, first, because it represents a rupture with existing assumptions, norms, and values, and will thus imply some sort of unlearning. Second, a change of archetype will also imply a radical change in structure and strategy. A study of English municipalities in the 1970s and 80s was able to detect two different archetypes. In one group the researchers placed municipalities that looked much like professional bureaucracies. The organization was grouped according to professional skills, evaluation and control were conducted by peers, units were loosely coupled, and recruitment was based almost solely on formal competence.[179] The other group consisted of municipalities that looked more like divisionalized firms, or – using the researchers' original labelling – "corporate bureaucracy". The structure was more centralized, the grouping was to a larger degree based on programmes or clients (market), many coordinating mechanisms were applied, there was a clear hierarchical line from leaders to employees, and recruiting was based as much on personal skills as professional knowledge and education. During the 1980s, the researchers observed a movement where many of the professional bureaucracies changed into corporate bureaucracies. This was classified as a radical change, a change from one archetype to another. Furthermore, they observed that "major organizational change, or passage between archetypes, is less common than is inertia–archetype stability."[180]

The main reason for this according to the researchers,[181] with support from others, is that archetypical change is much more difficult than change within the context of an archetype. Such findings also send important signals to those working with planned change as they show that the radicality of change may have a significant impact on the probability of succeeding with the change effort.

INCREMENTAL OR RADICAL? BOTH, PLEASE.

Much of the traditional organizational development (OD) literature seems to be based on an idea that continuous incremental change decreases the probability of radical change.[182] The previous discussion questions such an assumption. Some changes are just not possible to plan for, and thus not possible to adapt incrementally to. Great shocks in the market or technological discontinuities are not possible to predict. Thus all organizations must be prepared for shocks and ruptures. This represents a great challenge for change agents, something the following should make clear:[183]

> The dilemma confronting managers and organizations is clear. In the short run they must constantly increase the fit or alignment of strategy, structure, and culture. This is the world of evolutionary change. But this is not enough for sustained success. In the long-run, managers may be required to destroy the very alignment that has made their organizations successful. For managers, this means operating part of the time in a world characterized by periods of relatively stability and incremental innovation, and part of the time in a world characterized by revolutionary change.

Organizations have to change continuously to improve within a set framework, configuration or archetype. But dramatic and unpredictable events happen, and there is no way to control them. In such instances, it is of no use incrementally changing what one is accustomed to doing. Radical change becomes necessary. New technology has to be acquired and put to use, and the old technology has to be discarded or unlearned. Old structures must be left behind, and new models must be designed. Old values and norms must be reconsidered, and new ones have to be internalized. Organizations may have to change their basic strategies, develop new products and markets, rearrange the structure, and build a whole new culture.[184] Such changes are really dramatic, and much research indicates that it is hard for organizations to survive such change attempts.[185] Organizations must be able to change both incrementally and radically to survive in the long run.

Recent research, however, points to a paradox concerning incremental and radical change. It seems that the better an organization is at changing incrementally, the less capable it is of changing radically.[186] A much talked-about example is found in the phenomenon called "disruptive innovation".[187] Such innovations might be technological in nature, as in the case of Uber by using telephone applications to outcompete traditional taxis. Or they can be related to business models, as when Norwegian and Ryanair challenge the whole airline industry by only offering low-fare trips. And they can be political, as they are in the case when German authorities opened the door to banning the use of diesel-driven cars in all large cities in Germany, thus threatening the entire, and very powerful, German car industry.

Hearing these stories, one question unavoidably pops up: Why didn't a resourceful and skilled company like SAS foresee the market that the airline Norwegian stepped in to exploit? Why didn't large car companies like BMW and Volkswagen predict the coming of electric cars? How could the taxi business not see the possibility of apps? Why is it that it seems to be mostly outsiders – like Tesla, Uber, and Norwegian – with no experience from the business who manage to see and exploit the opportunities created by technological, market, and political changes?

One explanation is found in what has been labelled "the productivity paradox",[188] the "competency trap",[189] or the "success syndrome".[190] The better one is at refining existing activities, the harder it gets to leave something you have refined into perfection. When someone succeeds in becoming the "best pupil in the class" it is very tough being confronted with the idea that what you master is not of any use. The problem with being the best is that it is so hard to accept no longer being the best. It is like going from the top directly to the bottom.

Instead of accepting such change, they will resist it with all possible resources.[191] At the same time it is necessary to accept ruptures – the ability to go through with "creative destruction"[192] and destroy what one masters – as an integral part of long-term survival.

This dilemma or paradox is often referred to as "exploitation" versus "exploration".[193] Organizations good at exploitation and at refining what they already know and do will increase productivity within the given framework. Increased productivity will probably increase income through the "milking" of known products and markets. At the same time, such a focus on increased productivity seems to make organizations less apt to see new opportunities, or to explore. Thus they often lose new opportunities because they have developed a blind zone for new things. On the other hand, we find organizations good at exploring and seeing new opportunities. But these organizations will often lack the ability to convert opportunities into practical and commercial activity. Many innovative organizations are characterized by personnel losing interest in the product once it is designed. To exploit the innovation is treated as "boring" and "not challenging enough". This dilemma is illustrated in figure 3.5.

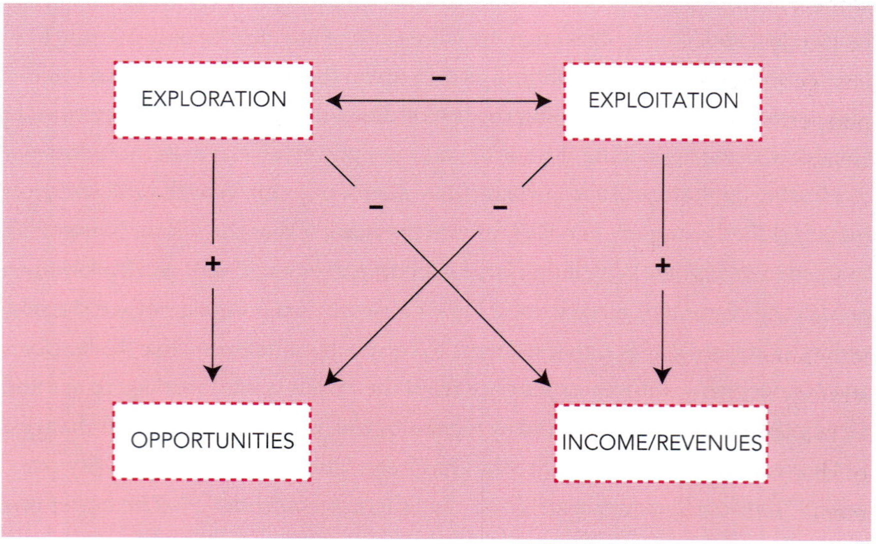

FIGURE 3.5: The productivity paradox – the dilemma between exploitation and exploration[194]

The productivity paradox makes us aware of organizations' tendency to develop systematic biases in their span of attention. Organizations may survive a long time based on innovation, but at some point in time opportunities must be transformed into products and services that someone is willing to pay for. And organizations may thrive, for a period, on exploiting a certain technology or market, but to survive in the long run they also need to seize new opportunities. As a consequence, organizations seem doomed to go through crises. The productivity paradox has receive a considerable amount of scientific attention in the last few years. It is almost a search for the Holy Grail to see whether it is possible for organizations to master both exploitation and exploration at the same time. We will delve more deeply into this matter in chapter 8.

Summing up

The main message in this chapter is that change is not a uniform phenomenon. Changes can and will affect different aspects of organizations. Thus this chapter, hopefully, makes it clear that changes may differ, not only from organization to organization, but also within the same organization. Some changes are cultural, some are technological, and others may be structural. And changes may even be purely symbolic. The content of change will necessarily affect any choice of change strategy, as it will represent the main levers of change.[195] If we uphold the perspective of organizations as systems, we must acknowledge the possibility that change in one element will have consequences for other elements. Still, it is possible that different changes may include a different number of elements. Some changes may be limited to a few aspects, while others will be system-wide changes.[196] These insights should inform any choice of change strategy. Changing an organization's culture should require a different strategy than attempts to change structures or strategies. And system-wide changes must surely demand another strategy than more limited and incremental changes.

In addition, the scope of change should surely have consequences for the choice of change strategy. This chapter has delved into two general types of scope – incremental and radical. Incremental change is adjustment of the current organizational form, improving the balance and fit between elements within the framework of a system, an archetype, or a configuration. This is a change path characterized by convergence.[197] Radical change must follow a different change path, as it represents a break with everything the organizations knows and probably loves. Between these two ideal types, we will find a wide range of variations.

Knowing the scope of change is essential to planned change. Radical change will imply a strategy where many elements are "attacked" at the same time, and that the change strategy is comprehensive and massive. Radical change will affect many interests, and one should expect mobilization of strong counterforces. A more incremental type of change is probably possible by addressing single or a few elements at a time, and adjusting through small steps. In short, radical change will be more difficult to succeed with than more incremental change. The micro-foundations of such a claim are to be found in the processes spurred by a change initiative. This is the topic of chapter 5.

Chapter 4

Where is change taking place? The change context

One of the questions that has received most attention within research on organizational change is: Why do some organizations succeed with change, while others do not?[198] One possible answer is, of course, that those attempting to change did not choose the right strategy, or that leadership in the change process was lacking. These rather obvious types of explanations, although they may be correct, may hinder us from seeing that different organizations have different possibilities for change. Change may be easier to implement in some organizations than in others. Some organizations may have a better capacity for absorbing impulses from the environment,[199] some may be more capable of learning from experience,[200] some may be more flexible,[201] and some may function in environments that are more open for change.[202]

Thus we need a more detailed specification of where change is taking place, and what the change context is.[203] As discussed in the first chapter, one can argue that organizations first and foremost are created with an eye for stability and predictability, not flexibility and change. In and around any organization there will be a set of "stability forces",[204] making it easier or more difficult to change the organization. A metaphor could be the difference between changing a lump of clay and a rock. The rock is hard and difficult to change, while the lump of clay is easy to shape. At the same time, the possibility to change an object will depend on the outer context. The lump of clay, for instance, will get harder to form the lower the temperature is in the room.

Organizations thus consist of both an internal and an external context. The *internal context* refers to characteristics of the organizations, while the *external context* refers to characteristics of the organization's environment. Context is important because it can either facilitate or limit planned change. Planned change may be very difficult in some contexts, and more easy to conduct in other contexts. Our challenge is then to define these characteristics. It has been indicated that organizations have their "characteristic level of change", or put somewhat differently: "Each organization has its own unique comfort zone with respect to the rate and tempo of change. (…) When a change exceeds this comfort zone, action will be taken to resolve the discomfort."[205]

This "comfort zone" may vary from organization to organization because of variations in the internal and external contexts.

The internal context

The starting point is an assumption that organizations are different, even though they can be described by the same theories, concepts and language.[206] A hospital represents a totally different context than a consultancy firm, and a clothes shop is quite different from a garage. The structures vary, personnel have different backgrounds, and informal power relations and organizational culture will probably vary as well. These differences make it difficult to treat organizational change only in generic terms. How change happens, what is perceived as dramatic or incremental, and the possibilities of succeeding with planned change will vary from organization to organization. As Henry Mintzberg says, it will be a totally different thing to change a professional bureaucracy than a machine bureaucracy. In the following we will discuss central elements of the internal context in more detail.

TECHNOLOGICAL CONTEXT

Organizations perform different tasks, using different technologies or tools. A producer of tubes for the oil and gas industry needs employees with a high level of competence on steel constructions, as well as expensive machines. A hospital requires employees with long formal training to be able to perform complex surgery, as well as expensive machines for scanning and x-rays. Investments often represent barriers to change in the sense that the larger the investment made, the harder it is to change.[207] This is a general insight; the more you have invested in a relationship, the harder it is to end it; the more you have paid for a car, the more difficult it is to admit that it is not very good or practical; and the longer you have attended a study, the harder it is to break out and start studying something completely new.

The concept "sunk cost" entails this phenomenon. "Sunk cost" means something like investments already made.[208] All organizations make investments in people, machines, routines, and knowledge that are difficult to sell or to transfer to other tasks or functions. Hannan and Freeman express this as follows: "An organization's investments in buildings, machinery and specialized personnel represent assets that are not easy to transfer to new tasks and functions. The way these investments (sunk costs) limit adaptation is obvious."[209]

Smelters, for instance, invest in large buildings usually located physically close to a power plant and a harbour, in large production machines, and in specific routines to run the processes. A negative change in demand for the smelters' products will produce a difficult decision situation.[210] Making a change may imply buying new machinery, or moving to a new location, necessitating new buildings. The old machines and buildings will have little value as they are hard to sell, and the competence of the workers is not much sought after in the market. At the same time one can never be sure that new investments will be profitable. In such cases, it is normal to "wait and see" and "hope for the best". Decisions to change are postponed as long as possible. The investments have introduced slowness into the organization.

Many organizations will also have made investments that are highly specific, that is that they are tailor-made to particular products and particular customers. Asset specificity denotes the degree of coupling between an organization's investments and a specific set of products and customers.[211] In situations of high asset specificity, change is difficult because the technology is tightly linked to a limited set of products and customers. One example of such a situation is found in the reactions of organizations involved in the weapons industry after the end of the Cold War.[212] The fall of the Berlin Wall in 1989 and the disintegration of the Communist regime sparked a general disarmament in all Western countries. Many organizations in the weapons industry wanted to transfer their production to civilian products, but soon found out that the technology was very difficult to transform. Instead of changing – a process that would have been prohibitively expensive for some and simply impossible for others – the industry invested large sums in lobbyism to persuade governments to refrain from reducing the military budgets. To summarise, it could be claimed that the more investments an organization has made, and the higher the asset specificity of these investments, the more difficult change will be.

STRATEGIC CONTEXT

An organization's strategy can in general terms be defined as the specific mix of products and markets on which it concentrates. In much of the classic strategy literature it is assumed that organizations with the ability to prioritize and select, and to maintain these priorities and choices over time, will outperform those trying to please everyone.[213] Organizations unable to choose one strategy will soon find themselves "stuck in the middle" without the possibility to exploit the benefits of any of the strategies. One example is to be found in organizations trying both to be exclusive (differentiation strategy) and to produce as cheaply as possible (cost leader strategy).

Recent research, however, indicates that the success of choosing and holding on to one specific strategy is dependent on the organization's need for change.[214] Such a strategic choice locks the organization onto one track, and enables it to exploit this single track. All resources and all attention are focused on one market and a sett of products or services. The more specific a strategy is, and the longer one holds on to it, the more the organization has invested in that specific strategy. Thus, as with sunk costs and asset specificity, it becomes hard to break out of the chosen strategy. In situations when disruptive innovations emerge, organizations with strong and focused strategies will probably have considerable problems adapting to them. Organizations combining strategies may, on the other hand, more easily change from one strategy to another when the situation demands it.

STRUCTURAL CONTEXT

As early as the 1950s researchers identified a strong link between an organization's structure and its ability to innovate and change.[215] Innovative organizations were labelled as "organic", characterized by fluid structures, flat hierarchies, and little standardization. These organizations were contrasted with the "mechanistic" structure, a structure with strong bureaucratic characteristics, displaying limited abilities for innovation. This distinction in structures was further developed by Henry Mintzberg (1979) in his work on organizational configurations. One of Mintzberg's main points is that different configurations have different abilities to innovate and change.

On one end of the scale we find the machine bureaucracy with several structural characteristics hindering change. First, this is a structure based on rules and routines, or what has been called "frozen experience".[216] By doing the same thing over and over again, one learns how to perform the task to perfection. To exploit this knowledge, it is usually formalized in written rules and routines, making it impersonal and as such possible to transfer to new employees. This mechanism makes machine bureaucracies extremely efficient in repeating the same task every day for a long time. But strong standardization also entails important weaknesses, especially in respect to organizational change. One such obvious weakness is how a strong focus on rules and routines over time makes it more difficult for employees to see new things, things that do not fit in with the rules and routines.[217] People became more interested in following rules than in solving problems, a phenomenon sometimes labelled as the "bureaucracy sickness".[218] Thus, a strong focus on rules and procedures seems to complicate adaptation to changes in the problems to be solved or in the environment.

Second, a heavy reliance on rules and procedures will also create and reinforce an internal focus. The focus for both leaders and employees will be on the production process, how to exploit existing machinery and competence optimally.[219] Bureaucracies have a tendency to focus on the "static efficiency" – the efficiency of what one is currently doing – instead of the "dynamic efficiency" or being able to do different things when the necessity or opportunity arises.[220] This internal focus makes it less probable that bureaucratic organizations will be able to detect changes in the external environment, and they will thus be less able to adapt.

Third, there is a tendency for bureaucratic organizations to be centralized. It is regarded as dysfunctional and possibly disturbing for a smoothly running production process if employees use their own judgment. Deviations and irregularities must be detected on the shop floor, but the problem must be taken to higher hierarchical levels to find a solution. Thus, propositions for change coming from the operative core have to proceed through several hierarchical layers to be approved. Such centralization has been shown to be negatively correlated to the ability to change.[221] Decisions take time, and systems are so rigid that they hinder adaptation, or what we in the previous chapter called incremental change.

Thus it has become almost standard knowledge that machine bureaucracies are inert, while adhocracies are more continually changing.[222] Concurrently, there are empirical studies indicating that centralized, sometimes on the verge of autocratic, organizations change more often than decentralized structures, and that changes are often relatively radical.[223] The explanation is that in centralized structures, for instance where the owner is also the leader, there will be few possibilities to have an influence on the decisions made by the leader. Thus, leaders are able to effect changes, also radical ones, more or less on their own. Furthermore, centralization may also be a prerequisite for radical change as radical change will affect many, and may thus be expected to generate considerable resistance. Without a strong and powerful leader, such attempts at change may end up in endless negotiations, compromises, and, consequently, little real change.

TIGHT AND LOOSE COUPLING

Organizations will also vary considerably with respect to how tightly they are coupled to their environment, and how tightly coupled units and levels within the organization are.[224] Tight coupling to the environment implies that both individuals and organizational units are regularly in contact with external actors within their domain. For the individual employee, this may include attending external seminars; regular meetings with customers, collaborators and subcontractors; visiting other organizations; and participating in joint projects.[225] At the unit level, this can include units with special responsibility for scanning the environment, for customer relations, and for market analysis. Organizations tightly coupled with their environments will increase the probability of discovering changes in the environment, and thus of being able to adapt at an early stage.

At the same time, tight coupling with the environment may make radical change harder.[226] Tight coupling demands resources as it is time consuming and costly to devote people and units to external activities only. As a result, the external contact may be narrowed to only the most important actors and markets. Thus, tight coupling will only be carried out with limited parts of the environment, in turn making it harder to detect changes taking place outside these limited areas.

Tight coupling internally is the case when change in one part of the organization produces rapid and clear consequences for other parts.[227] A classic example is the production of cars (or any other physical product). First, the car must be designed, next, the bodywork must be constructed before the engine can be put into place, and then the interior can be installed. All operations have to take place in a carefully designed sequential process. If the sequences are altered, or one of the sequences does not work, the whole production line breaks down. Weak or loose coupling is found when what happens one place in the organization has few or no direct consequences for other places. One example of loose coupling is found in hospitals, where what goes on in surgery has little to do with what goes on in the psychiatric ward. The different units may be interdependent, but it is hard to find out precisely how.[228] Many modern organizations – hospitals, universities, consultancy firms, banks, and telecom companies – are in principle loosely coupled. It is difficult for employees in customer care in a bank to see how they are related to employees dealing in currency. Those employed in the currency department do not necessarily care much about what goes on in the private banking department.

In a change perspective, loose coupling may represent a benefit in the sense that changes in one part of the organization do not necessarily spill over to other parts.[229] This makes the organization quite flexible as changes can be made in isolated parts of the organization with necessarily involving the whole organization. The scope of change may be reduced. This is often claimed to be one of the main benefits of a divisionalized structure, or the M-form.[230] Decoupled divisions can operate more or less independently, and as a consequence are able to adapt and change independently. Each division may adapt differently to different tasks and environments as it is decoupled.

Loose coupling, both internally and externally, may also reduce the organization's sensitivity to "shocks".[231] External loose coupling gives the organization a broader perspective, thus making it easier to detect changes in diverse parts of the environment. Internally, loose coupling may function as a "shock absorber" as changes in one part of the environment may be isolated to a single area. At the same time, internal loose coupling may make it more difficult to implement whole system changes.[232] Adhocracies – most often complex and loosely coupled organizations – may thus have problems with the implementation of more system-wide changes. Tightly coupled organizations, on the other hand, may be easier to change radically as even small changes in one part quickly will spill over to other parts, and cumulate in a radical change.[233] This will not happen in loosely coupled organizations, where a small change in one part will not affect the other parts.[234]

As a partial conclusion, one may argue that loose coupling facilitates continuous and incremental adaptation, while on the other hand it makes it more difficult to implement radical system-wide changes.

SIZE AND AGE

Organizations vary enormously regarding size – most commonly measured as the number of employees – and age.[235] There is also a strong positive correlation between size and age, as most large organizations tend to be old.[236] Looking at size first, there is a tendency for large organizations to change less often than smaller ones.[237] One obvious reason for this is that the larger the organization, the higher the organizational complexity with many units, hierarchical levels, procedures and systems. Big organizations will also mean many people and groups, and thus many interests, perspectives and subcultures that may accommodate to change initiatives in a great variety of ways. Large organizations will also have long chains of command, increasing the probability of distortion of information, again making whole system change more difficult. Big size, in short, seems to make organizations less flexible.

On the other hand, there are those claiming that large organizations have a huge advantage in having more resources to devote to change than smaller ones. Huge resources will increase the change capacity in that these organizations will be able to invest more resources in the change process, and will have a larger portfolio of change opportunities.[238] However, most empirical studies conclude that big size is a hindrance to change.[239]

As already noted, large organizations are also old organizations, and it is difficult to differentiate clearly between the two. Age can be interpreted in a variety of ways. According to the notion of sunk cost, old organizations will probably have invested more time and resources in developing and refining systems and routines. Change often implies alterations in these systems and routines, a change that will most likely be resisted by those having invested considerable resources in developing them. High age also increases the probability that strong external actors will perceive the organization as important, as a carrier or symbol of essential values.[240] Change may be perceived by these external actors as representing a threat towards these values, in turn activating significant resistance. We will discuss this phenomenon more in detail in the section on institutionalized environments. In any case, it seems as though older organizations are, in general, more difficult to change than younger ones.[241]

HISTORICAL CONTEXT

As a consequence of an increased awareness about the importance of time in organization studies, focus has also been placed on the role of an organization's history in understanding change.[242] One central element of history's role in organizational change is expressed in the concept of "path dependency". This phenomenon is based on the fact that an organization's current situation is the product of a series of previous decisions. The challenge is that previous choices tend to limit current choices. Each decision made "locks" the organization to a certain path, thus making it increasingly difficult to choose other paths.[243] For instance, focusing on a specific product and a specific market also makes it more difficult to move to new products and markets. If the situation changes, for instance there is a change in demand for the organization's main product, it will be very difficult to change to provide another product.

The more an organization's history is characterized by success, the stronger the tendency is to lock into a specific path.[244] Previous decisions have been correct, and this is the reason why the organization is successful today. The combination of considerable investments represented by previous choices and the perception that this history is the reason for success may lead organizations into what has been called the "success trap".[245] Even though previous decisions have been successful, and thus the previous path has been successful, this does not necessarily mean that it will be successful in the future. However, a history characterized by success may result in organizational hubris, a feeling that one is unbeatable, and that change cannot be necessary.

As a consequence of the previous discussion, several researchers have pointed out that change, especially radical change, starts when the organization's history is characterized by poor performance.[246] "Change starts with results," as it has been said.[247] The reason for this is conveyed clearly in the following quotation:[248]

> Poor performance serves as a benchmark, alerting stakeholders and calling into question the effectiveness of prior strategy. When performance is unsatisfactory, managers engage in a 'problemistic search' to correct the deficiency, often comparing organizational performance to aspirations, and to performance within the industry. (...) Poor performance makes it easier to break down resistance to strategic and organizational change, enabling managers to make changes that would otherwise be politically arduous.

A history characterized by poor performance and bad results will thus be a factor increasing the probability of change. And vice versa: being unable to tell a story of poor performance makes change much less likely.

However, empirical studies indicate that the connection between performance and results is not as straightforward as described above. First of all, several studies show organizations that survive over long periods of time even if their performance is downright catastrophic. They are "permanent failures".[249] The reason for this is that organizations are, by many, evaluated not only on the basis of economic results. They are, as noted previously, carriers of important values. One example is the heavy industry in Norway and most other European countries. For decades, this industry was upheld by state subsidies, even though the industry lacked profitability and was harmful to the environment as well as to employees. These organizations, however, represented many important values, like jobs in the periphery, national symbols of historical development from a poor to a prosperous country, and the rich and historically important "workers' culture".

Results in themselves do not create change; it is how results are perceived and communicated that is the crucial part of planned change. Previous performance is to a large degree "constructed realities".[250] Thus, it is not the performance in itself that is important in understanding change, it is how the performance is interpreted.[251] Poor performance seems in many instances not to be interpreted as a need for more radical change. Rather, it is by many perceived as not doing what we are doing well enough. Instead of changing, increased efforts are devoted to improving the existing activities. This phenomenon has been labelled "escalation of the wrong course".[252] Poor performance is thus not sufficient to provoke change; one must also create an interpretation conveying clearly that the current way of doing things is wrong, and that a change is needed.[253]

Finally, we must take into account the change history of an organization, that is to what degree the organization has implemented changes previously. Traditionally, it has been assumed that organizations with extensive change experience will be better at changing than organizations without such experience.[254] The mechanism, it has been argued, is that organizations learn to change by changing, thus making them more adept at changing. Through previous change, the organization learns how to tackle current change. This assumption has, however, been challenged both theoretically and empirically.[255] Previous change in itself does not affect the ability to carry out changes in the present. Rather, it is the experiences organizations have with previous changes that are of importance.

If previous changes were perceived as successful, then organizations change less as it becomes less necessary to conduct further changes. However, if previous changes were deemed failures, then a need for new changes arises, and consequently organizations change more. When organizations with a history of many changes also carry out more changes later on, it is not because the organizations have learned how to change. Rather, increased change rate is caused by most changes being failures, and thus creating a need for new changes in the future.

RESOURCES

An organization's total resources – money, people, technology – will be tightly linked to its size. But with respect to organizational change, total resources are of less interest than slack resources. Slack or redundancy can be defined as the difference between the resources an organization needs to perform its tasks, and the resources it currently uses.[256] If the organization uses more resources than needed it has, per definition, slack resources. For us, the interesting thing to know is whether slack resources are a factor that hinders or encourages change. Two different perspectives can be applied to answer this question.[257]

One perspective is that slack resources hinder organizational change.[258] One reason for this is that slack resources can be used to cover up for poor performance, and thus to postpone change. Instead of changing, slack resources are used as a buffer to avoid change. Slack resources may also function as a "pillow" in the sense that central actors in an organization with slack resources may not feel the need for change. Put somewhat differently: "[R]esource-rich organizations are less likely to experience a sense of urgency regarding adaptation and more likely to perceive an increased (perhaps false) sense of security about the future."[259]

In this perspective, slack resources are viewed as a barrier to change as they make central actors in the organization less attentive to external and internal changes.

A contrary view claims that slack resources are necessary for organizations to succeed with planned change. In this perspective, slack resources are regarded as prerequisites for experimenting and testing out new ways of doing things. Organizations with few or nor slack resources will not have the possibility to experiment as they cannot afford to do anything wrong. Experimentation is per definition risky, and one needs to be able to afford failure to engage in it.[260] Slack resources provide the opportunity for experimentation. Second, it is possible that slack resources improve an organization's ability to exploit unforeseen opportunities.[261]

When such opportunities arise, the organization with slack resources may devote extra resources to grasping the possibility the opportunity represents. At the same time, slack resources may help organizations to resist and tackle crises. Both these arguments are central to Nelson and Winter's work on economic development. They show empirically that organizations with high slack resources are better at developing new processes, products, and services and at adapting the organization to changing environments. Thus, there is a self-reinforcing tendency for successful organizations to gain more slack resources, and thus to get constantly better at exploiting new possibilities. Smaller organizations with fewer slack resources will more often "die" in the sense that they are not resourceful enough to tackle crises or to develop new products.[262] Finally, it may be that slack resources in themselves encourage change.[263] Actors both inside and outside the organization may actively look for new ways of using the extra resources. As a result, slack resources may be invested in new activities.

Empirical research cannot, of course, give one clear answer to the question of how slack resources affect organizational change. This is because slack resources may function both as a barrier and a driver of change. Slack resources may make the organization less attentive to changes in the environment, but they may also help the organization to survive crises. Thus, slack resources seem to be essential for organizations' survival over long periods of time.[264]

CULTURAL CONTEXT

In studies of organizational culture in relation to change, most attention has been given to the unity and strength of the culture.[265] Once established, culture is essentially stable, and will only change slowly through socialization processes. There will, however, be large variations in the degree to which organizational culture works as a conserving force. Some organizations have strong and unitary cultures, while others consist of more fragmented cultures or several sub-cultures, and some may have rather weak cultures without any clear values and norms.[266] In recent research on organizational culture, it has become standard procedure to operate with three perspectives on cultural unity and strength. The first is called the integration perspective, referring to organizations with a strong and homogeneous culture binding people together. Differentiation is the second perspective, indicating a situation where the organization consists of several cultures, each of them strong and unitary. The third perspective is labelled as fragmentation, referring to a situation where culture is ambiguous, shifting, and volatile.

The integration perspective applies to organizations characterized by a strong and unitary culture on the verge of being a "big, happy family".[267] Organizational members share the same basic assumptions, values, and norms, and they employ the same premises when making decisions. For the members, the organization is more than just a place of work, it is a place they like and respect, even love, and would be willing to fight for. In his now classic writings, Philip Selznick (1957) noted that the main task for top management was not to administer the organization, but to infuse it with value to make the organization a distinct entity. Several modern organizational studies – the most famous probably being Peters and Waterman's book *In Search of Excellence* – have shown strong, unitary cultures to correlate with success.[268] The mechanisms are numerous, for instance that a strong and unitary culture works as a powerful motivator, that it can base coordination and production on trust instead of control and supervision, that it creates a common language that facilitates communication, and that it creates a robust feeling of direction that gives the organization a solid strategic thrust.[269]

The challenge is that a strong and unitary culture may function as a barrier to change. Culture is a way of seeing the world, and the stronger this way of seeing is, the less open it often becomes for new ways of seeing things. Attempts to change the culture may be perceived as a threat, as an attack on the community and the community's reason for existence. Thus, strong resistance may be activated. In his study of what he termed "groupthink", Ian Janis[270] shows how a group with strong cultural unity reacts with aggressive resistance to what is perceived as threats against the supremacy and existence of the group. Changing a strong and unitary culture may demand extreme measures, and the possibility of success is often small.[271] The stronger and more homogeneous a culture is, the more attempts to change it will be met with resistance. This may produce what someone have labelled as the culture paradox:

> The lesson is a simple one: organizational culture is a key to both short term success and, unless managed correctly, long-term failure. Culture can provide competitive advantage, but as we have seen, it can also create obstacles to the innovation and change necessary to be successful.[272]

Consequently, organizations characterized by fragmented or weak cultures may be easier to change. Several cultures will represent several views of the world, and thus a wider variety of impulses, the stronger the tendency is for diverging points of view to meet, and the less locked the organization may be to a single path.[273] It is food for thought that of the 36 organizations highlighted in the famous book by Peters and Waterman, none of them was listed among the top 10 of Fortune 500 – a list of the largest businesses in the US – in 2008 ranked on the basis of shareholder profits. Several of them had "died", some had experienced bankruptcy and emerged as different firms, and most of them had lost their leading position in their markets.[274]

Still, cultural strength and unity must be treated together with the content of culture.[275] Change and flexibility can be the main values in an organization's culture, something that an increasing number of organizations seem to be understanding. Or as indicated in the following:

> Research indicates that cultural strength can be both a benefit and a drawback. Under conditions of stability, strong cultures will support the organization's strategy and contribute substantially to good performance. But if environments change, a strong culture may become a burden. If not, the culture emphasizes ability to adapt.[276]

Strong cultures emphasizing flexibility and change may thus work as drivers, not barriers, for change.[277]

INFORMAL POWER STRUCTURES

Organizational culture is closely linked to informal power structures in organizations. By informal power, we mean the power located outside the formal hierarchy or the right to participate in formal decision processes. The source of such power can be specific knowledge. It could also come in the form of informal leaders who are perceived as idols, "natural leaders", or people with charisma. Or it could be people or groups who control critical tasks in the organization.[278]

Power in itself does not necessarily impact on an organization's general ability to change, but it is of critical importance to actors implementing planned change. As noted several times earlier, planned change is based on the notion that "someone" – a change agent – initiates and then implements change. Only rarely will there be total consensus on the need for change, and the way change should be implemented. If everybody agrees, power is of less significance.[279] When there is disagreement, informal power structures will deeply impact the possibility for change agents – often coupled to the formal leaders – to succeed with change. In organizations where much power is located in the operative core there will be problems with implementing top-down change processes. Such a discrepancy between formal and informal power is found mainly in two types of organizations.

The first of such organizations is the professional bureaucracy. One of the main characteristics of this configuration is that much power is located at the professional level, among professors, doctors, and specialists.[280] The operative in these organizations will have both great informal power and a large degree of formal power through decentralized decision authority. Work conducted in the operative core is complex, and difficult to evaluate and monitor for others than peers. Thus it becomes difficult for formal leaders to see if change is taking place at all. The tasks the professional controls are critical, so threats to "work more slowly" or "refuse to work overtime" will have critical consequences for the organization. Moreover, skilled personnel are usually a very scarce resource, posing a big problem for the organization if people quit their jobs. The final element is reinforced by the fact that most professions control the recruitment to the profession, for instance by limiting admission to the professional course of study.[281] Professionals are also highly interested in maintaining the status of the core knowledge of the profession. Thus it has been claimed that professions "have tended to be reactionary forces rather than progressive, dedicated to preserving traditional entitlements and characteristics."[282]

Professions are backed up by powerful organizations that are experts at influencing external actors and decision makers like politicians and the media.

The second type of organization where power is not primarily located among the formal, hierarchical leaders is the adhocracy. One the main characteristics of this configuration is that it handles complex and "fluid" tasks. The employees in the operative core are the most critical resource in the organization, whether it is a research laboratory, a consultancy firm, or an art firm.[283] Attempts to give orders in such organizations will usually be met with ignorance and forbearance. Some may quickly threaten to move to a competitor, or establish their own businesses.[284] Trying to conduct top-down change processes in such organizations is probably destined to fail.

On a more theoretical note, we will argue that the stronger the concurrence between formal and informal power is in an organization, the better the possibility there is for leader-driven or top-down change strategies. This will be the case in, at least, machine bureaucracies (much power in top management and staff), divisionalized firms (much power in the corporate management) and the simple structure (much power located with owner/entrepreneur). This is not the same as saying the top-down change will always be successful in these organizational types, only that the probability of success is higher than it will be in adhocracies and professional bureaucracies.

Table 4.1 shows the informal power in the five basic configurations, and thus the possibility to succeed with leader-driven, top-down change.

TABLE 4.1: Configurations and power structures

CONFIGURATION	POWER LOCATED WITH...	POSSIBILITY FOR LEADER DRIVEN CHANGE
Simple structure	Leader, owner, entrepreneur	Great. The leader runs the organization as his/her own.
Machine bureaucracy	Top management, staff (technostructure)	Great if top management are supported by staff.
Professional bureaucracy	Highly skilled/educated operative core	Small without support from the professionals and the professional organizations.
Divisionalized structure	Corporate management, headquarters	Great with respect to strategic change, small regarding internal change in each division
Adhocracy	The individual employee	Small, without support from the operative core

One special case should be given additional attention: What if it is the formal leaders in organizations where they have substantial power who resist change? Several researchers have pointed to the fact that leaders have invested quite a lot in the organization, especially those who have been in the organization for a long time.[285] These leaders will have a tendency to defend previous choices, even if performance is poor and indicators hint that the strategy does not work. Often, these leaders will argue that "we have to wait until the strategy is really implemented". In such situations, change is not very likely without a change in top management. This seems to be especially important in situations where radical changes are necessary, and where this necessity for change is caused by previous decisions made by the leaders. Empirically, we find a clear correlation between radical organizational change and leader turnover.[286]

External context – stability and institutionalization

Organizations are located in different environments, and these environments will affect the possibility of implementing planned change. First of all, all organizations are working in a a field or domain.[287] These environments consist of: a) customers and clients, b) cooperating organizations, c) competitors or organizations performing similar tasks, and d) regulating agencies, both public and private. Changing an organization that is tightly regulated by government agencies will probably be quite different from changing an organization that is more or less unregulated. Change in a nuclear power plant will not be the same as change in an ice cream factory. Moreover, all organizations are embedded in specific local, regional, and national contexts, and in different cultural frames.[288] Different national cultures, traditions, and laws will affect how change can happen (process), and what type of change that is viewed as legitimate. Changing a division in Malaysia is not the same as changing a division in Norway, even if it is within the same firm.

In the following paragraphs, we will operate with a distinction between two types of environments. The first is what we have labelled "technical environments", that is the elements in the environments that directly influence the organization's capacity to conduct its tasks. This is connected to access to important resources like technology, skilled workforce, sales which are affected by competition, allocations over public budgets, etc. The second is what we label as "institutional environments", or the environments that provide the organizations with legitimacy and support.[289]

TECHNICAL ENVIRONMENTS – DEGREE OF STABILITY

Focusing on the technical environments first, one environmental characteristic seems to be of utmost importance for organizational change: the degree of *stability*. James Thompson (1967) was one of the first to classify different types of environments and their effects on organizations. For classification, two dimensions were applied: complexity and stability. Complexity refers to the diversity of actors in the environment an organization must relate to: customers/clients, competitors, public agencies, and collaborating partners. Complexity is of less importance to change. Stability is about the rate of change in the environments, or the level of uncertainty the organization must tackle. In turbulent environments organizations will experience quick shifts among competitors, in technology, in demand, and in cooperative relations.

The degree of stability can be linked more specifically to a set of environmental characteristics.[290] The first is about the degree of competition, or the number of organizations operating in the same market or field as the focus organization. The higher the number of organizations, the stronger the competition. Competition will be further intensified if competitors are more or less equal in size and market share.[291] In some market niches, the situation may be characterized as "hyper competition".[292] The stronger the competition, the stronger the external pressure for change. And the opposite: the less competition, the lower the external pressure for change.

The above discussion on competition and change is based on the existence of a mechanism giving feedback from the market. Many organizations, especially public and voluntary, do not, however, operate in markets. The goods and services provided are more or less free of charge, or at least heavily subsidized. Examples are schooling, hospitals, and social support. With prices close to zero, demand will be unlimited as customers are not forced to evaluate benefit in relation to costs. One special characteristic of these organizations is that they get little, or at least rather vague, feedback from the market.[293] This makes it harder to decide whether change is needed or not. Some indications can be collected from benchmarking or user surveys, but such feedback will always be slower and more ambiguous than market feedback influencing economic indicators directly. Monopolies may find themselves in a similar situation.[294] Such organizations do not get any clear responses from the market, as customers do not have any choice. It is thus impossible to know whether the customers are satisfied or not. In any case, unclear or vague signals from the market will probably create less pressure for change.

INSTITUTIONAL ENVIRONMENTS – REGULATIVE ELEMENTS[295]

As noted previously, organizations are also dependent on legitimacy and support from their environments to survive in the long run. The actors providing this legitimacy are often termed as an organization's institutional environment. Institutional environments have usually been regarded as conservatory or furthering stability.[296] One important part of the institutional environment is the degree of regulation.

One regulatory element is connected to the degree to which an organization is under some sort of public agency control. A hospital must comply with a long list of laws and regulations that in many instances make it difficult to conduct change.

A firm producing furniture must also comply with public regulations, but these will usually be weaker and less comprehensive. How extensive the regulation of an organization is will clearly impact on its ability to change. Public laws and regulations will work in a conservatory fashion as organizational change also must entail change in the regulatory framework. This will clearly involve more actors with diverging interests and world views, and will probably slow down and possibly stop the change process.[297]

There are also many influential professional associations regulating activities, especially in professional bureaucracies. Hospitals are again good examples of organizations existing in a highly professionalized environment. And professional associations, as noted before, tend to conserve the current situation. The role professional associations play, it is argued, is

> essentially a conservative one, in which coded prescriptions are reproduced through an association's ongoing day-to-day routines. This (...) role is the one usually assumed, albeit implicitly, within institutional accounts – hence, their portrayal of associations as mechanisms of conformity and reproduction.[298]

Even if the situation is more complex than the quotation above suggests, it is usually assumed that organizations related to strong professional associations will be difficult to change as organizational change will also imply some sort of change in the professional associations as well.

Another regulative element of great interest to researchers of organizational change is the number of employees who are organized in some kind of labour union. In Norway, this is usually measured through the relative number of employees who are members in LO, YS or other national labour unions. It seems to be a rather common assumption, at least in the American literature and research, to assume that labour unions are conservative, and thus a deterrent to change.[299] Some go to extremes, and claim that unions "have been conservative and generally content to maintain the status quo. Indeed, many unions seem to assume that they can handle problems best if they do more of what they have traditionally done."[300]

Unions, like professional associations, thus seem to function as barriers for change. Others argue that this is a too simplistic view of unions and professional associations, and that their role in change processes will clearly depend on what type of change one is talking about, the number of unions or associations that are activated in the change, and to what degree the unions and association are actively involved in the change process.[301] Studies of change processes where unions have been given active roles indicate that they may also function as important drivers of change.[302]

Thus it is impossible to make a general claim as to how labour unions and professional associations affect planned organizational change. Rather, we should be open to the probability that their role will vary according to the content of the change and the organization of the change process itself. In general terms, it seems as though unions and professional associations mainly work to obstruct large and radical changes, while they can play an important role in encouraging more incremental ones. And, most importantly, their role as barriers or drivers will probably vary a great deal depending on how actively they are involved in the change process. Nonetheless, organizations existing in strong regulative environments may find it harder to change than organizations operating in less regulated environments.

INSTITUTIONAL ENVIRONMENTS – NORMATIVE ELEMENTS

Organizations are also embedded in a larger set of regional and national values, norms, and assumptions, or what we will term a national culture.[303] National culture will shape the form of organizations, contributing to isomorphism or a homogenization of organizational forms within the same cultural framework.[304] One example could be the strong egalitarian values in Norwegian society, and how these have contributed to small pay differences, as well as small social differences, within Norwegian organizations. Attempts to contravene these norms will be met with dissatisfaction and protest in unions, professional associations, the media, and the general public.

In the now very well-known and frequently debated classification of national cultures elaborated by Geert Hofstede, six dimensions were identified as central to understanding culture:[305]

1. Individualism, or to what degree people perceive themselves as individuals or as part of a larger collective.
2. Uncertainty avoidance, or the willingness to accept risk and to experiment.
3. Power distance, or the acceptance of hierarchy and orders given by superiors.
4. Masculinity, or to what degree people embrace masculine values like competition and material awards compared to more feminine values like cooperation and care for the weak.

5. Time perspective, or whether people have a long- or short-term perspective on when results should manifest themselves.
6. Hedonism, or to what degree the culture accepts pure pleasure or, on the contrary, austerity and restraint.

The dominant values in the national culture will also most probably be important values in the culture of all organizations embedded in that culture. Not much research has been carried out on how national values affect organizational change, but some research may be used to construct some hypotheses.

In a comparison of reforms to make public organizations more modern and effective, the conclusion was that there were enormous differences in how change was conducted, although the rhetoric on change was very similar across countries.[306] Norway, for instance, was labelled as the "tortoise", indicating a public sector changing incrementally and slowly.[307] One explanation proposed for Norway's reform path was that Norway as a country had large slack resources generated from the oil and gas industry, and thus did not need to change. Another, more cultural, explanation was that the Norwegian culture appreciated risk avoidance, a value emphasizing slow and small changes. As a third explanation, also cultural, the small power distance was highlighted as it complicates fast and comprehensive changes because many actors will be involved in the change processes. Hofstede's studies indicate that low power distance is one of the clearest cultural distinctions of the Scandinavian countries, implying that employees accept few or no orders from hierarchical leaders.[308] This situation probably reflects a long history of cooperation between capitalists and workers, manifested in formal cooperative arrangements between labour unions and employers' unions.[309] One reasonable hypotheses is thus that countries characterized by low power distance and high uncertainty avoidance will engage less in large and radical changes.

As we will discuss in more detail in later chapters, national culture will also influence clearly how organizational change processes can be organized, or at least what type of strategy is least likely to succeed. Change strategies based on hierarchical power will have less probability of success in countries with low power distance. Egalitarian countries will probably favour more collaborative change processes. In contrast, using classic Scandinavian ideals of collaborative processes may be less successful in countries with less egalitarian cultures.[310] Empirical studies also indicate that organizational changes focusing on individual level changes such as changes in incentive systems, individual jobs, and individual career opportunities meet a great deal of resistance in more collectively oriented cultures like those of many Asian countries. And collective changes will be met with resistance in more individually oriented cultures like that of the US.[311]

Furthermore, radical change may be harder to implement in some cultures. A study of attempts at implementing Business Process Reengineering (BPR) in a set of Chinese firms concluded that radical changes advocated by the BPR doctrine would be difficult to implement because 1) they would be perceived as "challenging destiny", breaking with a world view based on the world changing in long waves rather than punctuations, 2) it would be signalling extremely bad management from former managers, and thus they would lose all repute in the organization, family, and society, and 3) long cooperative relations with other organizations would be broken, something regarded as unacceptable violations of agreements.[312]

INSTITUTIONAL ENVIRONMENTS – COGNITIVE ELEMENTS

In most organizational domains or fields one will find a set of assumptions on how "correct", "good", or "modern" should look. Such assumptions are what we can label as institutional standards.[313] These standards say something about what a hospital, a school, a bank, or a university should appear, how they ought to be structured, what personnel they should employ, and what routines and procedures they are expected to use.

One such standard is the idea that modern organizations should be as flat as possible. Middle managers are to a high degree regarded as "unnecessary" costs. Eradicating hierarchical layers has been one of the mantras of modern structures.[314] In many instances, reduction of middle managers seems to be based more on a wish to appear modern than a measure to make the organization more efficient. Another example is found in the enormous rise in popularity of people or organizational units occupied with corporate social responsibility (CSR).[315] Currently it is almost impossible to find an organization, public or private, of a certain size without such people or units. These functions pop up in all organizations, no matter what actual or potential impact the organization has on the society in which it is embedded.

On the one hand, institutional standards represent some kind of pressure towards change, as all organizations within a field must comply with these standards, regardless of whether or not they are useful. On the other hand, institutional standards function in a conservative way, in the sense that it is impossible for an organization to carry out changes where the content or the process represent a deviation from the standards.

Context and change

Understanding the internal and external context is necessary for understanding what possibilities organizations have for planned change.[316] These possibilities will vary according to the context. Figure 4.1 illustrates the argument put forward in this chapter.

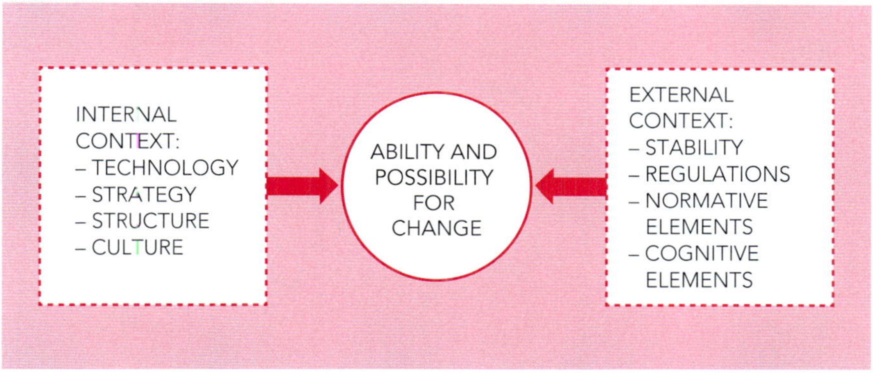

FIGURE 4.1: An organization's possibility and ability to change as a function of internal and external context

The context should be regarded as some kind of impersonal "forces" hindering or promoting change. From this we can deduce some basic and general assumptions about change, for instance that it will be easier to change small organizations than large ones, that it will be easier to change organizations in less regulated environments, and that change will be more difficult the higher the asset specificity of the organization's technology is, with regard to both hardware and competence.

Such general hypotheses are, of course, too simple. One way to make these assumption more detailed is to connect them to the content and the scope of change. A modification of one of the previous general hypotheses could be that it is easier to change small organizations incrementally, while it may be easier to change large organizations more radically. Furthermore, a strong focus on context may lead to a sense of determinism, that change agents are "locked" by the context. If we hold on to the idea that planned, intentional change is possible, a focus on context highlights how important it is for change agents to understand the context of the organization they are trying to change, and to adapt change strategy to the specific context. Only through an understanding of the organization – what type of organization is this? – and its environment – where is the organization embedded? – can the change agent be able to choose change strategies that fit the context, and thus to increase the probability of succeeding with planned change.

Chapter 5

How does change happen? The change process

Planned change starts, as emphasized many time before in this book, when someone – a change agent – takes an initiative to introduce change. There will, in planned change, always be some actors initiating activities to change the behaviour of employees, structures, or cultures. When focus is placed on the process of change, some elements become essential. First of all, change does not happen instantly; it is something that develops over time. Thus it becomes essential to understand the *time element* in change processes. Obvious questions in regard to this are: How long a time do have at our disposal? How do we sequence the process? What do we do first? What consequences would it have to start in a different way?

The second element emerging from a focus on the process is that planned change will always be an action taken by a specific set of actors or change agents. Someone must perceive the situation as something that could and should be improved. Central to all planned change are the words "someone" and "perception". Change agents are very rarely, if ever, all members of an organization, and thus they represent some perceptions of the situation, not all.[317] Thus it becomes essential to understand how people in the organization react to the initiative proposed by change agents. If large groups in the organization perceive the initiative as threatening, unnecessary, or simply stupid, the reaction will most probably come in the form of resistance to change.

To understand the change process, we must look more closely at the dynamic processes of action and reaction, more specifically how people react to change initiatives, and why they react the way they do. Change is not something abstract; it is a demand to leave something you know, and to do something new and unfamiliar. Change processes must thus be understood as series of interactions over time. In taking this view, we are also bringing organizational change to the microlevel, as the focus is set on individuals and groups, and how they react to change initiatives.

The time element in change processes

As pointed out in the first chapter of this book, time is an inherent aspect of change. Change is what happens between two points in time, and manifests itself in at least two different states. Still it is surprising to see how undertheorized the element of time is in the change literature, probably because it is so obvious.[318] However, a nuanced understanding of time is necessary in order to understand change, and essential to implementing planned change.

As a starting point, we will define two quite different perspectives on time: quantitative and qualitative time.[319] Quantitative time is the type of time we measure in seconds, minutes, hours, and days. In this perspective time is unidirectional in the sense that it only flows in one direction: forward. Time cannot be reversed. Treating time like this makes us aware of change processes as a series of events that unfold chronologically over a defined timeline. One example is an implementation of a new training programme at time 1 that will lead to new skills at time 2, that again will lead to changed behaviour at time 3. This quantitative perspective makes it clear that change processes are series of events that follow each other in time, and that are more or less connected. It is impossible to understand change without comparing now with previous states or events.

A qualitative perspective on time is not in opposition to the quantitative perspective, but rather it emphasizes how people perceive time. Seconds, hours, and days can be measured objectively, but that is not the same as saying that people perceive time in the same way. Or put another way:

> Time is not just 'out there' as neutral chronology, but also 'in here' as a social construction. (…) history is not just events and chronology, it is carried forward in the human consciousness. The past is alive in the present and may be shaping the emerging future.[320]

A good example of qualitative time is found in how different people – and the same person in different stages of life – perceive time. What seems like an eternity for a child may be the blink of an eye for an adult. What represents "ample time" or "in a hurry" will vary significantly from situation to situation. A qualitative perspective of time also introduces emotion to the study of time, as we perceive time as emotional highs and lows as well as second and minutes. Very few of us describe our history chronologically – "three years and two days ago I did that, four weeks afterwards I did that, etc." Rather, we describe it as a set of significant events, for instance "then I met him, then I took the exam, and that was the year the dog died". What we remember of our history is linked to the emotions we attach to specific periods of time. Periods where nothing happened that was worth remembering will soon be forgotten. Change is thus not only points in time that follow each other chronologically, but also events that we react emotionally to. Those events we remember, and those we perceive as important, will be those events that aer filled with some kind of emotion.

With the distinction between quantitative and qualitative time in mind, we can now delve more deeply into more specific elements of time and their relevance to planned organizational change.

THE TIME PERSPECTIVE OF CHANGE

Planned change is usually conceived as something with a beginning and an end, as some kind of project with a deadline. A basic question, if change is perceived this way, must be: How long a time do we need from beginning to end? A month? A year? Two years? Should the change be without a deadline? To answer such questions in generic terms is, of course, impossible. Still, we can bring two reflections on time perspective to the forefront.

The first reflection is linked to time and the content of change. It is probable that some organizational elements can be changed more quickly than others.[321] Earlier in this book we defined the content of change in terms of formal (strategy, structures) and informal (culture, informal power structures) elements. A specific characteristic of the informal elements is that they cannot be determined, and thus not easily designed. They are emergent, a product of interaction between people inside and outside the organization, and thus the outcome of a historical process. Informal elements may be influenced and shaped, but they cannot be decided. Cultures, especially core values, are per definition impossible to change quickly. Culture is the product of a learning process, and to acquire a new culture will, contain the following stages as a minimum:[322] 1) the old culture must be mapped to make values, norms, and assumption visible, 2) it must be shown how culture is expressed and manifested in artefacts, 3) new values and norms must be defined, 4) new artefacts signalling new values and norms must be taken into use, and finally 5) the new artefacts must be given content symbolizing new values and norms. A new culture will not be in place before values and norms are internalized by the members of the organization. This takes time. Cultural changes will thus probably need a long time perspective, and a change process focusing on training, education, and socialization.[323] Formal elements, on the other hand, can be changed much faster. In some instances, new incentive schemes, new group designs, and a new strategy may be decided in a short meeting by a small group of people. And if people do not comply with the formal changes, they can be "pushed" into following them by the use of incentives, or "carrots and sticks" like physical displacements, loss of bonuses, or restrictions on working time.

Such a blunt dichotomy is, of course, too simple. For instance, organizational cultures are usually organized in several layers.[324] Some values are core values, and some norms are regarded as more important than others. Other norms and values are more fluid and changeable, more often connected to a way of doing things. If cultural change is aimed only at changing the more superficial norms and values, it can probably be implemented quite quickly. Changing the core values or what we earlier called the "deep structure" will be much more time consuming as it will require a resocialization of organizational members, and maybe also a unlearning of previous values and norms. At the same time we must remember that organizations are archetypes, and that some structural characteristics may be perceived as important symbols of core values and norms. Such structural elements cannot be changed quickly as people will react strongly to swift attempts to change them.

The second reflection is mainly linked to the qualitative perspective on time. Whether people will start to change behaviour or not is not necessarily linked very strongly to the objective time at hand, but rather to a feeling of being pressed for time or having plenty of time. Some have claimed that one of the cardinal errors made by many change agents is lacking the ability to instil a sense of urgency or crisis.[325] A sense of urgency is produced when people feel that they are under time pressure, combined with a perception of dramatic consequences of not acting, for instance losing one's job or fearing for the existence of the whole organization. Time is central to definitions of both urgency and crisis. A crisis is per definition a situation where time is scarce, and there is a strong need for quick action.[326]

To establish a sense of crisis or urgency, a short time perspective is needed. At the same time, to produce human action and change, the perception of time must not be too narrow. A feeling of having too little time may put people in a "panic zone", resulting in apathy and a feeling that it is useless to try and do something. Change agents must create the right level of urgency, and strike a balance between being pressed for time and not having the possibility to act within the given timeframe.

We will end this section with a fascinating paradox related to time and the scope of change. In an earlier chapter we distinguished between radical and incremental change. These two types of change entail two implicitly different time perspectives. Incremental change is slow, takes a long time, and often has no deadlines at all. Radical change often happens quickly, almost brutally. The organization must react swiftly to survive. The paradox is that large, radical changes must often be implemented within a narrow time frame, while smaller and less dramatic changes can stretch over longer time spans. The challenge is that the most comprehensive changes often have to be conducted within a short time frame. Empirical studies indicate that quite a lot of radical changes occur quite quickly.[327] One reason for this may be that a dramatic shift in the environment of the organization will often be highly visible, and thus create a strong sense of urgency compelling the organization to act. The willingness to change becomes strong.

PROACTIVE VERSUS REACTIVE CHANGE

Most of us view change as a process following a specific rhythm or phases over time. At the first point in time, the organization is in balance, or "fit", internally and with its environment. Then something happens, internally or externally, that disturbs this state and brings the organization out of fit. These events thus spur

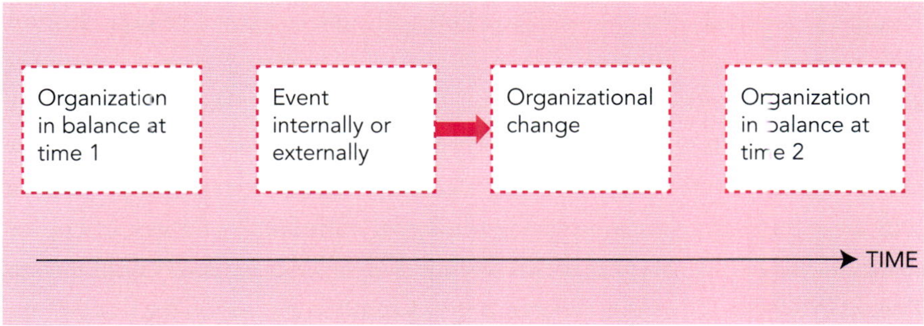

FIGURE 5.1: The sequencing of a reactive change process

the organization to start changing in order to obtain a new situation of balance. We usually think about change, as described above, as something reactive, as is illustrated in figure 5.1.

A reactive change characterizes a change process where change in or of the organization takes place as a reaction to events that have already taken place.[328] The organization is "forced" to change.

But there is a possibility for change to happen proactively, in the sense that organizations change to adapt to future events. Change is thus taking place before the organization is "forced" to change, and the change is based on some expectations of future events. Figure 5.2 illustrates this way of changing.

Such sequencing is grounded in an assumption that it is possible to predict and foresee the future, and thus to adapt before events happen. This way of thinking is normal in all types of planning, whether it is done in the form of trend analyses, scenarios, or other techniques.[329]

If proactive change succeeds, the organization will have adjusted to the new situation before any competitors, thus making it possible to reap the benefits of what has been called a "first mover advantage".[330] When the event occurs that makes it necessary for all organizations within a field to change – be it a change in demand, technology, or political regulations – the organization that has implemented a proactive change will already be adapted to the new situation. During the period when other organizations have to spend time and resources on changing, the proactively changing organization can reap the benefits of being the only or best one on the market.

Still, however positive the concept of "proactive" sounds, empirical studies indicate that changes seldom happen proactively. Or to be more precise: radical changes rarely happen proactively. Incremental changes occur somewhat more often proactively.[331] To try and look into the future is a risky business, and predictions often fail. Predicted events fail to happen, or something quite different from the expected happens. Organizations engaging in a proactive path of change are also involved in some kind of gambling, the and the risk of total failure increases.[332] No matter how thorough the planning is, the future is still uncertain. Another reason for radical proactive changes being so rare is the possibility that such a sequencing of change makes it difficult to build up a sense of urgency among organizational members. In a proactive state, there is no history of events to show that the organization "must" change. Instead of historical events, a sense of urgency must be created on the basis of narratives about the future. Such narratives will be uncertain; some may even perceive

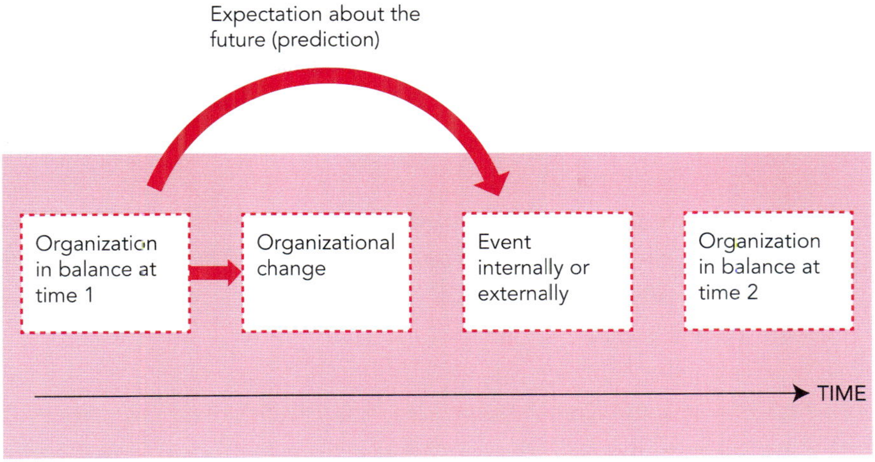

FIGURE 5.2: The sequencing of a proactive change process

them as fairy tales, and will probably fail in instilling a sense of urgency or crisis.[333] Most people will have a tendency to say "let's wait and see" instead of engaging in proactive change processes associated with great uncertainty and risk.

PATH DEPENDENCE

Treating change as a series of events taking place consecutively on a time line draws our attention to the possibility that events may be linked or coupled in different ways. Previous events may influence current and future events. Decisions we make today will probably affect the decisions we make tomorrow. Choices have a tendency to open up some new possibilities, as well as closing others. An example can be starting to study at a university. Once the decision to attend university is made, several possibilities open up. You can choose between a wide variety of studies. At the same time, this decision closes other opportunities. It makes it more difficult to do something other than studying. The more choices you make, the longer you stay at the university, the fewer possibilities you will have to choose something completely different. Leaving the university after one year is hard, but acceptable. After four years it is almost impossible.

A theory of organizational change must take into account that events at one point in time both open and close possible future choices. This phenomenon has been called "path dependency" (used in this book),[334] "historical dependency",[335] or "change tracks".[336] Events taking place early in the process seem to be particularly important in the sense of having a great effect on later events. For instance, decisions made early in the life of an organization have a tendency to be imprinted in the organization for a very long time.[337] The possibility of path dependence has deep consequences for change agents, or:

> like a decision tree, the trail of choices made by a system rules many options out, at the same time as it rules mutually contingent options in. This characterization accords with organizational research on the tenacity of initial choices; (…) early steps in decision trees are the most fateful.[338]

As indicated by this quotation, the sequence in which decisions are made or events take place will have an effect on how the change process proceeds. Most theories on planned change operate with a sequence of phases in the change process – for instance Lewin's unfreezing, moving, and refreezing – with a diversity of techniques to use in each phase.[339] However, extremely few theories address the possibility that some techniques may be very difficult, if not impossible, to use after other techniques have been applied earlier on in the process.

An interesting insight emerging from this discussion is the tendency for decision opportunities to narrow down in the course of a planned change process. The more choices that have been taken, the less room there is for later choices. Organizations get locked into a path. Figure 5.3 illustrates this phenomenon.[340]

A planned change process will always have a rather clearly defined starting point stating what should be done first. One example could be a decision to invite all employees in an organization to a two-day seminar to discuss the challenges the organization faces and invite suggestions as to how to meet them. By starting with such an arrangement, expectations are created for future events. By inviting everyone, expectations are raised that also the rest of the process will be characterized by involvement and participation. This situation puts pressure on the change agents to organize future events in a similar way, even though there may not be enough time, or the change content is not very well suited to broad discussions. The more choices are made in constructing a broadly participative process, the more difficult it may become to change the strategy into a more narrow, top-down process.

The connection between events in time opens the door to the possibility for change processes to move into positive or negative spirals, indicating that change may be a cumulative phenomenon over time.[341] The notion of positive and negative spirals is grounded in an assumption that the current event is a reaction to

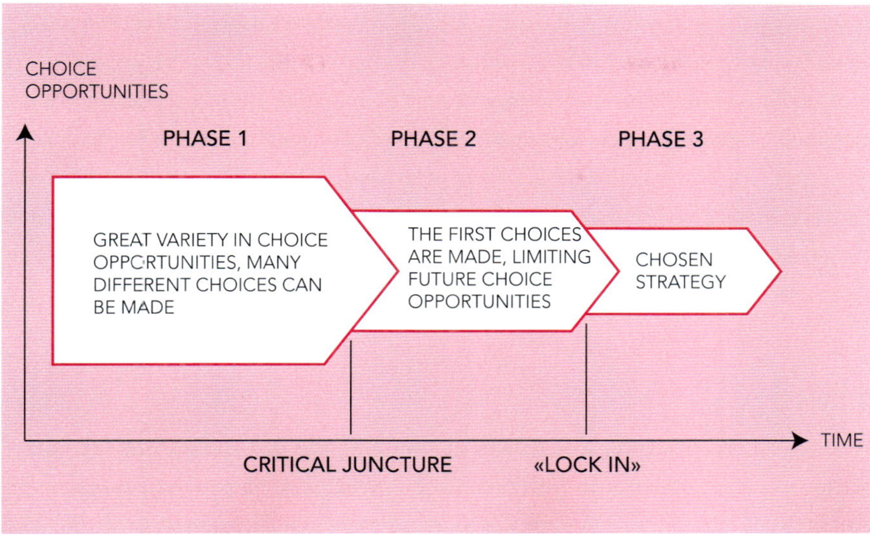

FIGURE 5.3: Change as a process of choices being gradually limited

previous events, and that good and bad experiences from previous events will determine the current reaction. Organization studies are full of examples of vicious or negative circles.[342] One classic example is the case where leaders intensified control over the works on the production line, only to have the workers react with ever more sophisticated ways of evading control, in turn leading to increasing control, etc.[343] Another example is where a group's decision is criticized, and then the group aggressively counters the critique instead of adapting to it, in turn increasing the ferocity of the critique, etc.[344]

Acknowledging the linkages in time also highlights the possibility of creating positively reinforcing circles of events. This is, in fact, a main element in what has been called "logical incrementalism".[345] The ability to detect and communicate small and early "victories" in a process is important in creating a sense of success. "Small victories" create a positive psychological state, providing the process with energy and thrust, which in turn prepares the ground for more radical changes. Thus, a good sequencing of a change process may create a psychological climate supportive of change. And if many small changes follow each other in a planned and logical way, the result may be rather radical change.[346]

However, not all events are linked as tightly as in the previous examples. In many change processes it is difficult to establish how events are linked, and what they mean for each other. In such cases it is important to remember that time is just as much about perceived time (subjective) as chronological time (objective). Links between events are thus not necessarily always something that exists, but are just as often something that is constructed. For change agents, this activates the possibility, and perhaps the necessity, of moving the change process in the desired direction – of being active interpreters or sense-makers of links between events. In some instances, it may be beneficial for the change agents that events are perceived as decoupled, as having nothing to do with each other. In other instances, a perception of tight coupling is most beneficial for the change agent.

TIMING

A focus on the time element makes us aware of the fact that events take place within a certain time frame with certain characteristics. Although days may seem similar, they vary over time. One day all employees may be present, while the next day a third of the staff is away at a seminar. How a change process unfolds will probably vary significantly depending on which of these two days was chosen as the "launch". The placement of events in time is what we call timing. A measure implemented at one point in time might be a success, while the same measure implemented at another time may fail miserably.

In the context of planned change, timing is essential. Change agents must be highly aware of parallel events taking place in the organization when they are planning for the sequence of the change process. As organizations engage in change processes, they still have to maintain ordinary activities.[347] And ordinary activities consist of a series of organizational procedures following a certain rhythm, or unfolding in a specific set of sequences. Examples of such rhythms can be budgeting, winding up summer vacations for staff, monthly reporting of results, etc. Change processes always demand time and resources of those involved, people who in most instances must also take care of their ordinary jobs in a satisfactory way. If activities connected to the change process coincide with periods of heavy work load for the people involved, attention will be drawn away from the change process, possibly bringing it to a halt.

Furthermore, there is seldom only one change process going on, at least in large organizations. Change is, for most organizations, not a one-off event. Empirical studies indicate that organizations often engage in several, parallel change processes, and that these only to a limited degree are viewed as connected to each other.[348] Introduction of new IT systems are run in parallel with regrouping, which again is run in parallel with new routines for registering work hours. Thus, the same people will be involved in several change processes, a situation that may put a quite severe strain on some. If change projects are not coordinated or timed in relation to each other, employees may experience what has been called "exaggerated change", a experience that is often translated into negative psychological states like apathy and change cynicism.[349] If such a perception takes hold in the organization, the whole change process may be threatened.

Change often represents a stress factor for the involved parties, and radical changes have a tendency to wear out those involved. As a consequence, it may be sensible to let periods characterized by comprehensive change be followed by periods of relative stability. Stability will make it possible for the organization to "rest", to regain social relations and stable working conditions, and to acquire a deeper knowledge of new tasks and routines.[350] The ability to establish a good "rhythm" of change, where change is followed by stability, is an important capability not only for change agents, but also for leaders in general.

Finally, we must admit that not everything is possible to time rationally. Things just happen, without the change agents being able to predict them. Sometimes they could have been predicted to a certain extent, but weren't. One example is the turnaround currently going on in the airline SAS. A large change programme for cutting costs was established in 2012/13.[351] This programme would require downsizing and reduction of salaries for most groups. At the same time it was announced that the salary of the CEO of the company would nearly double. Even though the two events have little to do with each other, they were coupled by media and employees, creating considerable discontent, and not making the start of the change process any easier. In 2016, it seemed as though SAS had learned its lesson as a new step in the cost-cutting programme was announced.[352] At the same time, a reduction in the salaries of top management was announced, and this reduction was relatively greater than that of the employees. The example clearly shows how events are perceived as being linked. In other instances, coincidental events are impossible to predict. A change process could coincide with a natural catastrophe, a highly unlikely political decision like the outcome of the Brexit referendum in the UK in 2017, or with the sudden exit of central employees.

Reactions to change initiatives

Why are some change initiatives met with enthusiasm, while others only meet silence or disdainful comments? The types of reaction provoked by change initiatives are essential in understanding the probability of succeeding with planned change. For most change agents, the main challenge is often perceived to be negative reactions or resistance to the change initiative.

Research on reaction to change initiatives is mostly divided between those who focus on resistance and those who are more interested in support for change.[353] Research on support for change is quite new, and can be divided into two subtypes: studies on commitment to change[354] and studies on readiness for change.[355] These two research traditions have so many similarities that they enrich each other, and should thus be treated in parallel. Research on resistance is much older and in fact more common, and might be traced back to central figures like Kurt Lewin (1951).[356] Classic voices in the organizational change literature like Chris Argyris and Donald Schon claimed, for instance, that change would almost without exception activate "defence mechanisms" in individuals and groups in organizations.[357] According to these researchers, everyone has a tendency to think in terms of gains and losses, and to assume that all others think the same way; we tend to avoid negative feelings, and we do not want to lose face. Organizational change offers plenty of opportunities for activating negative feelings, producing losses, and losing face.[358] As long as this is almost part of human nature, resistance to change will be the normal reaction.

COMMITMENT TO CHANGE

Support for change – or commitment to change – is usually divided into three subtypes. Even if it is not stated explicitly, these three types also indicate varying degrees or intensity of support.[359] The implication is that support can range from weak and unstable to strong and stable. The three types are illustrated in figure 5.4.

Continuance commitment is related to a) the investments made by the individual in the organization, and b) the alternative options an individual has outside the organization. Investments made in the organization refers to the time and resources people put into the organization, for instance in building knowledge, networks, and status. The more one has invested, the higher the cost of leaving. Resistance to change will put these investments at risk, as one may come out of the process as a loser. The second point is connected to the possibility of leaving

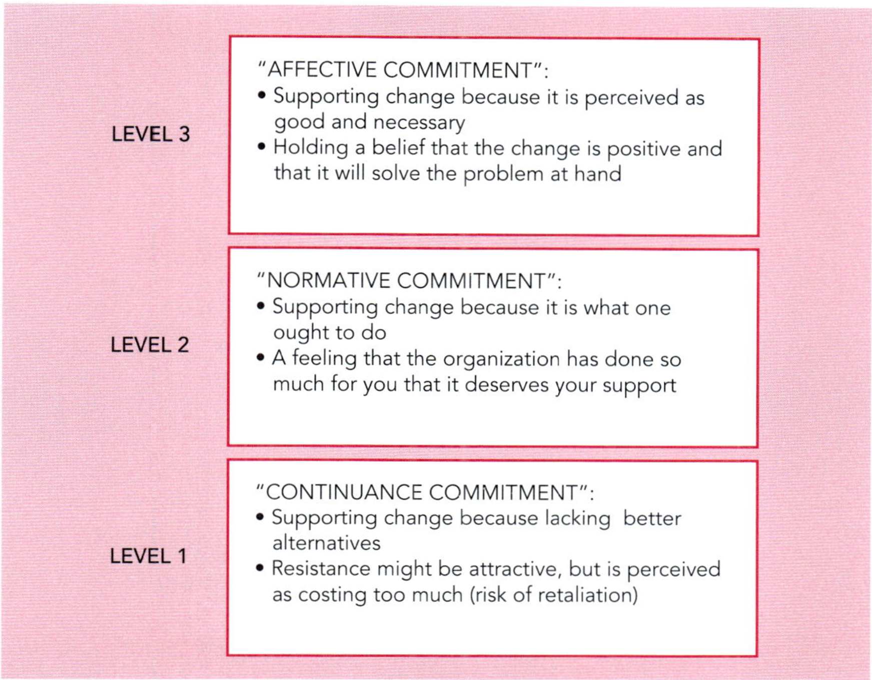

FIGURE 5.4: From weak (continuance) to strong (affective) commitment

an organization without the cost being too great. An individual having plenty of opportunities on the job market will not as obliged to support the change as a person with more limited job opportunities. In short, people support the change because they feel, in a way, "locked into" the organization.

Normative commitment to change is grounded in a feeling of reciprocity, that one has to recompense earlier benefits given by the organization. Some organizations may have stretched rules and regulations at one point in a person's career, for instance in periods of illness in the family. This creates a "sense of duty" to reciprocate by supporting the change, but it does not necessarily imply that the change is perceived as good or necessary. Finally, people are affectively committed if they also believe the change is good and necessary. This type of commitment contains a certain element of enthusiasm. This is definitely a strong type of support, and people with this kind of commitment to change will probably function as active drivers in the change process.

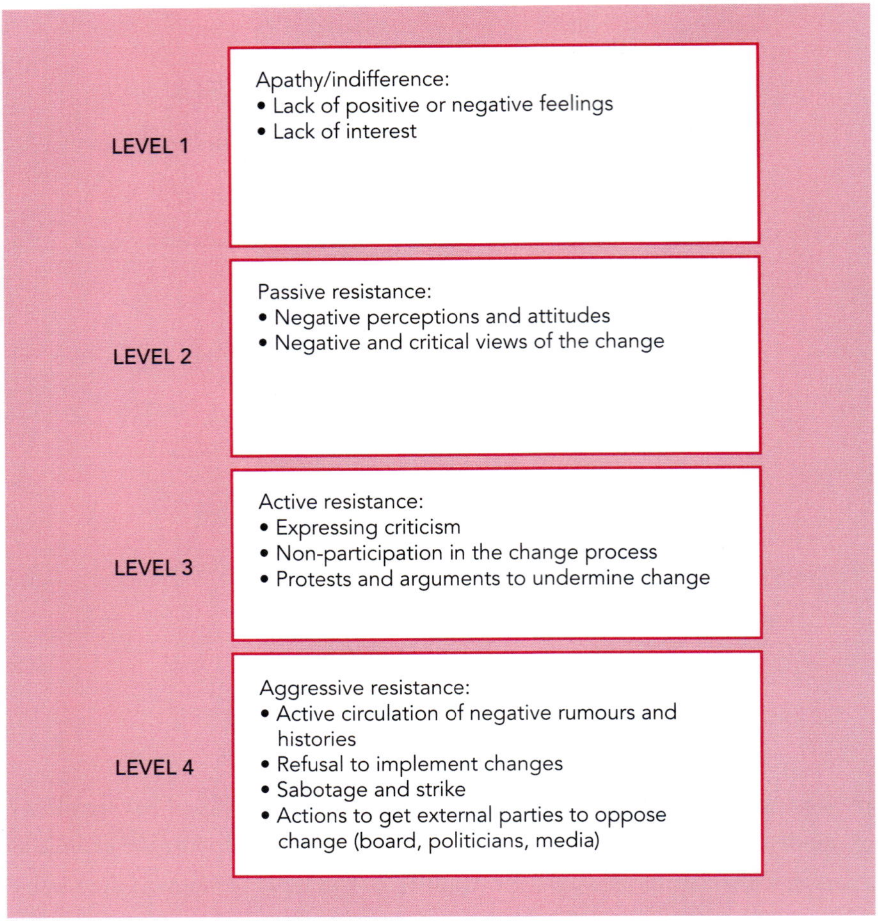

FIGURE 5.5: Different levels of resistance, from weak to intense

RESISTANCE TO CHANGE – TYPES AND PHASES

Resistance to change, like support for change, may be seen as having varying degrees of intensity. These levels are illustrated in figure 5.5.[360]

Level 1 represents a relatively mild, and probably very common, form of resistance. Some have labelled this form of resistance as the BOHICA syndrome, meaning "Bend over, here it comes again". A further description of the phenomenon is as follows: "Bohicans are survivors. Guided by the biblical passage 'This, too, shall pass', they stay low, line the bunker, keep their options open, smile, nod at the right times – and wait."[361]

Change processes are slowed down, almost to a halt, and the blame is put on unforeseen complications or the lack of necessary resources. Difficulties in measuring whether change has really been implemented or not is exploited, so that one can claim that change has been implemented without this really being the case. This skewed information about whether or not measures have been implemented is used actively to postpone changes that are difficult or impossible to control. Bohicans merely say that change has been taken care of, while they are actually only waiting it out to see if it will pass when change agents lose interest or devote their attention to other parts of the change process.

At level 2, resistance becomes more visible and open, first manifested in the voicing of critical comments and the questioning of both the need for change and the relevance of the measures to be taken. Some may take it even further, and threaten to quit the organization.[362] At level 3 resistance become highly manifest in strong critiques of the change initiative and/or process, sometimes even externally in union settings and local media. Peaceful demonstrations might also be included here, such as taking a collective, five-minute pause in all work, or through some kind of "go slow" action. At this level, the first coalitions and alliances are created, with the aim of hindering or stopping the change process.

At the final level, we find a type of resistance that is not limited to only critical comments and counterarguments. At this level, it becomes equally important to undermine the arguments of the change agents, lowering their status and legitimacy and questioning their motives. Is the objective for change really for the best of the organization, or is it only for the benefit of a few owners? Moreover, at this level many of the activities of the organization will become "political" in the sense that action is taken by several actors to influence other decision makers outside the organization. At the most extreme level, resistance can take on the form of "wildcat strikes" and sabotage.

SUPPORT AND RESISTANCE – A MODEL

Support for and resistance to change are phenomena that can be plotted into a two-dimensional space. The first dimension describes the degree of arousal or activation, while the second describes the type of valence the change represents for members of the organization, positive or negative. The result is displayed in figure 5.6.[363]

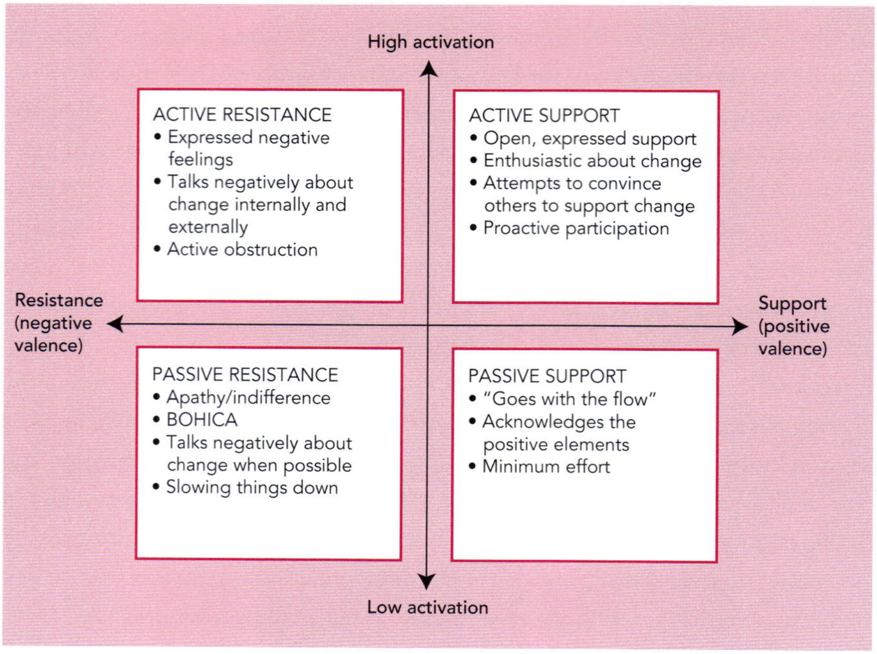

FIGURE 5.6: Different types of reactions to change initiatives classified along dimensions for activation and positive valence (support) / negative valence (resistance)

For the change agent, resistance will make the implementation of change more difficult, and will thus work as a "counterforce". The stronger this counterforce is, the less the probability of succeeding with change becomes. Support for change will, on the other hand, work as a driving force, and thus increase the probability of succeeding with planned change. These conclusions may seem obvious, but they are important as they indicate two main tasks of any change agent: a) creating support for the change, and b) reducing the resistance against change. To be able to do this, it is essential to understand the reasons for support and resistance. Even though there may be different grounds for support and resistance, there are several good reasons to deal with them concurrently.[364]

Causes of support and resistance

It may seem unnecessary to repeat, but still we would like to emphasize the fact that the organization, and thus organizational change, is about humans. Organizations consist primarily of individuals and groups of individuals. To understand why change initiatives are met with support and/or resistance we have to understand how change affects individuals and social relations. In the following, we will go through some of the most important elements in understanding why humans react as they do to change initiatives.

1. PROFESSIONAL AGREEMENT/DISAGREEMENT

One reason why people resist change is that they disagree on professional or substantive grounds. As noted previously, neither the analysis of the need for change nor the solution proposed, is an objective phenomenon. Thus, one common reason for resistance is that someone does not agree with the change agent with regard to the need for change ("What's the use of a new data program? The old one works fine, thank you!"), or does not accept that the solution proposed will solve the problem. One example could be a municipality deciding to outsource some of its services to cut costs. It is not hard to find studies, or experiences from other municipalities, that will support the notion that this will cut costs, and studies that show the opposite. Or studies that show no effect, or varying effects depending on what services one studies. As a consequence, a discussion of the effects of a proposed change will emerge. Such a reaction is pointed out as quite common by Brunsson and Olsen in their writings on reform in the public sector:[365]

> The reformees may resist reforms because they disagree with the reformers in their definition of "good" results or solutions. (...) When they adopt a negative stand on a reform, they may be doing so because practical experience (...) tells them that the proposed reforms are based on faulty premises, are self-contradictory or even destructive to the operations in question.

Agreement on substantive or professional grounds with the proposed change is one of the main reasons for support of change initiatives.[366] When people inside and outside the organization accept the change agent's understanding of the need for change and the causal mechanisms between the proposed solution or change and the effects, the probability that they also will support the change initiative increases. Professional disagreement, on the other hand, is a very common and important source of resistance. Still, professional disagreement may work as a "smokescreen" for other, more hidden reasons.

2. FEAR OF THE UNKNOWN

It is quite common to point out fear of the unknown as the most important reason for resistance to change.[367] Faced with change, people often ask themselves questions like: "What will happen to me?" or "Will I be able to tackle this?" Such questions rarely have clear answers, a situation often perceived as stressful. Stress is often perceived as a negative emotion, something most of us try to avoid.[368] The lack of clarity "makes it difficult for people to focus on the future and direct their energy at working toward the future. Instead, the free-floating anxiety is left to feed on itself."[369]

As a consequence, people will try as far as possible to reduce the level of anxiety. The easiest way to do so in a change process is to maintain the *status quo*.

Fear of the unknown varies enormously in intensity. The most dramatic for members of an organization is the fear of losing their job. This is clearly one of the main reasons why change efforts aimed at digitalization and automation are so often met by resistance.[370] Behind the concept of "new technology" lurks an assumption of reducing costs by replacing humans with machines. Thus the "fear of technology" is often a fear of losing one's job. Such fear is moderated by the opportunities that people have on the job market. Older people, those with little education and those with skills very specific to one task and one organization will have few alternatives, and thus the fear of losing their job will be very strong.

Another aspect of fear is the anxiety of not measuring up.[371] Change often implies new jobs and new ways of working that demand new knowledge and skills. Thus fear will be connected to the ability to cope with the situation. One starts to wonder whether one will master the new task, or be able to handle the new technology. Again, this seems to be a fear that often arises in relation to "new technology". Many people are unfamiliar with working with databases and new channels of communication. This may create a situation where people become afraid of losing face, of being regarded as "old timers" who have "passed their expiry date".[372]

It is interesting to note that the removal of fear in a change process, if it is possible, does not in itself create support.[373] Fear of the unknown may create resistance, but the absence of such fear does not create support.

3. LOSS/GAIN OF GOODS

Organizational change most often represents a win/lose situation. Some people lose, while others win. One prominent example is how organizational change affects career opportunities. A central element in all organizations is different career ladders, and organizational change may alter these.[374] The number of leadership positions is cut in half, for example, when two departments merge. Some people may perceive this as a threat to their upward mobility. Thus, some people may oppose the merger because they see that their personal career opportunities are reduced. But organizational changes represent a plethora of possibilities for losing benefits and goods. People may lose their office, their free parking, or their treasured working hours. Many changes implemented in the public sector in the past few decades have been aimed at increasing productivity by introducing elements of competition that were not there before.[375] In most instances, and as is intended, competition leads to higher stress and more job strain. That many of these reforms meet resistance must in part be understood in the light of how they increase the pace of work, the intensity of competition, and stronger control.[376]

But changes may, of course, also create positive opportunities for benefits and gains. The possibility of positive benefits is probably an important factor in creating support for change, and in line with the many recommendations to use incentives strategically in planned changes.[377] Such incentives can range from the possibility of a higher salary, via better offices and canteen food, to better physical working conditions, and many other things. Some empirical studies still question how efficient material incentives are in creating support for change.[378] Expecting benefits makes it more "costly" to oppose change as no change implies the loss of benefits. Thus, continuance commitment to change may be strengthened. Positive incentives may also be perceived as an effort on the part of the organization to improve the lives of its members, possibly strengthening the normative commitment as well. However, there are few studies indicating that incentives play any important role in promoting affective commitment.[379]

4. LOSS OF IDENTITY

Organizational change is often associated with a reshuffling of tasks and responsibilities, as well as moving physically to new buildings and offices. People have a tendency to become emotionally bonded to both tasks and physical places and objects. Mastering a task is a confirmation of one's capabilites and one's value for the organization. Physical buildings and offices are not merely spaces to work in, but for many they represent some kind of "home". Offices are customized to the people working there, and are given a personal touch through furniture, pictures, and other objects. People build identities in the process of mastering a task and customizing the working place. Organizational changes may represent threats toward these identities. Or as Bolman and Deal point out: "When a relative or a close friend dies, we feel a deep sense of loss. Unconsciously, we have the same feelings when a computer replaces old procedures, a logo is changed after a merger, or a new leader replaces another."[380] Fear of losing one's identity may lead to a resistance to change.

5. EXTRA WORKLOAD

Resistance may also be caused for more obvious and mundane reasons than the ones listed above. One such reason is based on the fact that change costs energy and time, and many people in the organization may have to put in an extra effort, at least for a limited period.[381] As change has to take place while the organization conducts "business as usual", many employees and leaders may experience that they acquire a double work load. In short, people have to phase out old tasks and routines while learning new ones at the same time. For instance, an old archival system cannot simply be discarded during a short period of time. Rather, it must be slowly dismantled as the new system is constructed. During the transitional period, both systems must be operated at the same time. Such situations lead to increased work pressure, overtime, and stress, which many people will resist.

Closely connected to the phenomenon of increased work load is the need change creates for investments in new knowledge and skills.[382] New technologies, tasks, and procedures will require some kind of training. For many employees, this will imply periods of training, even schooling, which is in many instances a process that must take place while they are still conducting ordinary work. This will mean an extra effort for many, which at least some people may react negatively to. This problem becomes even more accentuated if people not only have to learn something new, but also to unlearn something old and well established.[383] One example is a change currently taking place in many schools, where teachers are shifting their way of teaching from the principle of "one teacher – one class" to working in teams with other teachers for several classes. This change is not just about learning a new way to work, but also unlearning the old system where the individual teacher had much more autonomy. For many, this may be a painful process that will be opposed.

6. BREAKING UP SOCIAL RELATIONS

Losing established social relations may be an important cause for resistance. In a now classic study of the coal mines in England it was clearly mapped out that change was followed by increased turnover, intensified labour conflicts, and a strong increase in sickness absence.[384] All these activities were interpreted as being signals of resistance to the changes. One of the main reasons for this resistance was that the automation of the production process resulted in a social fragmentation in the sense that colleagues lost contact with each other in their daily work.[385] Workers became isolated, and lost an important element in making work meaningful. Organizational changes often imply regroupings of people, by either splitting up or merging units. Some people will thus lose contact with not only colleagues, but also friends, and at the same time they have to build new social relations with unknowns. The social connectedness is thus, at least for a period, broken, something that may be perceived as highly negative, thus leading to resistance.

The reactions to breaking up social groups and relations will, of course, depend on how good relations were in the existing groups. For people experiencing a poor social working environment, organizational change may represent a possibility to improve the situation. In this way, the change may be perceived as good, not because it is good for the organization, but rather on the grounds of being good for some individuals.

7. VIOLATION OF PSYCHOLOGICAL CONTRACTS

Closely linked to social relations we find the construction of personal, informal, and unwritten agreements between people working together, often labelled "psychological contracts", that appear in every organization and group.[386] Violation of such psychological contracts is an important reason for resisting change. A psychological contract is developed through constant interaction among individuals. In the course of this interaction, people learn what is expected of them by the others. One learns how to perform work, when to do things (and not to do things), what to say and how to say it, and much more. Everybody that has experienced starting a new job knows that one has a tendency to be rather withdrawn and "invisible" for the first few weeks. During this period, one observes what goes on, what others say and do, and one adapts. As noted above, change will in many instances imply reshuffling people, meaning that one must learn to work with unknown people. Consequently, new psychological contracts must be negotiated. This is time consuming, and sometimes actually stressful. Many will perceive the negotiation of new psychological contracts as something negative, which they will try to avoid. However, the fact that people do not have to negotiate new psychological contracts does not create support for change.

8. POWER STRUCTURES ARE ALTERED

At a certain point in time, organizations can be regarded as rather stable power structures, a distribution of control over resources, the right to participate in decision processes, and the availability of information.[387] Organizational change will also affect such structures. Power structures can be both formal – connected to the formal hierarchy and formal decision rights – and informal. Informal power is, as discussed earlier in this book, connected to the control over critical tasks, availability of information, personal charisma, and knowledge. People controlling critical tasks may stop the functioning of the whole organization if they do not perform their tasks correctly.[388] One such example is air traffic controllers, who easily can shut down a whole airport by not doing their tasks. The access to information, to some extent determined by personal competence, physical location, and social network, will give some people an upper hand in negotiations, and also the possibility to influence who knows what in the organization.[389]

Change in the formal hierarchy will be a direct threat to the influence of those occupying these positions. But also less obvious changes – in tasks, physical location, the right to participate in certain decision arenas – will affect the power structure. People may lose control over a critical task, or be moved to an office located outside the informal information flow in the organization. People do not necessarily react negatively to losing power in itself. Rather, loss of power is resisted because it contributes significantly to the ability to shape one's own job, working situation, and autonomy.[390] Loss of power will make the situation more uncertain as one becomes more dependent on the actions of others.

Some will, of course, gain power in the process of organizational change, again moving these individuals to support the change. This, however, is not necessarily support on the grounds of believing in the change, and finding it good and necessary. People supporting the change because it increases their power are supporting it on egotistical grounds, not organizational ones.

9. THE SYMBOLIC ORDER IS ALTERED

The power structure in any organization also carries a symbolic side, a structure of symbols conveying status, prestige and esteem. Things are not just what we see; they also carry a deeper meaning.[391] Recently, a name change in Statoil – one of Norway's largest organizations – to Equinor has spurred a quite intense debate. For many, this discussion will be met by a shrug of the shoulders, and remarks like "it must be horrifically expensive to change all those logos!", or "what was wrong with the old name?" Delving more deeply into the issue, it becomes clear that the name change also symbolizes a change of direction for the whole company. "Oil" is taken out of the name, giving a clear signal that Statoil is defining itself as a producer of energy, not only oil and gas. It also conveys a signal that Statoil is toning down the emphasis on fossil fuel, thus reducing the status of the traditional focus area for the whole organization. The future is not oil and gas, but renewable energy. Such a change will also have repercussions inside the organization, as those working in different fields will have their status altered. Those working with renewable energy will be part of "the future", while those working within Statoil's traditional field suddenly represent the – possibly unpleasant – past.

And status is the central concept here. Where one sits in the organization, what kind of clothes one is allowed to wear during a working day, what computer one is allocated, etc. are all symbols saying something about a person's status in the organization. An attractive and spacious office, located close to the leaders, symbolizes power and influence, although this may not be reflected in the formal status. Physical elements are particularly important as symbols conveying status, as they are easy to see.[392] This can be described as follows:

> Ordinarily when space is reorganized people invent all sort of reasons why their future plans involve the use of all the unused space, why secretaries need private offices, and the like. (...) It takes serious mobilization of political power in an organization to reallocate space.[393]

Such resistance may be grounded in a real need for the physical space or area, but just as often it may be a struggle over the symbolic order and rank. Again, we find little evidence that maintaining one's symbolic order is a driver for change, creating support. It only creates resistance when it is threatened.

10. EXTERNAL ACTORS

Organizations are, as noted several times before, deeply embedded in their local environments. Such embeddedness may dramatically hinder, or at least slow down, change. First, most employees in an organization live with their families in the local environment. Physical relocation or downscaling, with loss of jobs as a consequence, will in turn affect families that will have to move and children who will have to change schools, and has many other ramifications. In 2018, a Norwegian specialist committee proposed a transfer of a wide spectrum of national government's tasks to the regional level: the counties. In practical terms, the consequence of this would be that approximately 5000 employees would both have their formal status changed, and would have to move geographically. As could be expected, the reactions from the organizations being affected were vehemently negative, many of them pointing to the consequences associated with moving whole families to other geographical areas of the country. In addition, local politicians, afraid of losing jobs in their local area, mobilized to influence decision makers in Parliament, ministries, and other central agencies. And, of course, the media were activated. The reorganization triggered, long before it started, counterforces in the local environment of the organization.

Second, many organizations are not just treated as a job and a place to work. Many of them carry a symbolic value, and thus they constitute an important part of an area's identity. The shutting down of a local brewery is perceived as closing something genuinely local, something that defines the local community. In such cases, large and dramatic changes will be opposed not only by people inside the organization, but also by the general population in the area.

Organizations may also encounter stability forces from customers, users and partners. One blatant example of this was the spectacular failure of an attempt to introduce "the new Coke" as a response to the increasing success of Pepsi.[394] The change was met by unanimous protest from customers, claiming that changing "Classic Coke" was close to blasphemy. Due to the vehement protests, Coca-Cola quickly abandoned the change. Similar attempts to change have been experienced in Norwegian hospitals over the last decades. Attempts to centralize hospitals, and thus to liquidate small, regional hospitals in favour of larger ones, have been met with protest marches, the establishment of local interest groups with the objective of stopping the change, and fierce debates in local media. Many of these attempts have been discontinued.

Positive resistance

Resistance to change is usually perceived as a negative phenomenon. Opponents to change are often characterized as "old fashioned" or "museum guards".[395] Such labels may obscure the fact that resistance will, in many instances, be a highly positive phenomenon. Resistance often manifests itself in critical comments on the need for change, and whether the change really represents a solution. As noted at the start of this book, change is always uncertain. Mapping a clear and objective need for change, and knowing with certainty what consequences a change will produce, is not possible. There will always be different opinions concerning these elements of change. As an implication, we must acknowledge that change agents may be wrong. They are not "angels of truth". Resistance can thus be a reaction to a change initiative that is not very well grounded in reality, that is not thoroughly reflected on, or simply based on a feeling of having to act. Furthermore, one can never be sure that an organizational change will solve the problem that is the reason or argument for change. Knowing whether or not a change will work is not possible before the change is implemented. This is clearly stated by Jeffrey Pfeffer, who says: "[A]t the moment a decision is made, we cannot possibly know whether it is good or bad. Decision quality, when measured by results, can only be known as the consequences of the decision become known."[396]

Consequently, resistance should be viewed as a continuous debate on current conditions and on how problems can be solved. Supressing critical comments by labelling them "resistance" is thus a dialogue-limiting act.[397] Such limitations are particularly problematic if they are set before a decision is made to go through with a planned change. Planned change must usually be decided or at least sanctioned through formal decisions. Resistance before such decisions are made should, as far as possible, be treated as discourse rather than resistance. It is the resistance taking place after legitimate decisions are made that should be regarded as problematic.

If we accept ambiguity, and that there are different perspectives on reality and that we cannot be certain which one is the most correct, discourse is a way of producing common understand. In this way, resistance is a positive phenomenon in the sense that it may provoke a more thorough reflection on the change, evaluating more alternatives and consequences. Furthermore, change process that does not meet any resistance can seem, in fact, quite ominous. It may indicate that everyone agrees and enters wholeheartedly into the change process. But it may also indicate that no one really cares, that employees and leaders, as well as external stakeholders, are apathetic as to what the organization does, and thus indifferent to what happens with the organization.

On a final note, it is easy to defines resisters and supporters as two distinct, opposite groups. Such a notion is probably far from reality, as lines between support and resistance are probably blurred and constantly changing. Change processes will clearly take on political characteristics, but not in the way that one can define two clear fronts. Conflicts may play out along many different dimensions, over a wide variety of issues. Some will agree that change is necessary, but they will disagree on solutions proposed. Some will oppose the whole idea of change, while some will believe that a certain amount of change is needed. Support and resistance will, in many change processes, represent a rather blurred line.[398]

From understanding to leading change processes

This chapter's discussion of time, resistance, and support is essential in understanding attempts to start planned changes in complex social systems. It is probably impossible, in practice, to imagine a change plan that will be followed to the smallest detail. The reason is, of course, that social systems are impossible to predict perfectly. Something unexpected will always happen. Social systems are undetermined.[399] Once a plan is laid out, people can start to act strategically to prevent the plan from working if they do not appreciate or agree with it. Unplanned things happen, because people may act to undermine the plan. Moreover, parallel and unpredictable events will occur as change proceeds, changing the premises laid down for the original plan. It may the environment of the organization that changes in an unforeseen way, for instance that a new competitor emerges in the market, or a person central in the change process quits.

In one of the most well-known attempts for planned change – the socio-technical experiments in England during the 1960s and 70s – one of the researchers noted the following: "The project showed in great detail how unanticipated and uncontrollable events in the broader as well the immediate context can influence outcome in the later stages."[400]

Insights like these are probably even more relevant today. Organizations, as social systems, have probably not become less complex during the past few decades. Claiming that change processes are impossible to steer perfectly does not negate the possibility that such processes can be influenced or channelled in a desired direction. The idea of planned change is based on the notion that it is possible, at least partially, to influence processes in certain directions.

Successful management of planned change is to steer processes so that change initiatives are transformed into better results. Understanding the driving forces of change, its content and scope, its inner and outer context, as well as the complexity of social system processes, will increase the probability of succeeding with planned change. Expressed quite simplistically, a good change agent must be able to create support – even enthusiasm! – for the initiative, as well as being able to manage resistance in an adequate way. Creating support and lowering resistance are closely connected with the change agent's ability to interpret and communicate convincing analyses of the need for change, and that the change proposed is urgent, correct and beneficial. Managing resistance includes predicting counterforces that will be activated during the process, and finding ways to counter these forces. Concurrently, good change management implies understanding the context in which change is taking place, and thus adapting to both internal and external specificities. Finally, a change agent has to understand and acknowledge the dynamics inherent in any change process, including how events and processes are connected, as well as the importance of timing and how to meet unpredictable consequences.

Knowledge of the four elements in the conceptual model of change – driving forces, content and scope, context, and change process – will constitute the basis for the next topic to be covered: planning and leading organizational change.

Part III

From understanding to action – conducting planned organizational change

Chapter 6

Strategies for change

It should come as no surprise following the previous discussion that organizational change is extremely complex. This complexity has prompted the claim that:

> Organization change is some kind of chaos. The number of variables changing at the same time, the magnitude of environmental change, and the frequent resistance of human systems create a whole confluence of processes that are extremely difficult to predict and almost impossible to control.[401]

Nor should it be surprising that change processes may look chaotic.[402] Many forces, both inside and outside the organization, are activated both to promote change and to resist it. The outcome of this "fight" is highly uncertain.

Still, most of us will cling to the idea that change is, at least to some degree, possible to steer and manage. If we abandon that assumption, it is easy to sink into a kind of determinism and paralysis, thinking that "it's no use trying; it won't work in any case". To support the notion of the possibility of planned change, we find several organizations that have managed to change as a result of planned change initiatives, although it is highly variable how successful these changes have been.[403] Such empirical results indicate that planned change is possible. The following assumption is a premise of this book: Planned change is possible if 1) the right change strategy is chosen, i.e there is a fit between the change strategy chosen and the type of change that is intended, and 2) change is managed correctly, in other words there is a fit between the change strategy chosen and the leadership style of the leader of change.

This underlying notion indicates that several change strategies and leadership behaviours exist. Looking at change strategies first, we will define a change strategy as "a unique combination of means through which to accomplish a desired change in a certain context given its unique features and challenges."[404]

Planned change is not one strategy, but many. Still, to make the following discussion transparent and easy to follow, we will operate with two main strategies, two main ways to organize change processes. The two types should be treated as ideal types in the Weberian sense, indicating that they are ideals and not empirical descriptions. Rather, they should be regarded as something to which one can contrast reality. In the real world, the two strategies will overlap. In this chapter they have a primarily analytical function.

Each of the two change strategies corresponds with two approaches to leadership. The two types of leadership will be the focus of chapter 7. In the final chapter, we will conclude with a contingency perspective on planned change where we discuss under which circumstances one strategy and leadership type should be preferred over another. As an answer to the question of which is the best strategy, the answer will be the classic "it depends".[405] Such an approach is needed as an alternative, and more realistic, way of treating attempts at planned change rather than much of what dominates the popular management literature, where "the one best way" is commonly preached.[406]

Two main change strategies

It is highly probable that all organizational change, even in the same types of organizations, will look different. Sometimes it may even be very hard to find commonalities between two changes. The radical merger of Norwegian municipalities from 2018 to 2020 is extremely different from the municipalities' continuous work to reduce sickness absence. Still, both processes can be defined as organizational change. In this chapter, we will start with the idea that two basic change strategies exist. The first will be labelled "E", where the E stands for "economic". It is described as follows: [407]

> (...) E has as its purpose the creation of economic value, often expressed as shareholder value. Its focus is on formal structure and systems. It is driven from the top with extensive help from consultants and financial incentives. Change is planned and programmatic.

The other strategy is labelled "O", where the O denotes "organization". The description of this strategy is as follows:[408]

> (...) O has as its purpose the development of the organization's human capability to implement strategy and to learn from actions taken about the effectiveness of changes made. Its focus is on the development of a high-commitment culture. Its means consist of high involvement. And consultants and incentives are relied on far less to drive change. Change is emergent, less planned and programmatic.

Each of these change strategies has unique attributes making it highly distinctive. The differences can be systemized along six dimensions: 1) the main objective or focus of the change, 2) the role of formal, hierarchical leaders in the change process, 3) the main content (levers) of change, 4) how change is planned and sequenced, 5) how motivation for change is spurred, and 6) the use of external consultants.

Strategy E

Strategy E is based on the idea that change is something that is driven primarily by a small group of people, usually the organization's top management. This group perceives a problem or an opportunity, they see there is a need for change, they develop solutions to tackle the problem, and they implement the measures to solve the problem. The main driving force is usually top management, and thus the strategy looks like something called a "commander model",[409] or some kind of "dictatorial change".[410] It is also similar to traditional top-down theories of implementation with its focus on how a small group can control the implementation of programmes and policies.[411] Change is basically treated as an analytical, rational process based on set goals, the identification of possible alternatives and their consequences, and choosing the best possible alternative.[412] The process of change is planned well in advance of the implementation, and the change process will have a clear starting and ending point. The ideal type is illustrated in figure 6.1.

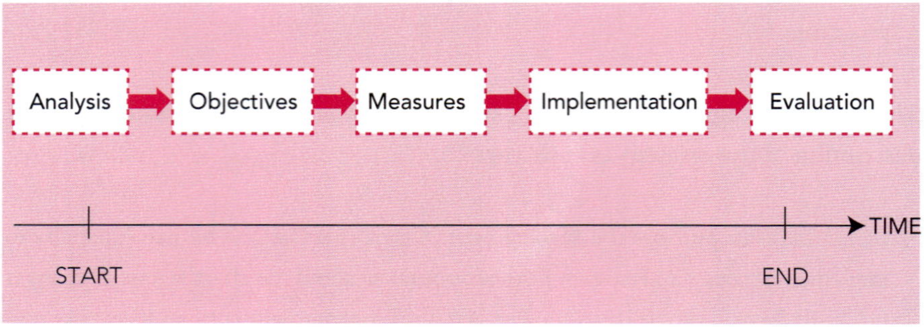

FIGURE 6.1: Change as an analytical process with a clear start and end

The separation of analysis, objectives, and solutions may be blurred, but the main point is that these activities take place *before* change is implemented.[413] A change process will thus have several similarities to a project, defined as a time-limited activity. This is also why this type of change strategy can be called episodic.[414] Now, let us analyse this change strategy along the six dimensions described above.

MAIN OBJECTIVE OR FOCUS OF CHANGE: VISIBLE, QUANTITATIVE OUTCOMES

The main objectives for this kind of change strategy are the visible outcomes that can be related to the change initiative. In most cases, these outcomes will be defined in relatively narrow and quantitative terms (as numbers). For organizations operating in a market, focus will be placed on quantitative indicators representing return on capital, or elements that are visibly linked to return on capital. Change is initiated mainly when economic results are less than satisfactory. Reasons for initiating change can thus be loss of market share, decrease in orders, increase in production costs, or falling stock values. Economic indicators will be evaluated as more relevant than other indicators like growth or market share. By focusing on quantitative indicators, change agents will get clear and "objective" feedback on whether the change works or not. This makes it easier to determine whether one should continue the change process as planned, change course, or even terminate it.[415]

Economic, and often quantitative, indicators are less valid for organizations not operating in a market, which will mean most public and voluntary organizations. According to classic economic theory, such organizations should maximize the public value. In a representative democracy, this will in practice mean the value of the electorate. Assuming that politicians act as rational actors, and that they – or at least the political parties they are members of – seek re-election, one will seek results that are visible for the voters.[416] Visible, quantitative results are also important for politicians, providing information on whether the change produces results that can be conveyed or "sold" to the electorate.

Public organizations will find it difficult to define income and cost:[417] they do not operate in a market where goods or services are traded for a price, and they will in many instances find themselves in situations of complex and contradictory goals and foci. Still, results can be quantified. Results can be defined as the number of patients on waiting lists at hospitals and how long they have to wait; results could be the number of patients treated in the course of a year, the number of students graduating at a university, or the cost of a kilometre of road built. If it is difficult to measure results, proxies can be used, such as change in the formal structure, change in staffing, or change in resources provided. Current Norwegian examples of such changes in the public sector are the "municipality reform" between 2016 and 2020 resulting in a reduction of municipalities from 428 to 356, the so-called "neighbourhood police reform" in 2017 ending with the elimination of 126 police stations, or the introduction of a norm for teacher-pupil ratio in Norwegian elementary schools in 2018. Such changes are highly visible, and it is easy to measure whether they have been conducted or not.

Focusing on simple, easy to measure, quantitative results also makes it easier to avoid one of the main pitfalls of planned change: trying to drive change by focusing on ambiguous, hard-to-measure outcomes and processes.[418] Such results, usually in the form of written descriptions, are much harder to communicate and measure than simple, numerical indicators. In sum, this will make it harder to keep a strong focus as it is difficult to differentiate the most important elements from those of lesser importance:

> The difficulty of connecting activities to the bottom line is complicated by the fact that most companies choose to launch a vast array of activities simultaneously across the entire organization. This is like researching a cure for a disease by giving a group of patients ten different new drugs at the same time.[419]

Some go as far as to claim that change initiatives should only focus on the final result or outcome of the change. Only one goal is important: the long-term creation of value. An organization unable to focus on this one goal will end up with an organization without goals. The well-known economist Michael C. Jensen, for instance, emphasizes that:[420]

> It is logically impossible to maximize more than one dimension at the same time unless the dimensions are monotone transformations of one another. Thus, telling a manager to maximize current profits, market share, future growth in profits, and anything else one pleases will leave that manager with no way to make a reasoned decision. In fact, it leaves the manager with no objective.

The simpler and clearer the objective, the easier it is to measure, and the easier it becomes to avoid goal displacement in the change process. One clear goal will make it much more difficult to shift focus to other, for some highly valued, objectives like growth, moving into a more luxurious market niche, or appearing as a hero or saviour. It will also make it harder for some groups to shift focus to more interesting and challenging tasks, higher prestige, or higher salaries. One the one hand, clear-cut and easy-to-measure results will sharpen the focus of both managers and employees in the organization. Feedback on clearly defined results can also work as an important motivating factor as it gives people something to strive for.[421] On the other hand, clearly defined results make it easier to supervise and steer the change process as it is easy to measure indicators of progress towards the final goal.

THE ROLE OF THE FORMAL, HIERARCHICAL LEADERS: TOP-DOWN PROCESSES

Top managers play a central role in strategy E. There may be several reasons for this; one obvious one is the access to information that is connected with occupying top, hierarchical positions.[422] Top managers find themselves squarely in the middle of any organizational information flows. Information from the environment will almost automatically flow in the direction of top managers as they are linking pins between the environment and the organization. Top managers will thus in many instances have the best overview of opportunities and threats present in the environments, giving them an advantage over other organizational members in registering a need for change. Lower hierarchical levels will not be exposed to external information in the same way, and may thus miss signals that should have spurred a change initiative.

Second, and closely linked to the access to information, top managers are usually those with the most comprehensive view of the organization. Managers of specialized units like departments and offices will often have a perspective limited to their specific unit, while top managers get information concerning all units.[423] Managers of more specialized units will be exposed to, and search for, specific information relevant to the limited task and responsibilities of the unit.[424] They will have a very good overview of information relevant to their unit, but – as a consequence of division of labour and specialization – less information about what other units do. Top managers are less specialized, and receive information from all units, probably making them more adept at making comprehensive decisions about organizational change, as: "senior leaders are less likely to have narrowly defined perspectives. They are also more likely to appreciate how the organization is an interlocking set of functions and systems – where changes in one will have implications for the others."[425]

Third, top management is the only group of managers that have the formal power and legitimacy to force through change. Their positions as top managers give them access to using incentives, mainly material and monetary, to overcome resistance. If the need arises to isolate groups to manage resistance, to reward individuals or groups that contribute strongly to the change, or to issue orders, top managers are the only ones capable of doing it.[426] They can also employ their formal power to set objectives, and to elaborate the indicators used to measure the change process.

Fourth, top managers are the only group in the position to engage in compromises as a result of negotiations taking place in the change process. As noted previously, resistance to change is almost inherent in any change process, and as it is naïve to believe that one group will have enough power to force through their solution, negotiations will be needed. In modern societies and organizations, power is distributed. In Norway, for instance, employees have great influence over changes in their own organizations, at least through the labour organizations. The same is the case for external actors like public agencies and professional organizations. In short, negotiation is necessary. While much negotiation on daily activities is usually delegated to lower hierarchical levels in an organization, it is hard to see that organizational changes, particularly more radical ones, can be delegated away from top management.[427]

Finally, one should not underestimate the symbolic function and power of top managers. They function as figureheads as they are highly visible both internally and externally.[428] The actions and words of top managers are strong symbols, giving them the possibility to exert symbolic power by exploiting their visibility.[429] What top managers say, how they say it, and what they do can have a deep impact on how organizational change is perceived by other members of the organization.

In most writings on planned change, even writings with a "bottom-up" perspective on change, the crucial role of top management support is emphasized.[430] However, for strategy E to succeed, top management support is not sufficient. Top managers must, for this strategy to work as planned, be actively involved in the change as change agents.

THE CONTENT OF CHANGE: STRATEGIES, STRUCTURES AND SYSTEMS

Initially, we sketched out a simple model on the content of change indicating that the content could be divided into two different types: formal elements like technology, structure, and systems, and informal elements like organizational culture and informal power structures. This distinction between the formal and the informal goes back a long way in the history of organization science.[431] Even if the elements are intertwined and almost impossible to separate clearly, strategy E will place its main focus on using the formal elements as levers to obtain better results. We see recommendations in literature indicating that successful change starts with formal elements, and is followed up by changes in the informal system.[432] Adherents of strategy E are by no means claiming that informal elements are unimportant, and some may even point to these factors as being more important than the formal ones to create real and enduring change. However, strategy E is based on an assumption that planned change should start with changes in the formal elements. There are several good reasons for such timing or pacing.

First, and perhaps most important, is that top management's direct control is mostly limited to formal elements. Investments in new technology can be decided on, training programmes can be started, and structures may be altered by merging units, splitting them up, decentralizing or centralizing decisional responsibilities, or reshuffling tasks and personnel. New goals and strategies can be decided on. All these changes can be determined in formal organizational arenas, and are thus changes that can be initiated quite quickly.[433]

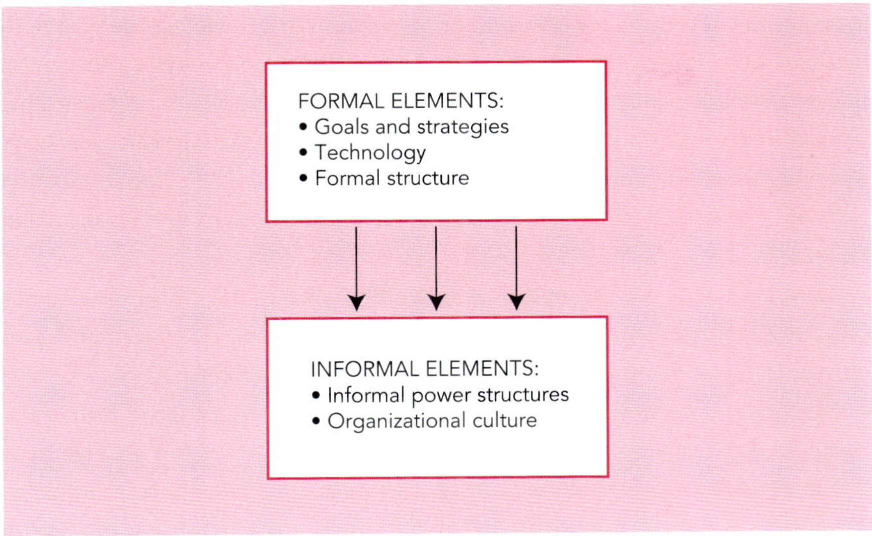

FIGURE 6.2: Strategy E – main focus set on formal organizational elements

Next, it is a well-established empirical finding that there is a correlation between structural change and behavioural change.[434] Structures, systems, and strategies function as normative standards for expected behaviour, and thus for the behaviour that can be rewarded or punished. In most cases, people in organizations will adapt to changes in the formal context. New tasks, altered relations, and new routines are all factors spurring behavioural change. Equally important is to acknowledge the links between the formal and the informal elements, as the archetypical perspective on organization makes us aware of. A structural change may affect informal power structures significantly. Restructuring as a response to accommodating new information and communication technology (ICT) has resulted in dramatic transfer of power from middle managers to the operative core and to top managers.[435] Furthermore, structural changes may directly alter channels of communication, changing the positions of people in the information flow of the organization. Restructuring may also end control of critical tasks by distributing them among more people and functions.

Structural changes may also create cultural changes. In many reorganizations, people are moved from one group to another, directly affecting interactions between individuals and groups. As a result, people gain new ideas and insights as they are exposed to new colleagues. Thus, one is forced to learn "how things are done around here". Changing people's structural position will also change their exposure to and search for information.[436] New positions will expose people to new people carrying new information, and they will start to search for information relevant to these people and the accomplishment of the task at hand. Over time, people learn to see things from "their position", and will thus develop new ways of seeing the world, an essential element in cultural change.[437] The connection between formal and informal elements in the lens of strategy E is illustrated in figure 6.2.

Focusing on formal elements does not imply ignoring the informal elements, only that formal elements are changed first, with the knowledge that theses changes will *over time* produce changes in the informal elements.

Moreover, one should not forget the symbolic effect of change in formal elements.[438] As with people's clothing, formal elements are – as top management – visible to actors both inside and outside the organization. People use clothes to signal who they are or want to be, and organizations use structure and strategy in the same way.[439] Investing in new technology signals being "modern", structural change indicates that the organization is aware of what is going on in the management literature, and goals and strategies are used to "flag" opinions that are viewed as "good". Changing formal elements signals an organization with the will and power to act, to do something to solve problems. Sometimes, organizations may be more interested in the symbolic effect than in any behavioural effects. Change becomes, as noted earlier, symbolic. Symbolic changes are conducted to increase legitimacy, in turn resulting in easier access to important goodwill and resources. So purely symbolic changes may be highly efficient. The problem is that changes in formal elements are hard to isolate as symbols only. Formal changes will have behavioural effects, and may thus create unwanted effects if the intention of the change is purely symbolic. A possible solution to such a problem is to intentionally decouple formal elements from behaviour. The organization indicates actions through formal elements, but actually does something else, a phenomenon that can be designated as "organizational hypocrisy".[440] In any case, the effects of changes in an organization's formal elements should not be underestimated.

PLANNING: FORMAL AND SEQUENTIAL

Strategy E emphasizes formal planning of the change process. Planned change is, as noted in the introduction of this book, regarded as a rational process, a process that is assumed to take on a linear form where phases follow each other logically and in time. Visions and goals must be set in advance in order to know the direction to be taken. Then measures are determined that will achieve the goal, the measures will then be implemented, and finally, rewards or punishments will be assigned and distributed.

Strategic analysis is central to such a model. Goals and measures are only legitimate if they are based on a sound analysis of the organization, both its environments and its internal conditions.[441] Analysis is important because it provides decision makers – here: change agents – with an overview of the "space of opportunities", that is the possibilities and limitations associated with initiating a certain change. The most commonly used analysis for this purpose is probably the SWOT analysis.[442] SWOT is an acronym for four fields of analysis, usually associated with choosing basic strategy for the organization. In a change context, a SWOT analysis will focus on the following elements:

S: Internal strengths, for instance support for the change, available economic resources, time, and more.
W: Internal weaknesses, for instance resistance to change, no acceptance of the need for change, lack of resources, and more.
O: External opportunities, for instance support from external stakeholders, media treating the change as legitimate, support from trade unions, and more.
T: External threats, for instance laws and regulations complicating the change, resistance from external stakeholders, uncertainty as to how competitors will exploit the weakness exposed in the change process, and more.

This analysis constitutes the basis for the choice of actions to be taken during the change process. In practice, this will mean a written plan where the change process is broken into several pre-defined phases. Each phase is determined with a milestone providing information about whether one is moving closer to the objective or not, and whether one should continue on the chosen course or adjust it. Every milestone is associated with an incentive, rewards or punishments. Figure 6.3 shows a stylized model of this type of change planning.

For each phase responsibility is placed, defining who is expected to do what, and when. Supplementary plans, providing information on measures, timeframes, resources and expected results, are elaborated.[443] Plans are formal and written, and are communicated to all levels of the organization affected by the change.

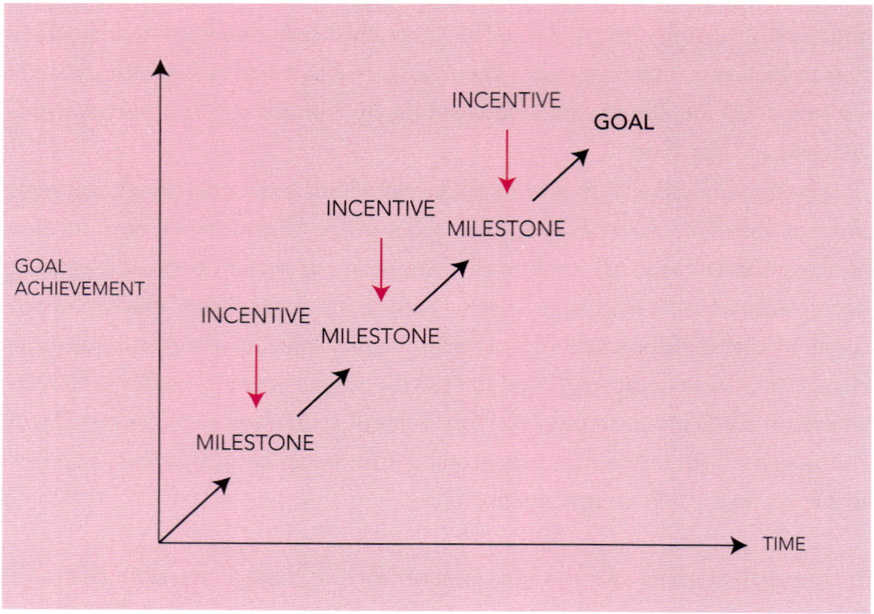

FIGURE 6.3: Change as a linear process consisting of phases and milestones

Comprehensive plans make it possible to supervise the process in great detail, and to intervene if things do not go as planned. Without such plans or pre-described "recipes", change may end up chaotic and unmanageable.[444]

Milestones are central to strategy E, as they represent points where the situation can be measured. Thus, it is the milestones that enable steering of the process. Knowing that one is being supervised, measured, and controlled at certain points during the change process can also "push through" change as this promotes discipline.

MOTIVATING FOR CHANGE: THE USE OF FINANCIAL INCENTIVES

The success of planned change processes is highly dependent on the acceptance, support and engagement of those who are supposed to change. Within the context of strategy E, financial or monetary incentives take on a central role. Monetary incentives – or more correctly: future expected rewards or punishments – are essential as a driving or motivating force to create change.

Central to the idea of incentives is that the prospect of future rewards will channel behaviour in the direction needed to obtain the rewards.[445] For such incentives to work, they must meet some basic requirements. First, incentives should be designed so that individuals are appreciated for what they are doing for the organization.[446] One example could be receiving a bonus if standards specified in a milestone are met. Second, incentives should strike the best possible balance between individual, group, and organizational incentives. Using only individual or group incentives may intensify competition among individuals and groups, and it may strengthen egotistical considerations. This could harm organizational change, at least where one is expecting collective change. Third, rewards must be perceived as realistic. If demands are set so high that it is impossible within the actual resource and time frame to meet the standards defined in the milestones, the result may be demotivation instead of motivation.

Used appropriately, incentives can be effective in both reducing resistance and increasing support. The main reason for this is that incentives may harmonize views so that what is good for the organization is also defined as good for the individual or group. What is good for the organization "trickles down" to individuals, motivating them to actively take part in working for the change.[447] As efficient incentives are based in expectations about future rewards, it is necessary to outline these incentives and the standards to be met to obtain them *before* the change process starts. If not, they cannot function as motivators and a driving force for change.

CONSULTANTS: EXTERNAL SPECIALISTS

Most planned organizational changes involve some kind of assistance from external consultants, usually representatives from larger consultancy firms. As organizational change in general seems to have become more common, consultancy activities within this field seem to expand.[448] Within the framework of strategy E, consultants usually take on an "expert role" or a "doctor–patient role".[449] In its most extreme form the situation may be as described in the following:

> When the organization has a problem, bring in the expert consultants. Tell the consultants where to look, (...) then turn them loose. The consultants know their business and have been called upon to handle many similar problems. They work in a calm and deliberate way, drawing people out, listening, and forming conclusions. Afterwards, only a few trusted executives review the results of their investigation and make the necessary decisions.[450]

The authors label this form as the "mafia model", as it resembles a model where an almighty leader calls on a troupe of professional assassins to finish the job. Apart from the negative associations activated by this label, this seems to be a much used model for how consultants are used in planned change processes.

Hiring external consultants to do much of the job is associated with several benefits.[451] One is that external consultants, as "outsiders", will have a more impartial view of the organization than "insiders". People who have been in the organization for a while will often develop "blind spots", indicating that they do not see things because they are too accustomed to seeing and experiencing them. External consultants may be less hindered by such blinders, and may thus be better at arriving at the right diagnosis.[452] Another benefit is that external consultants are specialists in organization and management, a field of expertise that people working in an organization often lack. Again, this will make the consultants better at making correct diagnoses and choosing appropriate solutions to the problems. Finally, external specialists may have a better capacity to take a holistic view of the organization. People who have been in an organization for a while, both leaders and employees, will usually develop more parochial views as they will focus on elements that are close to what they work with on a daily basis. External consultants will most often employ analytical tools forcing them to take into considerations all aspects of the organization, for instance through the use of the well-known 7S Framework used by McKinsey.[453]

Another characteristic of the use of consultants is the tight coupling between consultants and the top-tier management of the organization. These consultants do not relate to everybody in the organization, but to a narrow group of formal decision makers.[454] In some cases, consultants may even take over the role of top management, as the use of "management-for-hire" seems to become increasingly common in, at least more radical, change processes.

The use of consultants within strategy E usually contains analysis of both problems and opportunities, as well as solutions and measures to be taken. However, it can also be more limited, for instance hiring consultants only to carry out the analysis. In any case, within this framework consultants play the role of the doctor diagnosing the patient and prescribing the correct medicine or treatment. Whether the patient takes the medicine or completes the treatment is not the doctor's problem.

Strategy O

This strategy, although it may at first glance appear to be the complete opposite of strategy E, is also grounded in an ideal of rationality. The main foundation is that problems can be analysed, goals can be set, and measures can be elaborated and implemented. Still, strategy O deviates from strategy E on several dimensions.

Instead of talking about change, this strategy is more about development. Change is not seen as episodic, but rather as a continuous and interactive process.[455] The process itself will have less clearly defined boundaries as the start and end points will be more ambiguous. This strategy has been described as "incremental"[456] or "participative",[457] or simply as "organizational development" or OD.[458] Change is not necessarily regarded as a linear process, but rather as a circular process where one small change fosters new changes. Figure 6.4 illustrates this perspective on change.

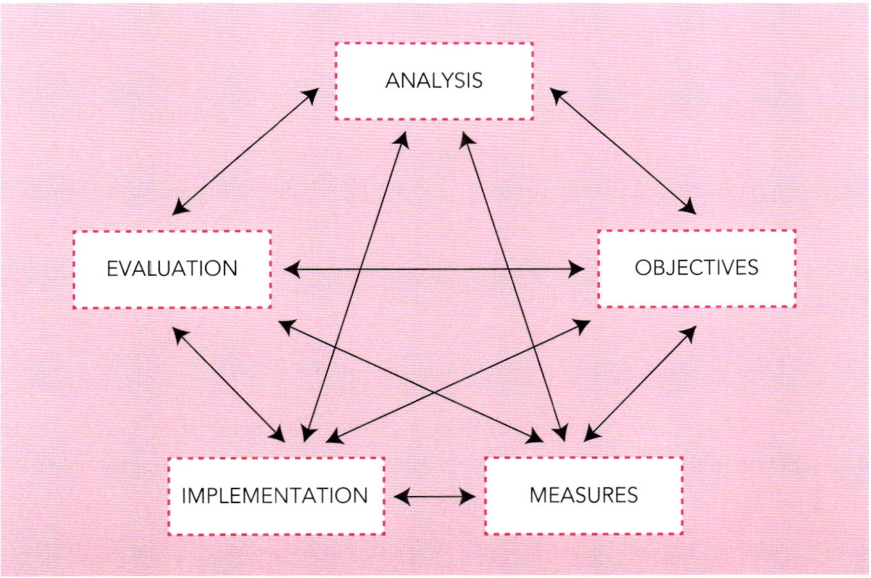

FIGURE 6.4: Change as a circular process with no clear start or end point

In contrast to strategy E, this strategy does not rely on a complete analysis of problems and opportunities, development of solutions, or measures to be taken before the change process starts. Rather, the strategy devotes more attention to uncertainty in the sense that it takes into consideration problems associated with developing a full analysis with solutions early on in the process. As the future is uncertain, and characterized by ambiguity, it becomes more important to be able to experiment, and to learn continuously from the results of experiments.[459]

MAIN OBJECTIVE OR FOCUS OF CHANGE: CAPACITY FOR LEARNING

The starting point of strategy O, although based on rationality, is clearly a critique and almost an anti-thesis to the narrow focus on economic and quantitative outcomes proposed by Strategy E. Organizations are not simple machines designed for production, and thus cannot be redesigned every time someone is dissatisfied with the production. Rather, organizations should be regarded as living organisms in constant movement. As organizations and their environments are in constant movement, attempts to design pre-planned change processes early on will face the danger of being outdated when they are implemented. At the time of implementation, there is a strong possibility that both the organization and the environments have changed in ways not possible to foresee. Thus, a new change process must be designed to solve the new problems that the first change process had not taken into account.[460] Instead of attempting to pre-plan changes, organizations should be enabled to perform continuous changes to adapt to ongoing changes both inside and outside the organization. This is only possible by creating a learning organization, defined as:[461]

> (…) an organization that is continually expanding its capacity to create its future. For such an organization, it is not enough merely to survive. "Survival learning" or what is more often termed "adaptive learning" is important – indeed it is necessary. But for a learning organization, "adaptive learning" must be joined by "generative learning", learning that enhances our capacity to create.

Such a view is not necessarily in conflict with strategy E's focus on results and outcomes. Strategy O is equally interested in what organizations achieve economically and financially. The difference is that strategy O focuses on the internal organizational processes necessary to achieve these results. The focus is more "inward", directed towards the human qualities and social processes that are necessary to create results.

To create learning organizations, one has to focus on the human side of organizations. Organizations cannot – per definition – learn; that is something only humans can do. Enabling organizations to learn will thus require humans who are willing and able to learn, and social relations where knowledge is distributed both within and between groups. Looking at individual learning first, one of the most influential theories was developed by Chris Argyris and Donald Schön (1974). Their starting point, based on a variety of empirical studies in diverse cultural contexts, is that human learning is guided by a set of basic "theories-in-use". The "theories-in-use" are basic assumptions on how to act, guiding the responses humans enact when faced with the consequences of their actions. Individuals are mostly not consciously aware of these "theories-in-use" as they are the result of a lifelong socialization process. Most humans' "theories-in-use" have some common characteristics: 1) define clear goals and act to obtain them, 2) try to win, avoid losing, 3) avoid negative feelings, both in oneself and in others, and 4) try to act rationally. Argyris and Schön claim that this way of thinking is dysfunctional in many situations, as it often leads to people defending their actions instead of learning from possible errors they made. As a consequence, humans learn to develop more sophisticated defence mechanisms instead of engaging in real learning.[462] Such learning is labelled "single-loop learning" or the Model I type of learning, and is described as follows:[463]

> People who behave according to Model I tend to develop group norms that support the model – for example, in the form of organizational structures and policies – and become accustomed to them. Model I conditions cluster and reinforce one another, whether the individual wishes them or not, and tension, inter-group rivalry, self-sealing attributions, or political lying become viewed as being as natural as apple pie. Once these phenomena become part of the social landscape, individuals see less need for changing them, and may even design ways to circumvent or adapt to these processes.

The core of this type of learning is to defend and reinforce the existing state, not to change.[464] Breaking out of the dysfunctional circles often created by single-loop learning means breaking down these defence mechanisms. This will be the first step in a move towards another type of learning, often termed "double-loop learning" or Model II. To be able to make this move from Model I to Model II type of learning, individuals must be made aware of the "theories-in-use" governing their behaviour. Only when they are explicated are they possible to change. And the only way to explicate them is to constantly confront people with how they act in specific situations, and to reflect on these actions and discuss them with others. This will in turn require an organizational climate characterized by trust and a feeling of support, i.e. that one does not fear being criticized and attacked when discussing one's actions. In this way the organization can move towards a situation where "theories-in-use" are constantly challenged and discussed.

This is by no means an easy task, as it is necessary to break down deeply ingrained defence mechanisms.[465] As noted, this will require a supportive and trustful organizational climate . And still this is not enough. In addition, one must create systems to ensure that individual knowledge is distributed to other individuals the group, and that group knowledge is distributed to other groups. This is what *organizational* learning is all about.

Peter Senge[466] put forward a list of measures necessary to create a learning organization. Two of them have clear similarities with measures needed to move individuals from Model I to Model II type of learning, namely constantly criticizing one own's mental models (very similar to what Argyris and Schön called "theories-in-use") and developing personal mastery. Personal mastery is about the ability to set and continually evaluate individual goals, an ability that requires a great deal of self-criticism. Furthermore, Senge emphasizes the need for system thinking, a way of thinking that sees organizations as consisting of interdependent parts. At the group level, there is a need to develop a capacity for setting common visions, and to increase the capacity for group learning, not only individual learning.

Group learning is, according to Senge, based on dialogue and discourse, that is, a free and constant exchange of meanings and opinions within a group. Such discourse rarely develops by itself; it requires training. The individual group member has to learn communication skills, both verbal and non-verbal, as well as central group processes that take place in all groups. One must learn how to handle conflict, and how conflict can be a productive force. In short, to encourage the development of learning, one must create a group where communication runs freely. The creation of such groups depends on their having the possibility to experiment, which in turn requires structural changes, most notably decentralization of decision-making power.[467]

Nonaka[468] completes this picture by focusing on the role of tacit knowledge in groups and organizations, beginning with the notion that organizations learn continually, even though they are not always aware of it. People observe each other, experiment, and develop personal theories on what works and what does not. Still, the knowledge created in this process is rarely consciously mediated to others in the group or the organization. And even worse: people are not themselves aware of the knowledge they acquire in such processes. For this knowledge to be usable for others, it has to be explicated and communicated. Knowledge must be transformed from implicit to explicit.[469] To further develop organizational knowledge, the organization must be able to develop systems to create interaction between the implicit and the explicit knowledge. Tacit knowledge must be explicated and communicated, for example through written rules or handbooks. And if the explicit knowledge is to be transferred from knowledge to action, it has to be internalized.

Development of organizational knowledge thus requires systems to make tacit knowledge explicit, for communication of explicit knowledge, and for internalizing explicit knowledge and thus transferring it to collective action. If an organization succeeds with this, it will establish a capacity not only to learn and adapt, but also to innovate. Strategy O focuses on exactly these processes: enabling individuals to learn, and creating groups that communicate well. As can probably be seen, this goal is much more vague and difficult to measure directly than Strategy E's strong focus on quantifiable results and outcomes.

THE ROLE OF THE FORMAL, HIERARCHICAL LEADERS: BOTTOM-UP PROCESSES

The role of top tier managers in the change process is not necessarily toned down in the framework of strategy O. Rather, it will take on quite a different, but still crucial, role. In this strategy, it is not the top level managers themselves who are expected to implement the change. Their role is, rather, to create enthusiasm for change, so that employees themselves want to play an active role in the change process. Or as Warren Bennis puts it: "If there is one generalization we can make about leadership and change, it is this: No change can occur without willing and committed followers."[470]

Leaders must create a sense of willingness to change, and furthermore an enthusiasm for change, an active wish for change to happen. This is only possible if top managers limit their roles to sketching out the general visions for the change, and in turn – through delegation and participation – facilitate the change by letting employees themselves develop measures and solutions they "own". Instead of giving orders and commands, leaders will have to be participative, supportive, and delegating.[471] Employees are the driving force of change, not the top management.

There are plenty of arguments for why such a leadership style is superior when it comes to implementing change. First of all, it is usually those at the operative level of the organizations who have the best ability to see what needs to be done. It is the operative core who engages in daily contact with the environment, and thus probably first will notice what need there is for change. Second, a participative leadership style will produce a wide variety of points of view on the change that is occurring. If we assume, as it recently has become more common to do,[472] that environments are becoming more and more uncertain, valid analyses of such environments will require a diversity of perspectives. Only through dialogue – the exchange of points of view and opinions – is it possible to obtain a valid and nuanced picture of both problems and solutions.[473] Engaging many groups and levels in the change process may thus contribute strongly to increasing the rationality of the process.

The two arguments above are first and foremost connected to how the analysis of problems and solutions can be improved by participation and inclusion. But it is probably a third argument that is even more important: that participation may contribute to decreasing resistance to change. As noted earlier in this book, resistance to change is a common phenomenon. However, what one should also be aware of is that resistance can be a product of how the change process itself is organized.[474] It is possible that

> if an employee receives an unfavorable outcome or loses a dispute, but believes that the decision-making process was fair, the decision will be perceived as more legitimate and the employee will be less likely to challenge the decision-making authority.[475]

Facilitating the use of participation and influence in the decision process will probably increase the legitimacy of the decision, in turn decreasing the resistance towards decisions that one does not favour. On a more positive note, it is also highly possible that participation will increase the feeling of "ownership" of the decision that is made. It is something that one has participated in producing, and not something that has been forced on employees with no possibility for them to influence it in any way. If people gain a feeling of ownership of a decision, it will be less necessary to use incentives to get people to engage in the change process.

A participative leadership style will require top managers to delegate power, both in the analysis of why change is necessary and what measures should be taken, and in the implementation of the specific measures. Such a leadership style resembles what has been labelled democratic leadership, as a contrast to a dictatorial or autocratic leadership style. The ability to delegate and to create participation becomes the key characteristic of leaders:[476]

> The top executive team that fails to involve these people (or their representatives) is running a high-risk strategy. The top team may have a more broad overview of the business; but in a complex organization with a dynamic technology base and diverse, turbulent, fast-moving markets, managers need some "good runners" to update them on what often isn't obvious from the lofty heights of the hill. Also, (...) when it comes to making strategic change happen, the top team is quite impotent without the mindful, motivated commitment of an informed work force.

In strategy O, the top managers delegate authority, consult employees from all levels of the organization, and make decisions that are products of processes with broad participation from many groups and hierarchical levels in the organization. At the same time, top managers should be aware of important group processes that may stall the change, and should thus be able to step in to resolve conflicts, to coach, and to "train" participants in the change process.[477]

THE CONTENT OF CHANGE: INDIVIDUALS, GROUPS, AND CULTURE

Strategy O clearly focuses on the human side of the organization. Successful organizational change is seen as being completely dependent on whether people in the organization want to change, and on their ability and capacity to change. Focus is then moved from the formal elements of structure, strategies, and systems to individuals and human relations. To obtain organizational change, it is thus necessary first to focus on:[478]

- Interpersonal competence, or competence in communicating and interacting with others
- Individuals' emotions and values
- Relations between groups and the ability to handle tensions between groups
- Ability to cooperate and to function as a team
- Ability to handle conflict in other ways than by the use of hierarchy and formal power.

These elements have led some to label this strategy as an "educational change strategy".[479] Individuals must develop competencies for how to interact with others, groups have to learn how to interact and cooperate with other groups, and the organization must develop common norms, values, and assumptions on what the organization "is". Measures to be taken in the change process are thus directed towards what has been labelled the "deep structure" of the organization, namely basic assumptions and skills, social relations, and cultural elements.

At the individual level, measures will usually take on the form of training, either as pure education or in the form of skills training. A highly debated technique is the so-called T-group, proposed early on by Chris Argyris as a powerful tool in organizational change and development.[480] T stands for "training", and had in its practical execution strong similarities with a type of sensitivity training where the aim was to develop personal understanding of how one functioned in relation to others. Similar techniques encompass role analysis, or life or career planning.[481]

At the group level, the focus is set on group processes, for instance how cooperation in a group is influenced by emotions, and how productive cooperation can be constructed. Some techniques are aimed at improving relations between groups, for example through "mirroring tools" or dialogue conferences to improve communication between groups.[482] To enable groups to learn from their actions, Peter Senge has introduced the concept of "micro worlds". This concept is based on a notion that we live in organizations that are

> complex systems (where the) consequences of our actions are neither immediate nor unambiguous. Often they are far removed from us in time and space. (…) We learn best from experience, but we never experience the consequences of our most important decisions. How, then, can we learn?[483]

Establishing a "microworld" may solve some of these problems. This is done by constructing a realistic situation – for example, changing a routine, establishing a new task group, or setting up a project consisting of several organizational departments – on a small scale. Practically, such situations may be enacted through diverse forms of role play, experiments, or – as is more and more common – computer simulations. In such deliberately constructed situations, feedback will come more swiftly and clearly than it does in the real world. This will enable people to see the consequences of their actions more clearly, and can facilitate a more direct, experience-based learning.

At the organizational level, strategy O focuses on the organization's "softer" side: the cultural elements of assumptions, values, and norms. Tools and techniques to change the culture will include the use of physical symbols, storytelling, and the establishment of myths, histories, and heroes that convey the wanted change signals.[484] To change culture in a planned way also requires a plan for socialization, or how new values and norms shall become a natural part of the lives of the organization's employees.[485]

The main logic behind strategy O is an assumption that durable change has to come from within; it has to be something that is wanted by the members of the organization, not something that is forced upon them. Research on organization is chock-full of examples of changes in formal structures and systems that have little or no enduring effect on the behaviour of the organization.[486] Structural changes may become superficial changes with, at best, minor consequences for actual behaviour, and may thus end up primarily as symbolic changes.[487] Another important element in strategy O is the clear signal it gives that it is the employees – the individuals – that are the crucial part of the change. Such a focus will also make it more likely to produce changes that not only benefit the organization, but also the individuals working in the organization.[488] Such signals will in themselves create enthusiasm and involvement, and may increase the possibility that changes are good for both the organization and the individual. The strong emphasis given by strategy O on the

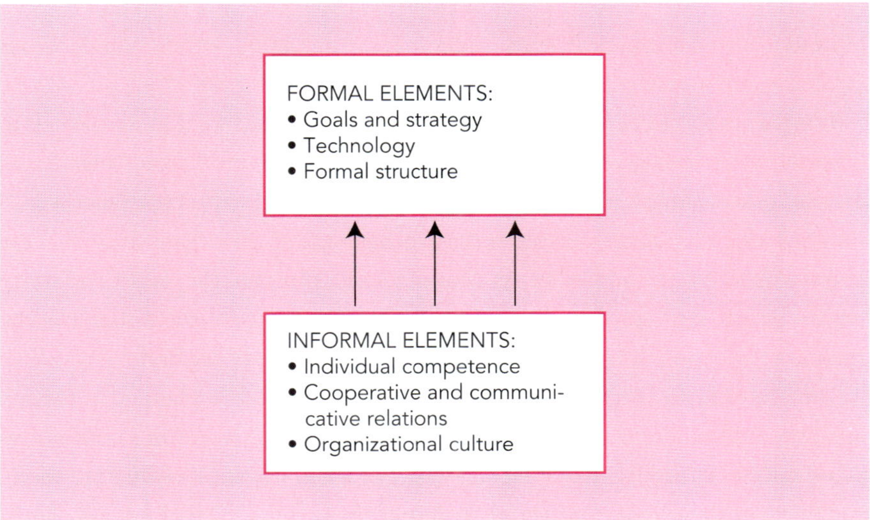

FIGURE 6.5: Strategy O: main focus on the organization's informal elements

possibility for employees to participate actively in the reshaping of the organization, and thus to increase their possibility of self-realizing, makes it basically humanistic.[489]

One should not be lured into thinking that strategy O totally overlooks formal organizational elements. Rather, it is a strategy where changes in the formal elements follow logically as a consequence of changes in the individual and cultural system. It is a matter of timing. First, one should focus on changes in the "softer" elements, and then the formal elements should be adapted to the changes in individual skills and norms, cooperative relations, and culture. Figure 6.5 illustrates this idea.

Strategy O's main philosophy is that behaviour should be changed first, and then followed up by changes in the formal elements. As a consequence, the idea that behaviour can be "pushed" in a certain direction by changing the formal elements of the organization is toned down. Structures and systems have limited capacity to change behaviour on a long-term basis, but they can represent barriers to reasonable action and interaction.

PLANNING: INCREMENTAL AND EXPERIMENTAL

Like strategy E, strategy O is based on having a vision and goal, a sense of direction and where one is going through the change process. But that is also all they have in common. Strategy O is based on an assumption that the most effective way to plan the process is to see the process as non-linear, as events and actions that do not necessarily follow each other in a sequential process. Planning is viewed as "a series of nested partial decisions in each strategic area interacting with similar decisions in all other areas and with a constantly changing resource base."[490]

It is the interconnectedness of all organizational elements that, according to proponents of strategy O, makes it impossible to make one "grand" plan based on one "grand" decision before starting the implementation process. Once a decision is made, it produces consequences in other parts of the organization that are impossible to foresee or predict. As a consequence, one runs the risk of ending up with a "grand" strategy that very quickly becomes unsuited to the situation as the situation has changed significantly from when the plan was decided.

Thus, some have argued that change processes should be planned in a more incremental fashion. Incrementalism is to treat planning more as a continuous process than a product. Planning is trying out small changes, evaluating them, and then decide whether one should continue along the same path or not. "Small steps" are the key elements. Planning in this fashion entails many potential benefits. First, it acknowledges that the world is complex, and that it may change even in a very short time perspective. Thus, it takes a realistic view of the human capacity for planning for the future. The planner taking such a stance is a "shrewd, resourceful problem-solver who is wrestling bravely with a universe he is to wise enough to know is too big for him".[491] Second, this is a strategy to optimize information. By taking decisions along the road, one waits until the last minute when one has optimal information, or at least the maximum information that is possible to gather at the given point in time. The longer the time horizon of a plan, the greater the uncertainty. Keeping the time horizon as short as possible will probably increase the quality of the decision.[492] Third, an incremental way of planning tends to dampen resistance to change. "Grand" plans often have a terrifying effect on people, because they are so all-encompassing. An incremental plan contains only an overview of the first few steps, an approach that many people may find less frightening.

The concepts of vision, experimentation, and evaluation are central to incremental planning.[493] Without any central steering or control the result may be a series of unconnected, small decisions, and will, as a consequence, not produce any larger change. Thus, some standards to which one can evaluate decisions are necessary. Such a standard is found in a vision, a strategic intention,[494] or "broad goals and policies which can accommodate a variety of specific proposals from below, yet give a sense of guidance to the proposers."[495]

Within the wide limits of such broad goals, it is possible to evaluate whether one is moving towards the goal or not. Taking many small decisions also facilitates experimentation. Small decisions often equal small risk, and thus it becomes less dangerous to explore whether something will work or not. Experimentation is also made possible because people usually do not invest as must time, energy, and prestige in small decisions as in "grand" ones. This makes it easier to abandon the decision if it proves to be impracticable. However, none of the above will work without some standards for evaluation. The incremental form of planning change processes is illustrated in figure 6.6.

As the figure illustrates, measures found to be within the upper and lower limits set by the vision are accepted after evaluation, while measures falling outside these limits are discarded. We see that measure 2 falls outside the limits, and is thus discarded when evaluated. Such incremental planning facilitates local initiatives, and enables the process to proceed through a series of "small wins" rather than "one big victory".[496] Moreover, planning becomes a continuous process closely

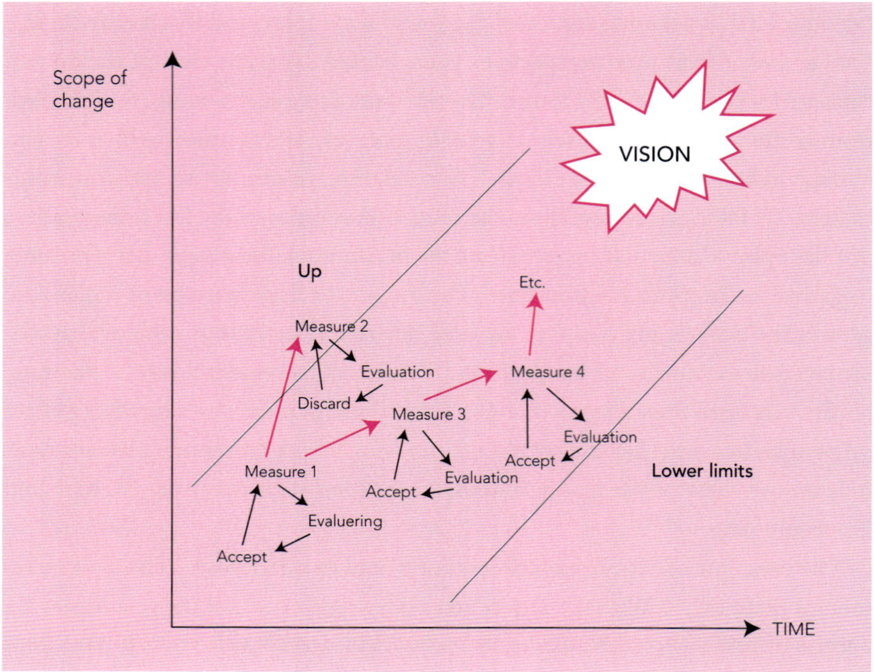

FIGURE 6.6: Strategi O: change as an incremental process

connected to concrete and specific measures, something which in itself is an effective means of creating change willingness in the organization.[497]

MOTIVATING FOR CHANGE: PARTICIPATION AND INTRINSIC MOTIVATION

Using financial incentives to create motivation for change is central to strategy E as people are "pushed" towards changing in the hope of getting a financial reward (or fearing some kind of financial punishment). Strategy O is more concerned with all the possible dysfunctional effects associated with using financial incentives as the driving force for change. One classic argument against using financial incentives comes from Fredrick Herzberg, who claimed that financial incentives at best could function as a "hygiene factor", that is, a factor that could help to prevent dissatisfaction, but not to create real motivation.[498] Motivation has to come from the inside, from a feeling that what you are doing is challenging, interesting, and fun.

Empirical research findings support the notion that people who are emotionally engaged in a change process contribute much more constructively to change than people who feel forced to support the change in fear of losing possible incentives.[499] Another argument is that financial incentives are a highly sensitive topic in most organizations.[500] There is a constant comparison between oneself and others in an organization concerning the level of financial compensation. If, as a result of this comparison, the distribution of compensation is perceived as unfair, negative feelings will be produced. Furthermore, if the differences in compensation are connected to the change process, this can in itself create negative feelings about the change.

With all the potential negative effects associated with the use of financial incentives, strategy O focuses on other ways to create motivation for change, ways that increase the desire to change.[501] To accomplish this, it is essential to create a sense of "ownership" of the change taking place. Probably the most frequently used tool for creating such a feeling is designing a change process characterized by broad participation and delegation of authority, and thus possibilities for employees to actively influence the ongoing change. Facilitating broad (as many people as possible participating) and deep (delegating authority to participants) participation is often regarded as the key to producing affective commitment to change.[502] Participation increases commitment to change in several different ways. First, simply being defined as a participant in the change will increase the feeling that one is actively engaged in designing one's own future. In turn, this will increase a sense of mastery, the feeling that one has the possibility to shape the process, and thus to avoid the most negative effects of the change process. Second, participation will always have a deep symbolic effect through being "included" as an equal, and by possessing a competence that the organization values. And third, participation may function as a sort of "unfreezing", preparing people for change. Through participation in the change process, people are – at least for a short period of time – removed from ordinary work, they are assigned tasks they do not usually perform, and they thus become directly exposed to change in practice. This may in itself create a greater acceptance of change.

To the extent that incentives are used in strategy O, there is a stronger focus on the symbolic than the financial incentives.[503] The change process is designed in a way that takes effects of symbolic acts seriously. Such acts could encompass different types of ceremonies, "burial rituals" to signal the loss of a task or a highly valued office, or handing out fake medals to change champions.[504] Or it could be arranging meetings to air feelings about the change, or "time outs" to drink beer at the local pub as a way to manage conflicts caused by the change process.[505]

Focusing on intrinsic motivation is not the same as ignoring financial incentives totally. Rather, strategy O is based on an assumption that financial incentives must always play a secondary role in creating motivation for change. However, incentive systems should be changed as a consequence of, in other words after, other changes in the organization to avoid dissatisfaction with a mismatch between a new organization and an old incentive system.[506]

CONSULTANTS: PROCESS SPECIALISTS

Strategy O does not entail the use of external consultants as "doctors", but rather as specialists in how to organize change processes. They are process specialists.[507] Such consultants usually ascribe to the following philosophy:[508]

> [I]t is the client who possesses the problem, and is assumed to do so through the whole change process. The consultant assists the client in handling the problem, but never takes responsibility for it. (...) The expertise of the consultant primarily entails involving the client in self-diagnosis, and enabling the client him- or herself to intervene to solve the problem.

There are several roles consultants working within this framework may take on, but three of them are crucial. The first is to function as a process designer, designing how the change process should be organized and sequenced.[509] More specific tasks will include setting up task forces, giving advice on who should participate in different groups and task forces, defining the topics to be handled in different groups, and setting up time frames and indicating expected results and deadlines. The consultant is not active in the discussions going on in the different groups. He or she is just setting up the framework in which the work takes place. The second is to take on the role of process assistant.[510] Performing this role requires the consultant to take part in the discussions taking place during the change process. Still, the consultant is not part of the discussion, but plays the role of moderator structuring the discussion, making sure that all point of views are aired, and supporting individuals in getting their views through. Another part of an assisting role can be to "feed" information to groups. Such a task is systematically covered in the concept of "action research", where the consultant works as a researcher to map effects of changes that have been decided and implemented.[511] The consultant is not part of the active discussion on what works satisfactorily or not, but limits his or her activities to providing information to the group. The third role is that of process maintenance.[512] The main task of the consultant is to prevent change processes from coming to a halt or breaking down. To do so, the consultant must be highly aware of conditions that may threaten the process, and make moves to prevent such events from happening. As it is not possible to prevent all crises, the consultant may also play an important role as conflict manager, mediating between different interests and proposing compromises.

Process consultants are not hired because of a specific area of expertise – for instance, knowledge about markets, structures, information systems, or leadership – but for knowledge about how change processes evolve, and because of their skills in interacting productively with the members of the organization. Instead of proposing solutions to problems, the main task of process consultants is to enable the organization to analyse and solve problems itself.

Strategy E and O – summing up

Table 6.1 sums up the main characteristics of the two change strategies:

TABLE 6.1: Overview of the main differences between Strategy E and Strategy O

	STRATEGY E	STRATEGY O
OBJECTIVES/FOCUS	Economic/quanititative results	Capacity for learning
ROLE OF FORMAL LEADERS	Instructions and orders	Delegation and support
CONTENT	Strategy, structures and systems	Individuals, groups and culture
PLANNING	Sequential, linear and analytic	Interactive, experimental and incremental
MOTIVATION	Extrinsic motivation, "stick and carrot"	Intrinsic motivation, participation
CONSULTANTS	External specialists, "doctors"	Process consultants

The elements of Strategy E will, for many people, evoke an image of a "hard" change strategy. The organization's needs – survival, profits, and the like – are the main focus, not the individuals working in the organization. Moreover, there is little or no room for participation and influence; the most important decisions are made by top management, possibly with the help of external specialists. The approach to change is analytic and based on formal plans, and there is little scope for human needs and emotions. The change is also concentrated on the formal elements of the organization: structures, strategies, and systems, and not on the "softer" side of social interaction and relations. Finally, the implementation phase receives significantly less attention than the preparatory or planning phase. The logic behind this is that those people responsible for analysing problems, suggesting solutions, and making the plan also have the power to enforce the change, even if it is met with resistance.[513] How this power is used – it could be force, expertise, or charisma, to mention some bases of power – is of less interest; the important thing is that a formal group of leaders can enforce the change in spite of meeting resistance from other actors inside and outside the organization. For many, Strategy E will also symbolize a rather negative view of people, where employees are regarded first and foremost as obstacles to change, and thus have to be enticed by positive or negative incentives,[514] and where human behaviour must be designed in order to obtain maximum return on capital.[515]

The main elements in Strategy O will be perceived by most people as more positive and "soft". Humans and groups, and their ability to learn and experiment, are placed at the fore. Employees participate actively, and thus influencs the change as much as – or more than –the top management. The strategy invites a more "playful" approach to change where a variety of small experiments are conducted continuously. Or, as James March puts it: "Playfulness is the deliberate, temporary relaxation of rules in order to explore the possibilities of alternative rules. (...) Playfulness allows experimentation."[516]

The implementation phase is also given much more attention in Strategy O, as it emphasizes that change is only possible if it is wanted or at least accepted by the members of the organization. As a consequence, change cannot focus exclusively on organizational needs like profits, but also has to focus on improved working conditions and social relations. The strategy contains a positive view of humanity.[517]

Even though many may find the characteristics of Strategy E "unpleasant", there is little doubt that quite a lot of organizational changes follow such a logic.

In a study of Australian firms, the researchers concluded that almost 70% of the changes were characterized by the use of hierarchical power.[518] Thus, "softer" strategies based on active and broad participation were used much less frequently. Moreover, there is little doubt that change strategies based on the use of hierarchical power also can be successful,[519] even though there is no lack of studies indicating that such strategies may also fail.[520] It is not a strategy that will work every time, under all conditions. The strategy may work as intended in some cases, and fail in others. The same can be said for Strategy O.

Chapter 7

Leading change

As noted in the previous chapter, the formal hierarchical leaders are central to both strategies E and O. Implementing change without the formal leaders "on the team" will most likely create serious problems. One obvious reason is that top managers possess the formal authority, and thus all the formal means of power that accompany the authority positions: determining pay levels, granting leaves of absence, and the like. As we discussed in detail in chapter 6, such means can be important in effecting change, but they can also be used by the top managers to sabotage a change they do not want to happen.[521] At the same time, formal leaders occupy positions that are highly visible, making it possible for them to exert symbolic power through what they say and do. This symbolic power can be used either to energize change or to undermine it.

Although chapter 6 discussed the role of formal, hierarchical leaders, it said very little about leadership. Change leadership is not necessarily a task exclusively executed by top managers.[522] Change leadership consists of activities conducted by what we earlier in this book labelled as change agents, and change agents may be other people than the ones occupying the formal leadership positions. We all have a tendency to equate "formal leaders" with "leadership". This tendency contributes to a blurring of an important distinction between leaders as people and positions, on the one hand, and leadership as activities and functions, on the other.[523] By maintaining this distinction, it becomes clear that there may be people in formal positions who do not act as leaders, while there may be people without such formal status who act as leaders.

There are several reasons why leadership – understood as special tasks and functions – will be particularly important during change processes. In more stable periods, organizations often run "on autopilot".[524] Rules and routines are followed, tasks are conducted as usual, and functions are coordinated through working standard procedures. There is little need for leaders to supervise, give orders, or motivate people. Change, on the other hand, represents an upheaval of this stability. Rules and procedures are changed, established views of how things should be are challenged, and old power structures are threatened. In such situations there will be an increasing demand for people who are able to make non-routinized decisions, to draw visions for the future, and to create order in a seemingly chaotic situation. Such a distinction is treated in much of the theory on leadership as the difference between administration and leadership.[525] Administration is viewed as making the existing activities work with the least amount of friction possible, while leadership is connected to changing the existing situation.

While strategies of change are different ways of organizing change, change leadership is primarily about the activities conducted by change agents – individuals and groups – in the course of the change process. Even though the distinction is not crystal clear, change leadership will focus on what individual leaders do as people, while change strategies are more focused on the organized context where planned change takes place.[526] Change leadership is thus about the actions taken by change agents to increase the possibility of succeeding with a planned change effort.

Leadership – "unfreezing" and implementing

Much of what has been written about planned change is grounded – explicitly or implicitly – in theories elaborated by Kurt Lewin.[527] Lewin's theory of change is based on an assumption that individuals and social systems seek stability or predictability. At the same time, he observed that both individuals and social systems changed, and concluded that it was possible to initiate and implement change in a planned way. Based on these assumptions, he then went on to elaborate the theory of "social force fields". In all social situations we face both driving forces and inertial forces. Driving forces are elements conducive to change, while inertial forces are directed at maintaining the status quo. A simple figure can illustrate the argument:

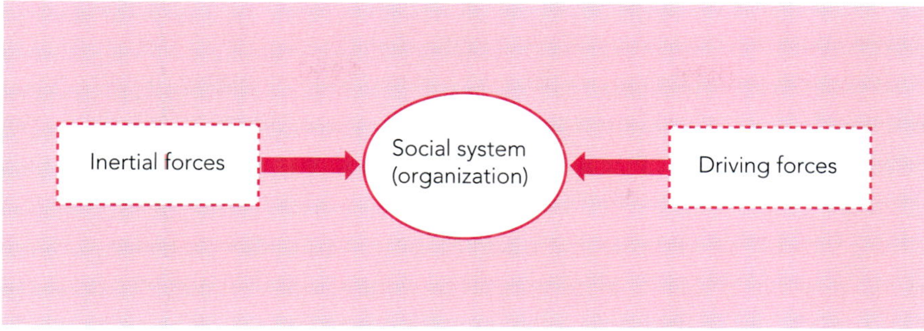

FIGURE 7.1: Organization facing inertial forces and driving forces

To make change happen, change agents must be able to make the driving forces stronger than the inertial forces. Even though this argument may be simple, verging on the simplistic, it conveys a very important message for change leaders: change can be effected in two different ways: either by strengthening the driving forces, or by reducing the inertial forces. Lewin sketched out what he labelled "change through three steps" in order to succeed:[528]; "unfreezing", "moving", and "freezing". Unfreezing is to create a sense of change readiness among the members of the organization, "moving" is the change of behaviour, and "freezing" is stabilizing the new behaviour in new rules and routines. The final phase could also be denoted as institutionalization.[529] The three steps are illustrated in figure 7.2.

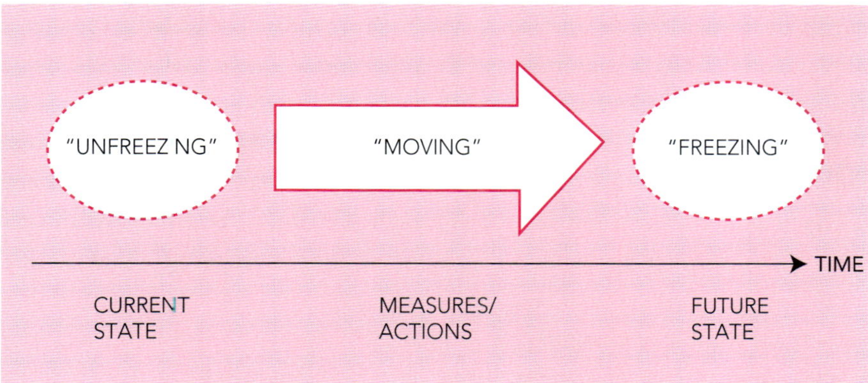

FIGURE 7.2: Lewin's three-step model for change

Change leadership is mainly about the two first phases: unfreezing and moving. To simplify, the leadership challenges can be boiled down to the following:

a. How does one create a climate for change, that is a situation where many, or at least the most central, actors perceive it as necessary to change (unfreezing)?
b. How does one act to implement the transition from the current to the future state (moving)?

Change leadership is thus equally important in the pre-change phase as in the actual phase of changing behaviour. In the following discussion we will make a distinction between the two, still acknowledging that the two phases are tightly interlinked and very hard to distinguish from each other empirically.

Unfreezing

Most theories on change leadership focus more on the unfreezing phase than the actual implementation phase, emphasizing the importance of the "change readiness" of the organization to succeed with planned change. The members of the organization, or at least a majority of them, must share the perception that "changes are needed and (that) the organization (has) capacity to successfully make those changes".[530] Such perceptions are not always present in organizations; they have to be created. In this process, the change agent will play a crucial role as "unfreezer". Whether the planned change effort succeeds or not will depend largely on the perceptions dominating the organization before the actual change is implemented. The more members of the organizations are ready for and seeking change, the higher the probability of succeeding.[531]

One central task for any change agent is to create a "change momentum" in the initial phase of the change process. This is done by instilling a feeling that change is urgent and necessary, and that it will represent an improvement of the current state.[532] To achieve this, members of the organization must perceive that:

a. they are capable of changing,
b. the change represents an improvement for the organization,
c. the top management is committed to the change, and
d. the change is positive for the members of the organization.[533]

In short, to be willing to support the change, members of the organization must perceive the change as urgent, relevant, and useful.[534]

FIGURE 7.3: Sensemaking and sensegiving as a process

URGENT, RELEVANT, AND USEFUL

Urgency comprises a combination of how the organization perceives its current situation and what the consequences of not changing will be.[535] The phenomenon includes a perception of the organization's history, or its evolution over time. It also includes a perception of the present in the form of comparisons with other comparable organizations, and it is connected to the future by the consequences of not changing. Urgency can thus vary from a perception that change is totally unnecessary and futile, to a fear of "death" (closing down) if measures are not taken. It is highly probable that readiness for change will increase as the sense of urgency increases. If one is standing on a "burning platform", one will do everything possible to escape.[536] One important task for change agents will thus be to create that feeling of urgency. In some situations, when the driving forces are clear and easy to communicate, this may not be a very tough task. If the change agent can refer to numbers indicating that bankruptcy is near, or to statistics showing that all key customers have left for a competing firm, creating a sense of urgency should not be difficult. It will be significantly more challenging when driving forces are more ambiguous and open to different interpretations. Examples of such driving forces can be feedback from some customers that quality is too low, or results of an internal mapping of working conditions showing that a small percentage of the employees find the working environment unhealthy. The more ambiguous the driving forces, the more important the role of the change agent to interpret the situation in order to create a sense of urgency.[537]

Relevance connects to a perception that the proposed change will actually solve the problem and move the organization out of the current untenable situation. The causal link between the solution proposed (the change) and the intended effects must be convincing. As with urgency, it will probably be easier to create readiness for change the clearer the link between the change and its effects is. In some instances a change may be rather obvious, for instance when new technology is introduced on the market. To be able to compete, all organizations must adopt the new technology, develop the necessary competence to use it, and change processes and structures to fit it. But many planned changes are characterized by a highly ambiguous link between the change and the intended effects, an ambiguity that may continue to exist long after the change process has been defined as terminated.[538] A current example could the proposal in Norway to amalgamate municipalities to reap benefits from economies of scale.[539] Is there an economy of scale in complex public services as we find in manufacturing? What are the unintended consequences of amalgamation? And could benefits from economy of scale be obtained through other means, for instance intermunicipal cooperation? In such situations, the role of the change agent as active interpreter of causal links between proposed change and effects becomes crucial.

Usefulness refers to the perception of whether the change represents an improvement over not changing. This is a serious challenge, because what is regarded as beneficial will depend on who is being asked. On an analytical level, there is a clear distinction between what is useful or good for the organization, on the one hand, and for individual members of the organization, on the other. As discussed in relation to resistance to change, it is not always the case that what is good for the organization also is good for the individual. For an organization to survive it may be very useful to close down a department, but this is a change that is very unlikely to be perceived as good by the people working in the department itself. The main challenge for the change agent is thus to be able to convey a narrative that the change will be good for both the organization and the individual members. In a situation where the future situation for the members of the organization is ambiguous, it is necessary for the change agent to create a vision of the future that they find attractive and feasible. Concurrently, it is important to create a perception that individuals will be able to master the change. As noted when discussing resistance to change, resistance will often arise from a fear of not being good enough, and of not having a place in the future organization. Thus change agents must provide, as far as possible, a sense of security about the future situation and how it is going to be achieved.

These three elements – urgency, relevance, and usefulness – are all about creating a common perception of the change in the organization. In practice it means nothing more than having good argument for why change is necessary, why a certain change has been chosen, and what effects the change will have for individuals and groups in the organization, and then to communicate this argument to the organization.[540] In other words, change leadership involves formulating an understanding of reality, or what Karl Weick (1995) calls *sensemaking*, and then to communicate this understanding, a process he labels as *sensegiving*. This line of thought is illustrated in figure 7.3.[541]

According to the figure, the first task of the change agent is to understand the situation. Next, this understanding must be communicated to others in order to trigger their own sensemaking processes. Change management in this context implies an attempt to steer or influence the sensemaking in the organization.[542] More specifically, sensemaking contains three central elements: interpretation of the past (history), images of the future, and contextualizing the present.

THE CHANGE AGENT'S SENSEMAKING – INTERPRETATION OF THE PAST

Interpretation of the past is based on an assumption that history will never be an objective entity. Rather, the past is ambiguous, vague, and uncertain, and different people will see and emphasize different elements of it. For example, it is not an easy task to claim that one school has performed significantly worse than another in the past few years by referring to standardized national tests. It could be argued that this is the result of unforeseen events, such as several years with an intake of significantly weaker pupils. Others could argue that the tests are not really measuring what they intend to measure, while others may point to the possibility that previous years' variation could be a stochastic process well within acceptable statistical error margins. Uncertainty and ambiguity leave room for multiple interpretations, and thus also for active attempts to create a specific interpretation of the past.[543] History can be made in someone's image, a process that has been labelled as "guided sensemaking",[544] "rhetorical use of history",[545] and "management of meaning".[546] In such situations, the change agent takes on the role of "interpreter of the history" who intentionally forms the history to fill specific functions.

Guided or managed sensemaking can take on many different forms.[547] One is to focus on elements in the past that could foster change. In a study of an attempt to change the deep structure or identity of LEGO, the researchers identified two ways in which history was actively interpreted.[548] The first was connected to a search for past changes that could be defined as failures, and thus as causes for the untenable present situation. The second was to go further back in the history of the company to look for LEGO's "real" identity, thus something that could be used as an ideal for what the company could become in the future. Or as Schultz and Hernes (2013, p. 19) phrase it: "Here, it is necessary not only to consider the future as uncertain but also to consider the untapped potential of the past to frame the future within the constraints of the present."

A main task of the change agent is thus to find examples from history to illustrate failures, indicating that not everything in the past had worked out as intended. By highlighting deviations from the dominating perception of the past it is possible to create a new understanding of the current situation. Such histories about deviations will – in the context of creating a climate for change – focus on what went wrong and what should have been done differently, but also on what has been lost and should be regained, something that will only be possible through change.

Just as important is telling the story of the organization's development until today. Such stories will imply a comparison of key performance indicators over time, for instance how processing time has increased, waiting lists have become longer, or profits are declining. The more clearly and unambiguously such negative trends can be described, the stronger the feeling of urgency, and thus the stronger the willingness to change.

It is also important to externalize the history, or, as John Kotter phrases it, "bringing the outside in".[549] To do this, the change agent must activate actors outside the organization to relate narratives about why the organization must change. These actors can be clients or customers, researchers telling stories about changes in other, similar, organizations, or a cooperating partner organization. The more legitimate this external actor is, the stronger the effect of his or her story.[550]. If a highly renowned doctor tells stories about how changes in her organization have made the hospital more efficient, the effect will probably be much stronger than if the same narrative were related by an economist or political scientist.

Dramatizing the story will also increase its efficiency. Karl Weick (2011) indicates that guided sensemaking has many similarities with the role of a poet or a writer of novels. In telling the story of the past, one can introduce a dynamic indicating what will happen if change is not undertaken. Such stories become even more powerful if it is possible to link them to other specific organizations where lack of change was followed by dramatic consequences. One example could be the story of a local hospital being shut down because of a lack of change, or a firm going bankrupt due to unwillingness to adopt a new technology. To create a sense of urgency it is important to paint a picture not only of what is wrong with today's situation, but also of the future if change is not undertaken.

It is quite common to claim that efficient change management includes creating a sense of crisis in the organization.[551] This is probably correct if the organization is in need of a dramatic change that must occur within a short time frame. But, as pointed out many times before in this book, many changes are less dramatic and more incremental, and lack a clear start and end. To kickstart such change processes, it is probably not necessary to create a feeling that everybody is onboard a sinking ship.[552] Still, change willingness is contingent on at least some degree of "unease". Once this "unease" disappears, even continuous and incremental change processes may come to a halt, and – even worse – produce a feeling of change tiredness or change cynicism.[553]

THE CHANGE AGENT'S SENSEMAKING – CONTEXTUALIZING THE PRESENT

Interpreting the past is necessary both for creating a feeling of necessity for change and – as shown in the history of LEGO's change – to point to something in the history that the organization must regain. At the same time it is necessary to paint a picture of a current situation that is untenable, combined with stories about how the organization possesses the necessary resources to complete and succeed with the change.

One forceful way to create a sense of urgency is by comparing the organization to other similar or comparable organizations.[554] Benchmarking is s strong technique for creating a feeling of necessity for change. Through benchmarking, it can be shown how the organization compares to other organizations on important performance indicators. This could apply to a university finding that the research output is much lower than at other universities it is competing with, or to a firm winning far fewer contracts than its closest competitor. As noted in the previous chapter, it is also a forceful technique to have external actors telling stories about the need for change. The more legitimate these actors are within the organizational field, the stronger the effect of these stories.[555] Such highly legitimate actors could be public authorities, professional groups, media specializing in the field, or strong and visible individuals acting as agenda setters. The more such actors there are expressing a need for change, the more it will become a natural part of the internal discourse in the organization, and the higher the probability of creating a sense of urgency.

Finally, contextualizing the present also contains stories about the resources the organization possesses, and thus the capability of the organization to succeed with the change.[556] This implies an interpretation of time available. There should be a general sense of time pressure, but still be apparent that successful change is possible. Finding the balance between conveying a story of time pressure and a story telling that it is impossible to change within the actual time frame is important (and difficult). Stories must be told about having necessary resources to conduct the change process in terms of competence, money, and time. In some instances, it may be necessary to tell stories about being willing to feed additional resources into the change process, for instance through financial incentives or extra staff for a period of time.

THE CHANGE AGENT'S SENSEMAKING – STORIES ABOUT THE FUTURE

As described in the two previous sections, interpreting the past and the present has focused mostly on how to create a sense of dissatisfaction with the current situation. It is directed at creating a picture of a situation one wants to escape from. Unfreezing is thus mainly regarded as consisting of instilling a sense of fear about what is going to happen if change is not undertaken.[557] But unfreezing could also be accomplished by another, probably complementary, technique: namely, painting a picture of a future state – a vision – that inspires people to change. This has been called inspiring leadership.[558]

Vision is a rather vague concept, originally linked to something religious, a revelation. However, in the context of planned change, vision is simply a way to conceptualize a literary description of a future reality. To be inspirational, this description must be both challenging and specific, and it seems to be most efficient if it can be conveyed in metaphors.[559] Efficient visions, that is, visions that create inspiration, are based on metaphors that make them "come alive", and contain an element of challenge. The vision must be something that is attainable, not merely a utopian story, but it also must require a great deal of effort to realize. Efficient visions are also inclusive in the sense that they transcend egoism or narrow self-realization.[560] Good visions are collective, linked to a common good. The famous speech by Martin Luther King Jr., which includes the famous words "I have a dream…", exemplifies a vision containing the above mentioned elements.[561] Imagining blacks and whites on the same bus was easy, but still every listener knew how difficult it would be to realize this state. At the same time, the vision appealed not only to narrow self-interests, but to a better society where everybody – both blacks and whites – would be better off.

At the same time, King's speech is a classic example of how words are used in efficient visions.[562] Repetition ("I have a dream...") is one common characteristic, often in the form of slogans that are easy to remember and repeat. Sentences and words are kept simple, so that all listeners can follow the line of logic. Visions are also filled with inclusive pronouns like "we" and "us". Finally, visions are generally highly abstract in the sense that they do not refer to specific current or past events that can be challenged on the grounds of correctness.

Discussing the visionary speech of Martin Luther King, Jr. in the context of ordinary organizational change may seem a bit over the top.[563] The main reason for most organizations to start change processes is the threat of losing out in the competition, and ultimately being shut down. Attempts by change agents to forge visions that are clearly there only to "decorate the reality" – for example, a firm labelling a change process as a way to "develop democracy" or an oil company's claim to change to "save the rain forest" – will quickly be ridiculed, and may have an effect that is the opposite of inspiring for change.

A somewhat less ambitious way of thinking about visions in change management is found in the literature on organizational learning. One of the most central theorists within the field defines a vision as a statement about "such fundamental questions as 'What are we?', 'What should we create?', 'How can we do it?', 'Why are we doing this?' and 'Where are we going?' In short, it determines how the organisation and its knowledge base evolve over the long term."[564]

Such a vision binds the organization together, defines what it should strive towards, and limits what needs to be done. The vision is also designed to attract attention, and thus to engage organization members in the well-being of the organization as a whole. To succeed, the vision must, at least to some extent, be based on the visions of the ordinary members of the organization. People are rarely interested only in making as much money as possible, but are equally concerned with having an interesting job, possibilities to learn and develop, and a good balance between family and work, and even with making the world a better place for all (altruism). The vision must be grounded in values that ring true and valid to members of the organization, involving something more than merely making money and having a good time. In order to accomplish this, visions should be developed as a dialogue between all levels of the organization.

To Peter Senge, efficient visions manage to introduce a "creative tension",[565] To do so, visions should create a gap between the current state and the described future. A vision is per definition a description of a wanted future, which has not yet come about. However, visions do not create any tension if they are not directly compared with a picture of the current situation. To create tension, change agents must be able to compare the future with the present and the past. Thus change management is, as noted earlier, connected to interpretation of the future in the form of a vision, the present in form of comparisons with others, and the past told as the organization's history.

Painting a vivid picture of the future is essential, but perhaps just as important is the ability to draw a road map for how to get there. Setting inspiring and challenging visions may work in a negative way for some people because they do not see clearly how they are going to obtain the wanted future.[566] Some may perceive the vision as unattainable, believing that they do not possess the resources necessary to succeed. If this is the case, people may be demotivated by the vision, and perhaps it might even foster resistance. In such situations it is important for the change agent to specify how the move from the current state to the wanted future will be carried out, and what the path to the future looks like. Of special importance is the change agent's ability to specify consequences of change for members of the organization, and what is expected from each of them in the change process. Specifying what is expected, combined with a description of the resources and support the organization will provide, is important in reducing anxiety due to ambiguity and uncertainty.

THE CHANGE AGENT'S SENSEGIVING – COMMUNICATION THROUGH WORDS

Once the message has been formulated, it must be communicated. Once change agents announce that a change process will start, this will trigger a discursive process in the organization.[567] The message will be registered by members of the organization, making it a part of both the individual and social sensemaking in the organization at large. How a message on planned change is formulated and communicated will clearly influence how the organizational discourse unfolds. This is, of course, difficult to control, and will vary from context to context (time and space). Still, it is important to reflect on how to formulate a message about change. More specifically, such messages can be communicated in a programmatic or participative way.[568] Programmatic communication is marked by the following characteristics: it originates from the hierarchical top management, proceeds in one direction only, is often communicated through formal communication channels and large gatherings, and is targeted differently towards different groups in the organization. Participative communication is more often based on the use of small groups, arenas where interaction and feedback is encouraged, and areas where there is little central control over what is communicated to whom. The two strategies have several similarities to what we earlier labelled strategies E and O. Programmatic communication will probably create a process characterized by action and reaction, and most probably in the form of resistance, while participative communication will probably encourage a process where interaction, experimentation, and incrementalism are more common.

Furthermore, it is essential that the message the change wants to communicate is contextualized to fit the organization, that is, to a language and form that are understood by the members of the organization.[569] In a study of 30 planned change processes, some researchers found that those that failed often entailed a "blindness" for the unique characteristics of the organization.[570] Those change agents who were more successful. had the ability to familiarize themselves with how the message of change would be perceived in the specific organization, and thus to understand how change would have practical consequences for the daily work of the employees.

More recent research has pointed to the efficiency of using narratives when messages about change are to be communicated.[571] A narrative of change is the formulation of a storyline posing a problem to be solved, what is needed to solve the problem, the efforts that people will have to put into the solving of the problem, and a "happy ending" describing the future desired state. It thus contains an interpretation of the past, the present, and the future. Storytelling is a classic rhetorical technique in efficient communication as stories often are easier to remember and retell than more factual arguments and descriptions. Good narratives about change may even become "viruses" that spread quickly in the organization, and transmit positive emotions about the change.

Several students of planned change have pointed out how common it is for the message of change to be under-communicated. As a consequence, the message does not reach some groups at all.[572] In very general terms, communication can take on two forms: words or actions. Communication through words can operate within a variety of channels.[573] Face-to-face communication is by most regarded as the richest channel in the sense that it allows for a wide variety of signals, and that response time is very short. If change agents want to communicate as efficiently as possible, they will have to talk directly with as many members of the organization as possible. Continuous communication of the change message will have a strong influence on the informal communication or the "daily chatter" in the organization.[574] Change agents must thus identify where the most important informal communication arenas are located, whether it is the canteen, the coffee machine, or the parking lot, and then be sure to attend these arenas with the intention to talk about the change. The more active a change agent is in doing this, the more the informal communication in the organization will be centred around the message of the change agent.

Still, it is very hard or sometimes downright impossible for change agents to communicate directly with all important groups and individuals in an organization. As a consequence, change agents will have to rely on other communication channels than face-to-face communication. Such channels will include intranet arrangements, internal newspapers or other written media, common e-mails, or a Facebook account.[575] To be efficient, it is important to repeat the message many times over a long period of time.[576] Communication redundancy – i.e. communicating too much – is, in fact, a better solution, even though some members of the organization may tire of the repeated messages. These recommendations are highly similar to how Kjell Arne Røvik (2007) portrays the efficient translator of change ideas. This translator is characterized as being:

- "multi-contextual, brave and creative" – or being able to formulate the message in a language that is directly relevant to the members of the organization.[577] The message must be conveyed in a language that members relate to and are familiar with;
- "patient" – that is, able to repeat the message until it becomes an integral part of the narrative in the organization;
- "strong" – as messages of change will often be met with resistance, it is important that the translator is capable of formulating good arguments grounded in facts.

In short, change messages must be communicated trough a plethora of channels, over a long period of time. No matter how well the message is formulated and grounded in facts, it will not have the intended effect without being efficiently communicated.

CHANGE MANAGEMENT – COMMUNICATION THROUGH ACTIONS

Communication of change messages through words will be inefficient if the messages are not supported and reinforced by symbolic actions. The change agent must thus also be very aware of his or her role as an example. The message to change agents is clear: just talking about change is not enough; it has to be supported by actions. Thus, if the change agent wants others to change behaviour, he or she must change behaviour first. Or phrased somewhat differently:

> When deep personal change occurs, leaders then behave differently toward their direct reports, and the new behaviors in the leader attract new behaviors from followers. When leaders model personal change, organizational change is more likely to take place.[578]

This puts symbolic leadership, understood as the change agent's being aware of the symbolic effect he or she has on the organization's members, at the forefront.[579] Symbolic leadership requires the change agent to have a relatively clear idea about what is identified as desirable behaviour in others in the organization. When this is clarified it is possible for the change agent to perform symbolic acts signalling how he or she wants others to act, as well as identifying unwanted behaviour.[580]

The first thing the change agent must do is to change his or her personal behaviour. If the change contains elements of cutbacks, the change agent must carry out cutbacks affecting him or her. If the change is about being more present for customers, the change agent must be the first to be out and meeting with the customers. Such symbolic acts will often be transformed into histories spreading quickly in the whole organization ("Do you know what she did?"). Even if it may seem a bit cynical, it is important for the change agent to be aware of the fact that only behaviour that is observed by someone will function as a symbolic act. Thus, it is not sufficient to perform such acts; the change agent must also ensure that the acts become visible and known to others.

An example of symbolic leadership through personal behaviour is found in the turnaround performed by the airline company British Airways (BA) in the 1990s.[581] The company had lost money during the two previous decades, and the service was so bad that the customers had rebaptized the company as "Bloody Awful". A new leader was hired, who immediately initiated a large-scale training programme for all 40,000 employees, called "Putting People First". The leader himself participated in 95% of the courses given, and was available for questions and talks during the whole course. Every time he took a flight with the company, he presented himself to the staff, and started to discuss how things were working. One time, when a queue formed due to delays, the leader engaged personally in serving breakfast to the customers. He also clearly conducted open structural changes, such as changing criteria for promotion from seniority to personal fitness for the position. The company was organized according to smaller groups (teams), so that they got to know each other much better, and thus could develop much closer working relationships. Incentives were changed from only quantitative indicators like the number of passengers and number of complaints, but also how employees treated the customers. In the year 2000, BA was named one of the best businesses in Europe.

The story of BA conveys a conscious and active use of the "power of example". The change agent will, as a visible person, affect what people think and the way they view the world, and can do that intentionally by sending out signals about what is good, desired and wanted.[582] That the leader attended the courses meant for the employees could have been interpreted in a negative way, for instance that someone could wonder whether the leader did not have better things to do with his time. Thus change agents should not trust symbolic acts alone. Even though it is essential to do what one says one is going to do, or as Karl Weick (1995) puts it: "Walk the talk", it may be just as important to tell stories about what one is doing and why one is doing it, which Weick calls "talking the walk". Talk and action cannot be separated; rather, they are tightly intertwined forms of communication. It is the interaction and reciprocal support of talk and walk that create the most powerful communication.

Much of what has been written in this chapter is similar to discussions on charismatic leadership. Charismatic leadership is problematic as it is often connected to personal "gifts of grace" that some simple possess and others do not. Charisma is regarded as being something one is born with, not something that is acquired through learning.[583] More recent research questions such assumptions, and points to the possibility that much of what characterizes charismatic leadership – except for the purely personal radiance – are techniques that can be learned.[584] Charismatic language, including the use of metaphors, histories, and anecdotes, as well as body language, is something that can be learned.

FROM UNFREEZING TO IMPLEMENTATION

Interpreting the past, contextualizing the present, envisioning the future and pointing out the way towards it, as well as communicating these elements through words and actions. Four basic elements in the "unfreezing" of an organization before the actual change process starts. These four central elements in change leadership is illustrated in figure 7.4.

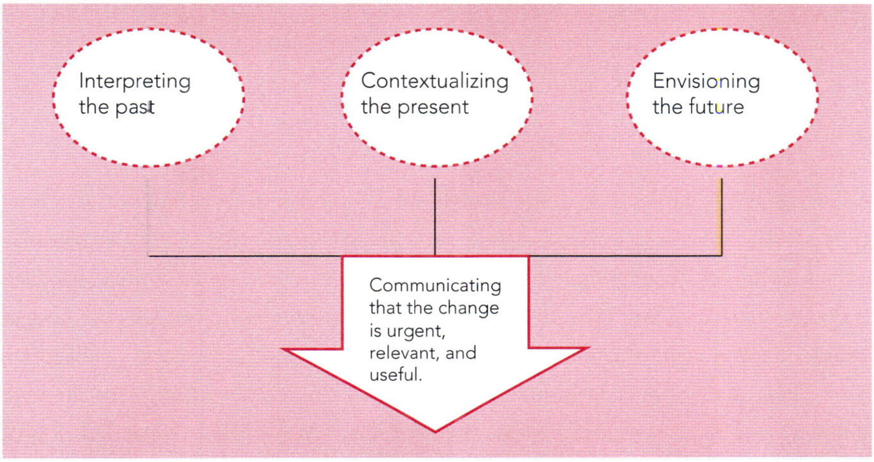

FIGUR 7.4: The key tasks of the change agent during the "unfreezing" phase

These four elements are all essential in creating a "climate for change", or what has been labelled "readiness for change". Extensive research shows that change leadership is essential in creating this readiness for change, or active support of the change initiative, and that lack of active change leadership may result in resistance towards change.[585] As noted earlier in this book, reactions to change initiatives can theoretically range from active support to active resistance. The role of the change agent in the unfreezing phase is thus to reinforce support while dampening resistance.

But how realistic is it to assume that one will succeed in creating a perception of the change as urgent, relevant and useful simply by being a good enough change agent? We all know that organizations are complex, ambiguous, and non-determined systems, and that attempts to steer them are highly risky projects. So, what if the change agent fails, and resistance to change is still dominating after all attempts to unfreeze the organization? Should the change initiative be forgotten and abandoned?[586] An if unfreezing is successful, will implementation work out on its own?

The answer provided by this book to both questions is a clear "no". Even if everyone in the organization supports the change, and finds it urgent, relevant and useful, there will still be a need for change leadership in the implementation phase. And if resistance is dominant, this is not a good enough reason to "pull the plug" and abandon the change. However, a situation where resistance dominates will require quite a different implementation strategy than if the situation is dominated by general support for the change.

Implementing change

Implementing change is about getting people to change their behaviour, and how they act and interact. For a change leader this will require the use of some kind of power to get other people to change the way the leader wants them to. Still, different situations will require the use of different types of power. In the course of this chapter, I have emphasized the importance of working to create a readiness for change, and, just as importantly, the possibility that the change leader may fail to do so. A change leader may thus find him- or herself in widely different situations, depending on whether the organization members support the change initiative or not.

For the sake of simplicity, we define two possible situations:

a. Central members of the organization support the change wholeheartedly, or at least passively.
b. Central members of the organization resist the change initiative, either actively or passively.

In a situation characterized by support, the main task of the change leader will probably be to enable people to change by removing barriers to change and by supplying resources to make change possible. We will label this type of change leadership "O-style leadership" as it overlaps clearly with the previously described "Strategy O". In situation b) it will be a change leader's main job to impose change in spite of resistance. We will call this leadership style "E-style leadership". The distinction between E and O leadership has several similarities to traditional two-dimensional, contingency theories of leadership, especially the distinction between the focus on relations and individuals, on the one hand, and focus on tasks and structures, on the other.[587]

E-style leadership: Handling resistance

In general terms, this is a type of leadership where the leader is less interested in reducing resistance than in finding out how resistance can be defeated. To do so, the change leader must create a solid foundation of power. As a consequence, this is a leadership style where the use of military language is prevalent. The organization is regarded as a "war field", and the process is characterized by a series of "battles" that are fought on diverse "battlefields".[588] In the following paragraphs we will outline the main elements of this leadership style.[589]

A. MAPPING RESISTANCE AND SUPPORT

Many change initiatives seem to fail because the change agent lacks the necessary power, and thus is unable to defeat resistance when it is encountered.[590] To be able to meet resistance, the change leader must implement a set of measures.

The first is to analyse the content of the change to get an overview over how different groups and individuals inside and outside the organization are affected by the change. Those affected the most are most probably also those activating the strongest resistance. As an example we can use a change process whose main element is eradicating several levels of middle managers. This will be a direct threat to the middle managers, and thus these groups should be singled out as the most probable to raise resistance. Although it is not always as easy to clearly map out who is affected as in the simple example above,[591] it is still important to have some idea of where resistance is most likely to appear during different phases of the change process. Just as important is to map out groups and individuals who are likely to support the change initiative. This is a kind of "political analysis" that many leaders seem to use more or less intuitively.[592] The change leader should not have preconceived ideas about who is for and who is against the change. The situation may change over time, so it is important to keep an open mind. The main point of a political analysis is to form a picture of supporters and opponents in the change process.

B. MAPPING POWER BASES

Having mapped out potential opponents of the change, it is essential to analyse the power bases of those individuals and groups.[593] An analysis of power bases consists of three main elements. The first is the analysis of the power of the change agent. To the extent that the power base is connected to material resources, the change agent needs to define what these resources are and the control one has over these resources. If the change agent also is a formal leader, he or she will at least be formally in control of monetary incentives like pay and promotion. In much of the American literature on change management, it is often assumed that formal leaders have more or less full control over these incentives.[594] This is far from the case in most European countries, end even less so in the Scandinavian countries. In the Scandinavian countries, arrangements for salaries and promotion are highly corporatized in the sense that they are the result of negotiations between employees' associations and employers' associations, often with the government involved as a third party. Such material incentives are thus not under the total control of the top level management.

The second element is an analysis of how valent the incentives controlled by the change agent are for those who may resist the change initiative. This analysis is based on a transactional view of the relation between the change agent and the "objects of change".[595] To be effective, the power base controlled by the change agent must be of interest for those upon whom the change agent is trying to exert influence. Having control over resources with no or little valence for the counterpart will be of little use if a conflictual situation arises. If the resources have high valence for the counterpart, they may also be highly effective, especially if this is a resource that is more or less monopolized by the change agent.

The third element is, as a mirroring of the above argument, the resources controlled by the people upon whom the change agent is trying to exert influence. One such rather common power base is a threat to leave the organization if an unwanted change is carried through. If the person is wanted in the organization, the threat to leave can be quite effective, especially if this person represents a capacity or competence that is hard to acquire elsewhere. Thus the change agent must take into consideration how great the probability of losing the employee is, and the cost associated with acquiring a replacement.[596]

Of course, analyses such as those described above will be infected with errors and approximations. It is impossible to predict exactly how individuals and groups will react to change initiatives, which power bases one controls, and which power bases can be activated by opponents. Still, such an analysis is important in getting a picture of how counterforces may be activated, how they can be used to stop the change process, and how the change agent can activate power bases to defeat resistance.

C. FORGING ALLIANCES

Taking steps to assure support for the change initiative is closely connected to the analysis of power and power bases. The main point is that it is necessary to forge strong alliances that are able to defeat resistance. One example of the effective forging of alliances is in the decision of Victor Norman, then Minister of Labour and Government Administration, to relocate state agencies from Oslo (the capital) to more peripheral municipalities.[597] This was clearly a radical change with negative effects for most leaders and employees in the affected agencies, as well as for powerful actors in the capital, Oslo. There was also significant resistance to such a change both within Parliament and from other ministers among Norman's own staff. One of the strategic moves made by the minister was to bring political representatives from more peripheral municipalities into the preparation for the final decision, knowing well that most of these representative were highly in favour of a geographical decentralization of state agencies. These municipal politicians put pressure on their own government representatives, thus "diluting" the resistance that could have been activated by other strong political groups.

The above example indicates how alliances have the capability to enable one actor, who is initially too weak to succeed with a change initiative if the resistance is too strong, to succeed if he or she can activate support from other groups. Also, by establishing ties with certain groups in an alliance, these actors are also prevented from joining in an alliance against the change. And, as noted explicitly in the example, alliances may split, and thus weaken, the resistance. Alliances may be created on a more long-term or permanent basis, but in change processes it is probably more common to create short-time, issue-related alliances.[598] Alliances can take on many forms, ranging from a "closed compromise" where the change agent presents a solution to the other members of the alliance and asks them for support in exchange for some other benefits or goods, to a more "open compromise" where the other actors are invited and included in the change process as active partners.[599]

The change "guru" John Kotter (1990; 1995) claims that one of the most common reasons for the failure of change initiatives is because the change agent has not succeeded in mobilizing strong enough support through an alliance to resist counterforces. To be sufficiently strong, the alliance should contain the most important formal power players both inside and outside the organization. Kotter (1995, p. 62), goes on to claim: "(I)n the most successful cases, the coalition is always pretty powerful – in terms of titles, information and expertise, reputations, and relationships." As indicated by the quotation, the members of the alliance not only possess formal, hierarchical power, but also represent a wide array of other power bases.

Finally, it is also possible, through changes in the formal structure of the organization, to reduce the influence of actors that may resist the change. This has been called, bluntly, "isolation",[600] or more elegantly, "selective inclusion and exclusion".[601] This could entail changing an individual's position so that he or she wields less influence over the process, for instance by losing his or her place in a central decision-making forum. Such measures, in Norway often called moving people "up and sideways", are not easy to use in a Scandinavian setting as employees and leaders are well protected against being displaced from their positions. Another way of regulating participation in change processes is through a instrumental use of timing and deadlines.[602] It is possible for the change agent to set deadlines that he or she knows will be difficult to meet for someone in the organization – preferably the person whose participation is undesired. It is also possible for the change agent to set up meetings during periods when one knows will be difficult for some people to attend. Used in this way, deadlines and timing can be powerful tools in structuring participation on the most central battlefields.

The discussion above shows how important it is for the change agent to think in terms of resistance and power before the actual implementation starts. It is a kind of "pre-launch phase",[603] taking steps to prevent counterforces from stopping the change initiative.

D. IDENTIFYING THE MOST IMPORTANT "BATTLEFIELDS"

All change processes consist of decisions that are taken over time.[604] Like a war taking place at specific battlefields, a change process involves "battles" taking place in different decisional forums. It is in these arenas that arguments for and against the change will be forwarded, that negotiations will be carried out, where voting will take place, and where there will be "tugs-of-war" between different groups with different points of views and interests.

As a consequence, it will be important for the change leader to try and channel the "battles" into "fields" (decision arenas) that he or she controls, or at least is familiar with. In practice, this entails attempts to steer decisions towards forums where the change agent can exert some control over the agenda, the participation, and the rules for making decisions.[605] The stronger control the change agent has over these arenas, the higher the probability that he or she will emerge as the winning part.

An illustrative example can be found in a radical change that took place in the global accountant and consultancy firm KPMG.[606] The main content of the change was an attempt to change the basic values of the organization, a change demanding intense debates over a long period, and at several hierarchical levels in the organization. Instead of arranging separate meetings for these discussions, they were integrated into existing meetings that were already planned. These were decision arenas where the top management could exert quite strong control. If new arenas had been constructed, including new rules and new participants, control over the outcome would have been much more uncertain.

Concurrently, the personal attendance and presence of the change agent in the most important decisional arenas is extremely important. Going to a meeting without being well prepared increases the probability of losing a battle. Being an E-style change leader thus entails being present and being prepared, especially for the rather tough debates and negotiations that will occur in most of the decisional forums during the change process. The change agent should also be prepared for continuous attempts at arranging "rematches".[607] Previous decisions will be challenged, and there will be constant attempts to alter them. Thus, it is essential for the change agent to be present throughout the whole process, in a variety of decision arenas where "rematches" can be decided. If not, the risk of "winning the battle, but losing the war" will increase.

E. DEFINING BRIDGEHEADS THAT MUST BE TAKEN

E-style leadership includes a strong focus on tactical targets in the change process. In a change process, it seems to be very important to "keep up the pressure". Interest and energy tend to wane in the course of a change process, making it important to set a series of milestones that have to be reached in a specific period of time. As Warner Burke expresses it:[608]

> A whimsical but illustrative comparison is that organization change is like losing weight. The first 5 or 10 pounds are easy, but the next 5 or 10 are much, much tougher. The early days of organization change, compared with later, are easy. People are excited and say things like "Finally, things are going to get much better around here." But a year later, the change effort may have bogged down, the excitement is gone, and fatigue has set in.

To keep up the pressure it is important to have the ability to refer to important bridgeheads that have been reached and taken. A bridgehead or a milestone presents an opportunity to tell a story about something concrete that has been achieved, not only the process of moving towards a vague future state. Such bridgeheads can be specific improvements in the production lines, the establishing of a new office abroad, or a new innovation. Such concrete milestones are clear indicators that the process has not stopped, and that the change agent still is focused on the change. Still, the change agent must be aware of the danger of mixing up a bridgehead with the final goal of the change.[609] If given the opportunity, opponents of the change will use any occasion to claim that the organization has reached its goals, and it is time to go "back to normal". If this happens, the bridgehead – intended to create energy and drive – may become give a sense of false security, slowing down or even stopping the change process.

F. CONTINUOUS SUPERVISION OF THE PROCESS

Any leader engaging in a "battle" must plan for the unexpected.[610] It may seem like a contradiction, but this is purely a reminder of the fact that things usually do not work out as intended. As a consequence, two things will be necessary. The first is to elaborate some alternative plans, or "what to do if this does not work out...". Such plans are, however, of limited use as the unexpected is, well, unexpected. Still, some alternative plans should be sketched out to avoid being in a situation where one feels that there are no steps that can be taken. More important is the constant surveillance of how the process of change unfolds. The claim has even been made that change agents should set up a "war room" where the process is continually observed and evaluated, and corrections are proposed.[611] Such an arrangement, perhaps even consisting of people with the unique task of conducting surveillance of the change process, can have several effects. First is the increased probability of detecting deviations from what has been planned, and thus the possibility to make quick corrections. Second is the improved ability to see if planned change activities have not taken place, and thus measures can be taken to get these activities back on track. The "war room" will be an element of constant disruption, an agency for keeping up the pressure during the whole change process. In addition, such a "war room" will have a strong symbolic effect by providing physical evidence of the importance given to the change, in itself something that will increase the pressure on the change process.

G. WILLINGNESS TO MAKE USE OF PRESSURE AND THREATS

E-style leadership is based on what in more traditional leadership theories would fall under the category of "directive supervision", based on a task focus, giving commands, and using formal power. For those using this leadership style, it is important to acknowledge that when people change their behaviour, it is not necessarily because they want to. They follow orders because they have to, not because they want to.

A directive leadership style is thus based on the use of punishment and rewards to make people change.[612] As a consequence, change in behaviour based on rewards and punishment is a "superficial" behavioural change that only will be maintained as long as a) the leader is capable of observing the actual behaviour of the subordinate, or b) the threat of a punishment or the expectation of a reward is maintained.

E-style leadership is thus based on different types of coercive power,[613] and consists of:[614]

> sanctions, encompassing actions such as threatening the target person's job security and preventing the target person from getting a pay rise, if he/she does not give in. The second one, blocking, encompasses actions such as threatening to notify an outside agency or threatening to stop working with the target person if he/she does not give in.

Leadership is based on threats in different forms.[615] However, to be credible, the change agent must also clearly display that he or she is not only able, but also willing, to realize those threats. It is a distinction between having the possibility to use a certain form of power (potential power), and actually using it (realized power).[616] Setting an example by using coercive power early on in the change process will always have a strong effect on those affected by the change.[617] Still, most leaders are hesitant to use this type of power as it activates negative emotions, both for the leader and the object the use of coercive power. But if the change agent wants to be taken seriously, he or she must be able to prove that threats can be transformed into action.

O-style leadership – inspiration and support

E-style leadership is grounded in a view of organizations as political systems characterized by groups with conflicting interests and the willingness to use power to reach their objectives. O-style leadership takes a quite different stance in looking upon organizations as being quite harmonic entities where there are plenty of opportunities for the sharing of common interests between individuals, groups, and the organization. Developing the organization is not possible without developing individuals and groups, and vice versa. A leader taking on the O style believes that people want to change, and that they see that what is good for the organization is also good for them.

In such situations, resistance to change will not pose a great challenge to the change agent. Rather, the change agent's main tasks will circle around empowering people, enabling them to change, and reducing barriers to change.[618]

A. INDIVIDUAL CONSIDERATION

Even if members of the organization are in favour of the change, it may still be difficult to clearly identify the role one is expected to play in the change process, how the change will affect oneself and one's colleagues, and how one can best contribute to the change. The potential energy that each member can bring to the process thus stands in danger of "getting lost in the crowd". If a sense of being left alone is spreading, the consequence may be anxiety and uncertainty, and perhaps apathy and passiveness.

To prevent such perceptions from spreading, it is essential that the change manager has the ability to undertake "individual consideration".[619] Individual consideration can be displayed by the change agent in a variety of ways, most commonly by being physically present, talking and interacting with the organizational members, using members' names when talking to them, and displaying knowledge of their role and work. Through such direct contact the change agents shows that he or she cares, which will have both a comforting and an inspiring effect. Inspiring because the member feels not only part of a whole, but also that he or she is regarded as an individual who makes a difference. Comforting because direct contact symbolizes a personal relationship that is a certain guarantee against being hurt or abused in the course of the change process.

It has been noted, probably very justifiably, that the possibility of direct contact between change agents and the members of the organization decreases dramatically with increasing organizational size.[620] Change agents in large organizations must thus compensate for the difficulties associated with establishing direct, personal contact. The most common form is to set up a team of change agents, and then to distribute responsibility for direct contact to members of the team. One should also be highly aware of the power of stories concerning the change agent's activities in the organization. A history of the change agent being "out there with the rest of us" is a strong symbol, often spreading quickly in the organization, and may function – at least partly – as a substitute for direct, personal contact.[621]

B. PROVIDING ENERGY AND RESOURCES

As previously noted, change processes demand energy and may put quite a heavy strain on many members of the organization. People must work extra hours in periods, they have to invest in new knowledge and skills, new social relations must be established, and new routines must be laid down. All these activities take time and energy. An important role for the change agent is thus to provide some extra resources during the change process.

In a purely instrumental perspective, change agents must be aware of the fact that changes demand resources, and that an important task of the change leader is thus to acquire these resources and distribute them where needed. This can be apply to somewhat obvious measures like hiring some extra workforce for a while, engaging consultants to act as supporters, putting in some overtime on the work plan, etc. All resources aimed at easing the stress caused by the change process will increase the probability of the process working more smoothly.

The change agent must also be aware how the marking of progress during the change process can provide energy. This may entail activities like sending a message or phoning a person who has done something special, coming to the canteen with a cake to celebrate an event connected to the change, or giving some flowers to individuals or groups that have done something to contribute positively to the process. Such attention has little material value, but the symbolic effect can be great.

The change agents should also be very aware that they themselves represent a source of inspiration and energy. The actions of a change agent will be observed closely, and everything he or she does will be a symbolic act that will be interpreted. Thus, the change agents should act in a way to symbolize the change, for instance by changing their office, eating lunch in a new place, or even reducing their salary. Such symbolic acts will often have a strong inspirational effect on others.

C. MOTIVATING LEADERSHIP

At the organizational level, one of the key tasks of an O-style change agent is to set up inspiring goals, connected to the uniqueness of the organization.[622] This is often about setting "hairy goals", characterized by being difficult or impossible to reach, placing little emphasis on measuring whether the goal is fulfilled or not, and deadlines that are changed and delayed. Such goals – even if they play an important role – are closer to visions than to goals meant to have a direct motivating effect on individual members of the organization. Individual motivation is more directly connected to the change agent's ability to formulate goals for each member that are challenging, measurable, and realistic.[623]

Challenging implies that goals should represent an intellectual stimulus for organizational members, forcing them to think in new ways. One often used technique is for change agents to ask members of the organization to scrutinize critically what they are doing, and then to propose improvements. Another technique is posing provocative questions like "What would happen if we did not do this?" or "Why is this the best way of doing things?" Realistic denotes that goals have to be obtainable with the time and resources available for each member of the organization. Research on the motivating effect of goal setting shows that goals that are clearly quite unrealistic may have a demotivating effect. People simply react by saying "this is impossible", and the result may be passivity. The realism of individual goals is also closely connected to individualized consideration. Individual members of the organization will have different resources at their disposal, both personal and organizational. Thus, goal setting must take such individual variations into consideration to tailor goals to different individuals and groups. Finally, goals should be, at least to certain extent, measurable. To have a motivating effect, it is important for all the people concerned to know whether they are moving closer to the goal, as well as knowing when they can celebrate having reached the goal.

D. DELEGATION AND SUPPORT

Delegation of power from the top tiers of the organizational hierarchy to lower levels is one of the main elements in strategy O as a change strategy. Change is based on decentralization, broad and deep participation, and involvement from all parts of the organization, not just the top management. A decentralized process implies that decisional powers are transferred from hierarchical leaders to middle managers and the operative core. Many of these are not accustomed to making decisions about changes in the organization. The change agent must thus play an important role in enabling people to make decisions, and must support them in the decision-making process. This is also a central element in the theory of transformative leadership.[624]

For some, having power delegated to them will arouse a feeling of being "thrown into deep water". The change agent must thus assure that those given responsibility for handling a situation they are unfamiliar with are given the necessary support to handle the situation. This puts a demand on the change agent's ability for individual consideration, so that support can be adjusted to different people in different situations. Change agents must work as "coaches" or trainers empowering members of the organization to manage the new situation they have been placed in.[625] Delegation of power is important, but the change agent must ensure that such delegation is used, and that it does not create unnecessary uncertainty and anxiety.

E. THE CHANGE AGENT AS "LINKING PIN"

Delegation of power is necessary if change processes are intended to contain elements of experimentation to foster learning processes in the way we described as an integral part of Strategy O. Learning is something that belongs to individuals.[626] Individual learning requires some degree of autonomy to be able to try out new things. To succeed in doing this, delegation and support are essential, but not sufficient. Individual autonomy may increase individual learning, and thus an increase in tacit knowledge, but not necessarily in organizational knowledge. Tacit knowledge must be externalized and communicated, which requires an environment where expressing opinions and views, as well as discussing different points of view, is encouraged. This, in turn, will require the establishment of teams that are at least somewhat autonomous. Internally, such teams must establish regular meeting points where opinions are aired and discussed, either face-to-face or virtually. In such a context, the competent change agent must play two important roles. The first is the role of "enabler", making it possible to externalize knowledge and exchange opinions. The change agent as "enabler" will play a role in asking questions, probing for the meaning in statements, and systematizing and critically scrutinizing available information. Moreover, the change agent must take on the role as "coach", where the most important element is to teach individuals how it is possible for the group to learn. Thus, the change agent must play an active role in disseminating knowledge within the group.

But knowledge should also transcend the group. If not, different groups will elaborate tacit group knowledge, which is not necessarily to the benefit of the organization. Groups learn, while the organization does not. The change agent must thus also play an important role as a linking pin between groups, externalizing knowledge in the group, translating it into language that can be understood in other groups, and communicating it to other groups through various communication channels.

F. THE CHANGE AGENT AS "TEACHER"

Peter Senge develops the idea of change agents as enablers and coaches, and argues that learning requires that someone take on the role of "teacher".[627] The teacher role is not one as disseminator of expert knowledge, but rather a person that poses questions to a group to encourage group learning. One important characteristic of such a leader is the ability to distinguish clearly between assumptions and facts. Most of us have a tendency to generalize on the basis of only one or a few observations. If, for instance, a customer claims that out product is too expensive, it is easy to conclude that this is a fact although it is not empirically verified. Such claims should thus be treated as assumptions, and should as far as possible be tested. Such an attitude will foster critical thinking, and can help in starting learning processes as people start questioning what are assumed to be facts. Another important characteristic is the ability to encourage and enable an open debate within a group. A good teacher will present his or her views in an open way, giving plenty of scope for criticisms and questions. This will also imply that one is able to explain how one has reached a decision, and the assumptions that are involved in the process of reaching a conclusion. A third characteristic is the ability to distinguish between people's theories in use and their espoused theories. People do not always act in accordance with what they say. An example could be people saying they generally trust others, but still they do not anyone borrow their belongings. A good change agent must have the ability to point out such discrepancies. Finally, a good change agent should have the ability to detect when people's defence mechanisms against change are kicking in. Handling resistance to change is thus a central ability of the change agent, as noted earlier. All the four characteristics mentioned above are really about the ability to observe the group, to pose critical questions in order to initiate reflexive processes in the group, and to foster openness in the discussion.

Senge also points to the importance of appointing "internal network leaders".[628] These people are members of the group, but will have a special responsibility for disseminating information, and thus knowledge within a group, to other groups. These network leaders are thus assigned to participate in discussions in other groups, a role demanding the same skills as discussed above. The role of top managers in creating learning groups is less direct, as most power to make decisions is delegated to the operative level and middle managers. However, as noted several times before in the book, delegation will not work if groups do not have the ability to use the power that is delegated.[629] To do so will require education as well as more direct support from top managers in the process. To make a transition towards a more learning organization, the structure must probably be flattened and become more fluid and organic.

Two leadership styles – two logics

Table 7.1 sums up the main characteristics of, and thus differences between, leadership styles E and O.

TABLE 7.1: The basic elements of leadership styles E and O

E-STYLE LEADERSHIP	O-STYLE LEADERSHIP
Map resistance and support	Individual consideration
Map bases of power (own and others)	Provide energy and resources
Forge alliances	Motivating leadership
Identify crucial battles	Delegation and support
Defining bridgeheads	The change agent as linking pin
Supervise the change process	The change agent as "teacher"
Willingness to enforce threats	

It is easy to conclude that E-style leadership is "hard" and "power based", while O-style leadership is more "human" and "soft". Such wordings, which may be perceived as "positive" and "negative", blur the fact that both leadership styles are based on the use of power, although they are very different types of power appealing to different sides of people. Quinn and Weick (1999) argue that E-style leadership (the "hard" form) is based on what they call "the logic of replacement". This is grounded in an assumption that people will not do anything unless they are compensated for doing it. This logic is illustrated in figure 7.5.

FIGURE 7.5: The logic of replacement – E-style leadership

O-style leadership is, almost as a contrast, based on a logic of attraction. This is a type of power where the leader is able to activate some resources that make people want to change their behaviour because they are attracted by what they can accomplish by doing so. This logic is illustrated in figure 7.6.

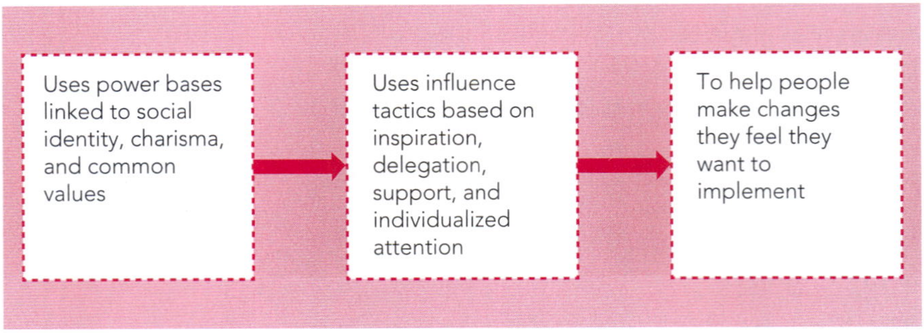

FIGURE 7.6: The logic of attraction – O-style leadership

The distinction between the two types of leadership is highly similar to the distinction between transactional and transformative leadership. In John Burns'

(1978) classic book, where the concept of transformational leadership was introduced, this was a leadership style closely linked to organizational and societal change. A transformative leader was less geared toward the existing state, and more towards creating common values that could bind people and groups in the organization or society more closely together. To do so, the leader should be able to formulate visions, to emphasize the larger meaning of what one was doing, and create enthusiasm for the main visions and strategies. Or, formulated in a somewhat different way:

> Transformational leaders seek new ways of working, seek opportunities in the face of risk, prefer effective answers to efficient answers, and are less likely to support the status quo. Transformational leaders do not merely react to environmental circumstances – they attempt to shape and create them.[630]

The transformative leader emphasises the symbolic aspect of being a leader, with a focus on creating common organizational values. Change in this perspective will necessarily focus on how it is possible to change the values and norms of individuals and groups. And values and norms are probably difficult or perhaps impossible to change through the use of force. A transformative leader must play on emotional strings, thus requiring a leadership style more centred around charisma, identification, and visions. The leader influences and changes the values of others through functioning as a source of inspiration.

A good transactional leader, on the other hand, will establish good transactional relations with members of the organization so that they feel there is a reasonable balance between contributions and rewards. The relationship between leaders and members is based on reason and intellect, and thus on rational calculation of benefits and costs. Change in such a relationship will take place when the balance between contributions and rewards is altered, for instance by pointing out that contributions are not sufficient to receive an increase in rewards. Additionally, the transactional leader must play the role as a good political leader in the sense that he or she must be well aware of the possibility of meeting resistance when proposing a change. Such leaders know that not all change will be met with support, and that there are many reasons for opposing change. To overcome resistance to change, such leaders will have to build alliances to increase their own power base, so that resistance can be counteracted. Knowing that some groups, either inside or outside the organization, will probably try to stop the change process at some point makes it important for transactional leaders to supervise the change process closely to be able to detect deviations from the plan.

It is easy to associate O-style leadership as being "soft", and thus as something positive, while we perceive E-style leadership as "hard" and thus negative. Such perceptions will probably lead us into a "trap" of thinking that there is "one best way" of leadership, in this example O-style leadership. We have a tendency to like phenomena that are characterized by harmony and are free from conflict and negative emotions, whether this applies to organizations or societies. In the leadership literature, we see a clear tendency to claim that transformative leadership is better than transactional leadership, even though the originator of the concept – John Burns – clearly considered the two types of leadership as complementary, not as adversarial.[631] Moreover, empirical studies indicate that the two leadership styles in fact support each other in the sense that good transformational leadership is difficult without also relying on good transactional leadership.[632] In fact, it seems as though leaders scoring high on transformative leadership also score high on transactional leadership. As a conclusion, it seems that organizations are in need of leaders who both can inspire and can use "raw" power, who have the ability to delegate and support, and to centralize and make "autocratic" decisions when needed. Within the context of planned change, this is merely an acknowledgement of the fact that changes may differ widely. Some are characterized by common interests, common values, and general harmony. Others are conflictual and dominated by coercion. Change agents must be aware that they can encounter all types of changes, and must thus be able to tackle several different types of change leadership.

Chapter 8

Change strategies – combinations and hybrids

The two previous chapters have presented two ideal models of change strategies and change leadership, while building on a rather simple dichotomy of change versus stability. This stands in some contrast to the first chapters where the complexity of change, as well as the rather opaque distinction between change and stability, was discussed thoroughly. Change, and organizations, are many-faceted and complex phenomena, and as a consequence it is impossible to preach "one best way" to change them.[633] Thus it is difficult to envision one change strategy and one style of change leadership that will work equally well in all situations. Empirical research also supports a complex view of change in the sense that it is difficult to support the notion that one change strategy and type of leadership is superior to another in general terms.[634] Change processes are messy, unpredictable, and full of surprises, where leaders "muddle through" with the resources and capabilities they have at their disposal.[635] And, just to make everything a little bit worse, we seem to lack sound empirical research on what constitutes good change leadership.[636]

This chapter will discuss some of these paradoxes in more detail. First, we will try to identify the conditions under which different strategies will or will not work well. Second, we will discuss whether, in situations where conditions do not favour any of the ideal change strategies clearly, combinations of strategies and leadership styles – hybrids – are feasible. Finally, we will discuss theories about whether it is possible to reconcile inherent conflicts between change and stability in the same organizational structure, and if so, how this should be accomplished. This discussion will be conducted under the heading of "organizing for change".

A contingency view of change strategy efficiency

Abandoning the idea that there is one best way of leading change leads us to what has become known as a contingency perspective. The contingency perspective is, arguably, the dominating perspective in modern organization theory,[637] and has even been labelled the "normal science" of organizations.[638] Even if contingency theory in its most axiomatic version does not hold a particularly strong position today,[639] the general idea that something is better or worse suited to a specific situation is well integrated into most theoretical approaches to organizations and thus organizational change. In its essence, contingency theory can be expressed as follows:[640]

1. There is no one best way to organize.
2. Not all the ways to organize are equally effective.

The claim of this book is that theories of change are no different from theories of organizations in this aspect. For theory E or O to be effective, it must be suited to specific situations or contingencies. Thus, the challenge is to define the important contingencies. Earlier on, the main contingencies were identified and made explicit in what was called "a conceptual model for change" (chapter 2, figure 2.7). Figure 8.1 repeats this figure, but with the difference that change strategy and change leadership are included.

The figure illustrates the importance of adapting change strategy and leadership to the driving forces, the content and scope of change, the context of change, and the change process. The general idea, derived from contingency theory, is that the better the fit between the strategy chosen and the actual change, the higher the probability of succeeding in the sense that the objectives of the change agent(s) are met. Let us first look at what will constitute the ideal conditions for the two strategies.

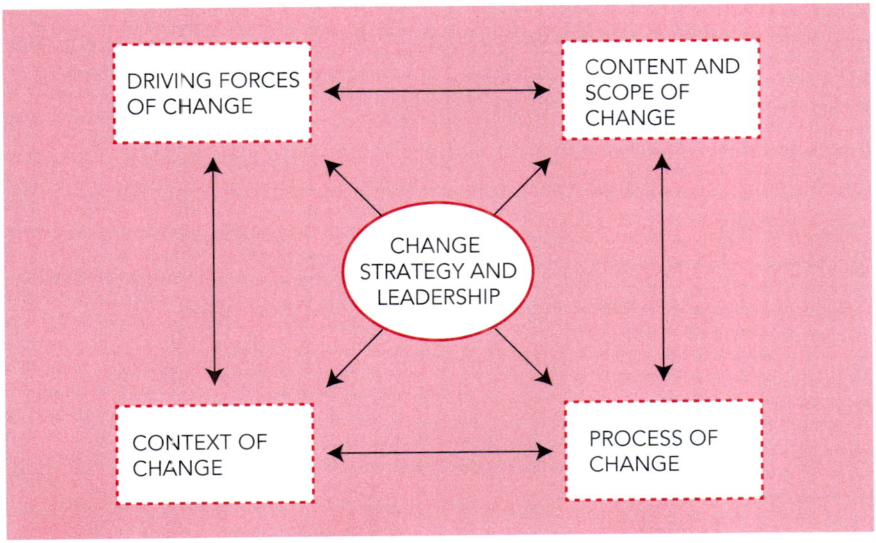

FIGURE 8.1: The conceptual model of planned change including change strategy and change leadership

The ideal conditions for strategies E and O

It has, in the course of the book, been emphasized that strategies E and O should be regarded as Weberian ideal models. Still, it is possible to imagine situations where the situation is close to ideal, where the choice of the best strategy should be rather obvious. To describe these ideal conditions we will use the elements outlined in the conceptual model.

A. DRIVING FORCES

Strategy E is probably best suited to situations where both the problem and the solution are quite clear and "objective" in the sense that it is difficult to disagree on them. Thus, the driving forces should indicate clearly that a change is urgent and relevant, in the sense that change is necessary and that it represents a realistic solution to the problems the organization is facing. It does not necessarily imply that the proposed change is perceived as useful, i.e. that all parts of the organization see the change as beneficial to them. However, the more clearly both problems and solutions are defined, the easier it is to design a change process based on clear, pre-defined goals, a stepwise plan with well-defined deadlines and milestones for reaching the goal, and thus possibilities to link incentives (both rewards and punishments) to achievement of objectives.

Strategy O will probably be a better choice in situations where the driving forces are more ambiguous. It is more or less implicit in strategy O that a stronger emphasis is put on exploration and experimentation, and thus on a trial-and-error process. This will in turn increase the probability of triggering continual learning at all levels of the organization, again requiring a strategy based on delegation, participation, and leadership focused on support and motivation.

B. CONTENT

Strategy E is basically directed at problems that are possible to solve by changing the formal elements of the organization: formal structure, strategy, and systems. Such problems will be connected to wrong mixes of products/services and markets, wrong business models (including pricing), or lack of strategic alliances.[641] The problems could also be associated with lack of coordination between organizational units, or decisions that are made too slowly or are not good enough. Or the problems could be associated with production processes that are unstable or producing output of low quality. It is possible to solve such problems through changes in the organization's formal elements, such as strategy changes, reorganizations, decentralization, implementing new technology, or redesigning processes.

Strategy O is probably better suited if the problems encountered are associated with cultural elements. Examples could be rude treatment of customers, lack of trust between departments, or a lack of a sense of belonging to the organization, resulting in high turnover. As noted many times before, culture is not something that can be decided; it has to develop over time. Such a change will require a process where a broad array of people in the organization discuss norms, values, and assumptions, and through such interaction change culture. Strategy O is a strategy that focuses precisely on such processes, enabling cultural change through participative processes.

This dichotomy is, of course, dramatically simplified. Several studies indicate that strategies highly reminiscent of strategy O have been used to change strategies,[642] structures,[643] and systems.[644] However, in these cases, changes in formal elements seem to take place after a cultural change has been completed. In a similar fashion, studies also indicate that change strategies focusing on formal elements over time lead to cultural changes.[645]

C. SCOPE

At first glance, it may seem as if strategy E is best suited to radical changes, while strategy O is better suited to a more continuous development, adjustment and refining process. Large and dramatic changes, for example in configuration or archetype, will necessarily have a large impact on many groups and thus interests. Thus, large-scale change will imply strong resistance, and will thus require a change strategy based on the power to overcome such resistance. Somewhat surprisingly, it is difficult to find empirical evidence that supports the idea that evolution (incremental change) and revolution (radical change) are closely linked to a specific strategy. On the contrary, it is possible to find both radical change through participative and incremental processes, and incremental changes with a significant use of coercion.[646] Strategy seems more connected to the time available than to the content of change, leading us to the next element in the discussion.

D. TIME

Strategy O is time consuming. Changes will not happen quickly when large groups are involved. Many groups represent many points of view and interests, so this strategy will favour a more incremental rhythm in the change process. During the course of this book, we have discussed the distinction between periods of relative stability and periods of turbulence.[647] Organizations may find themselves in periods of relative stability over quite a long period of time. During such periods, problems and challenges are at least somewhat possible to predict, and can thus be adapted to quite smoothly. Such changes do not challenge the "deep structure" of the organization. Rather, these changes are regarded as an extension of previous experience, and as such represents commonly accepted mental maps and beliefs.[648] Changes occur within a known framework. Such evolutionary change is slow, and is not caused by an imminent crisis.

More radical environmental changes have a tendency to "punctuate" the equilibrium that the organizations has developed over time.[649] Most punctuations are in their nature unpredictable. Organizations focus on what they know and master, which is usually what they have done in the past. Seeing the radical breaks coming is thus almost impossible.[650] Adaptation must thus take place within a short time frame. The organization must change quickly, or die. A short time frame will make strategy O almost impossible to use. Using a strategy based on incrementalism and broad participation when quick responses are needed will probably be highly dysfunctional. Time pressure will increase the need for quick decisions, again requiring processes with rather narrow participation limited to actors with the formal power to make dramatic decisions. A short time frame, something that is usually combined with more dramatic or radical changes, will probably require a change strategy like strategy E.

The effect of the degree of time pressure on strategy choice will probably be moderated by the available slack in the organization. As we noted in a previous discussion, having slack resources will dampen the feeling of crisis, and thus make it possible to choose a strategy more similar to strategy O even in a situation characterized by little time.[651] In general terms, we can claim that the more slack an organization possesses, the less impact time pressure will have on the choice of change strategy.

E. RESISTANCE/SUPPORT

If resistance to the change is fierce, strategy O is probably not a wise choice as it is grounded in a philosophy of harmony, that it is possible to find better solutions for all through collaboration and discourse.[652] An open and participative change process will have the benefit of reducing many reasons for resistance, like the feeling of being treated unfairly, of not having the possibility to influence your own future, anxiety, lack of ownership of the change, and lack of time to "digest" losses. Still, there are several other reasons for resistance, and in many change processes it is quite naïve to assume that all groups in an organization will support the change initiative.

In fact, an open and participative process may have a dysfunctional effect if resistance is strong.[653] Strategy O will imply the construction of several "extra" decision arenas where people in the organization can participate. These may be arenas for collaboration and common solutions, but can also function as arenas for "battles" between interests. Such arenas may constitute forums for people who want to resist the change, but do not have access to the ordinary decision-making arenas. The extra arenas for participation will thus lower the significance of the formal structure, an opportunity that will be seized by those opposing change.[654] As a consequence, the change process may evolve into a "cat fight"[655] or a "garbage can process".[656] If resistance is strong, there is little other choice than to choose a strategy resembling strategy E.

F. POWER STRUCTURE

Looking at the contextual factors, one can argue that the allocation of real power in the organization – both formal and informal – is the one having the strongest effect on the choice of change strategy.[657] Strategy E is based on the possibility for one group in the organization to implement – or impose – changes in spite of resistance. Thus the change agent must possess enough power, either in the form of authority – be it formal, professional, or personal – or control over incentives.

Many organizations are characterized by dispersed power, especially those often labelled professional bureaucracies, where most of the power is located in the operative core manned by highly educated and organized personnel, or in adhocracies, where power is located in the staff performing highly creative and specialized work.[658] Trying to change such organizations through something similar to strategy E will usually end up in failure. One of many examples of this is found in a study of implementation of reforms in the Danish and Swedish health care systems, where the researchers concluded that top-down processes (strategy E) only resulted in "(…) symbolic changes that did not change much in the daily routines".[659] On the other hand, what we have called the simple structure, the machine bureaucracy, and the divisionalized structure are characterized by several elements that favour the use of strategy E. In the simple structure much power is located in the owner or entrepreneur, in the machine bureaucracy it is located at the top levels of the hierarchy and the technostructure, and in the divisionalized structure most power is located at the corporate level.

The power structure is also determined, or at least strongly influenced, by the outer context, especially the institutional environments. Strong institutionalization, either through the regulative pillar in the form of rules and regulations or through norms and assumptions, limits the opportunity of the formal leaders to use strategy E efficiently.[660] Institutionalization will limit the possibility of using certain incentives, as they will often be regulated in laws and agreements, and supervised by professional organizations or public agencies. Perceptions of what is "reasonable use of formal power", grounded in the normative pillar of the environments, will also limit what actions change agents can take to enforce organizational changes. In some situations strategy O may be the only option, as it is the only strategy that is perceived as legitimate by central actors in the organization's environment, thus linking choice of strategy to national culture. The most important element of the institutional environment, in this context, is the degree of power distance.[661] Power distance refers to the degree of coercion that is accepted in a society. Empirical studies indicate that nations differ widely in this dimension. Countries with little power distance are found in Scandinavia, while countries in southern Europe, Asia, and the USA are characterized by significantly higher power distance.

It is likely that the use of strategy E will meet with much more scepticism and resistance in countries with low power distance than in countries with higher power distances. The reason for this is that "individuals measuring high on power distance readily accept hierarchy, are submissive to authority, and accept their social status."[662]

In countries characterized by smaller power distance, attempts to implement organizational changes through something similar to strategy E will probably be met with general scepticism. Thus, the claim has been made that E-type changes of strategy are poorly suited to use in the Scandinavian countries.[663]

The previous six dimensions do not, of course, represent all elements that should be included in a rational evaluation of which strategy to use for a specific organizational change. Still, they are dimensions of great importance when reflecting on the efficiency of a specific strategy in a specific situation. Table 8.1 gives an overview of the ideal preconditions for strategies E and O.

TABLE 8.1: Ideal preconditions for strategies E and O

DIMENSION	STRATEGY E	STRATEGY O
Driving forces	Clear and objective problems and solutions	Ambigous problems and solutions
Content	Strategy, structure, systems	Culture
Scope	Radical change combined with short time frame	Adjustment and incremental change
Time	Short time frame, time pressure	Relatively ample time, "slack"
Resistance/support	Resistance and conflict of interest dominate	Support and harmony of interest dominate
Internal power structures	Power concentrated at top level	Dispersed power
External power structures	Weak institutional environments (regulative) Acceptance for coercion (normative/cognitive)	Strong institutional environments (regulative) No acceptance for coercion (normative/cognitive)

In situations similar to the ideal forms, there is a strong probability that the use of the ideal types will function efficiently. So, what can be done if the ideal preconditions are not present?

Hybrid change strategies

Strategies E and O should be regarded as Weberian ideal models that are never, or very seldom, found empirically in their pure form. Thus, many change agents will probably find themselves in "unfavourable" situations where the ideal conditions for choosing either strategy E or O do not exist.[664] Change agents will have to make choices about change strategies in situations where some conditions pull in the direction of strategy O, while others are favourable towards strategy E.

One example could be an attempt to change the formal requirements for filling a leader position in a hospital. This is a type of change where one should expect quite a lot of resistance as such changes represent changes in the basic power structure of the organization. As a consequence, strategy O should be less suited as the whole process will be characterized by diverging interests and conflict. However, attempts to implement top-down changes in a hospital where much of the power is located at the operative level (doctors, nurses and other professional groups) may encounter serious problems. As power is not concentrated enough within one group that would be able to enforce a change, the change may risk coming to a halt rather quickly. Trying to implement change through strategy when one of the conditions – concentrated power – is not present is thus a risky project.

The situation described above will probably be highly recognizable to experienced change agents. Thus the following question will be posed: Is it possible to combine elements from both strategies? Are hybrid strategies, where elements from both strategy E and O are combined, feasible? Instead of treating strategies E and O as dichotomies, it is possible to regard them as extreme points on a continuum with several "middle positions" being possible.

In its "pure" form, strategy E could be described as a "commander model",[665] as "dictatorial transformation" or "forced evolution",[666] or as "directed change".[667] A change strategy with less use of open coercion, but still firmly classified as a pure strategy E, would be a strategy of manipulation where resistance is reduced through isolating important resisting forces from central decisional arenas, either by taking away their participations rights or by timing important decisions to periods when negative actors are occupied with other tasks.[668] Through isolation of change-negative actors, use of overt coercion becomes less necessary. Either way, it is a change strategy based on the use of coercion, either through order and command or through manipulation.

A strategy that will find its place as a type of strategy E, but with several elements resembling strategy O, is John Kotter's famous "8 steps for successful change".[669] The underlying premise for Kotter is that formal top management is the most central organizational group in any change process. As a consequence, his advice contains several hierarchical elements, as becomes rather clear when we take a closer look at his 8 steps:

1. Establish a sense of urgency
2. Form a powerful guiding coalition
3. Create a vision
4. Communicate the vision
5. Empower others to act on the vision
6. Plan for and create short-term wins
7. Consolidate improvements and produce still more change
8. Institutionalize new approaches

In addition to being inspired by Kurt Lewin's ideas about "unfreezing", "moving", and "freezing", the eight steps contain elements of both strategies E and O. The role of top management is emphasized, as is the need for a strong and powerful coalition. At the same time, the strategy contains elements central to strategy O, such as incrementalism, creating visions, delegation, and empowerment.

Moving further towards strategy O, but still placed within the category of strategy E, we find what can be termed "consultative change".[670] In such a strategy, the change agent – usually top management – will take the change initiative, present a solution, and propose a discussion of the change. In practice such change is organized as several working groups or projects where the discussions take place. The analyses and solutions produced by these groups are thus "fed" back to the top managers, who make the final decisions. The decisions made are centralized, while the preparation for the decisions is open to many actors inside and outside the organization.

A strategy that is difficult to place clearly within either strategy E or O is what we will label a "negotiation strategy".[671] The starting point for this strategy is an acknowledgement that change will have both beneficial and negative consequences, but for different groups. Thus the change agent should expect resistance based on diverging interests. Concurrently, there is an admission from all the parties involved in the change that no one part is strong enough to impose the change, or to stop it. To make change happen, the need arises to construct arenas for negotiations between affected parties. Arenas for negotiation will produce compromises, and the actual compromises will depend on several factors, such as the parties' interest in the topic which is the object of negotiation and the power they are willing to mobilize to ensure that their interests prevail. The role of the change agent in such a case will be to propose the change initiative and actively follow up the negotiations. The outcome of such a change strategy will depend on the negotiation ability of the change agents. In all Scandinavian countries, where norms for employee participation and influence stand strong, both formally (through national laws and national agreements) and informally (low power distance), such negotiation strategies are quite common.[672] The parties acknowledge that they have diverging interests, but also that they have a "common destiny" making it necessary for them to reach some kind of common, sensible agreement. At the same time, such processes may be somewhat centralized as compromises elaborated by the parties must often be sanctioned by the parties' interest organizations.

Moving on to the part of the continuum where strategy O dominates, but still containing elements of strategy E, we find what we will label a "participative strategy".[673] This strategy has several similarities with the "consultative strategy", but with one significant difference: in this strategy, groups set to analyse problems and develop solutions are delegated far more decision-making power. The groups are, within the framework of this strategy, semi-autonomous in the sense that they can make their own decisions. Just as important is the idea that groups will also have the possibility of trying out different solutions without seeking permission from top management. Such small changes may, if they are functional and good, spread "virally" in the organization.[674] In this aspect, the strategy will resemble the main ideas of incrementalism. In addition, great weight is given to the group process of reaching solutions, as this is regarded as an opportunity to create common views and interests. At the same time, each group will be clearly delimited to a specific area, thus operating under quite clear restrictions determined by top management. Delegation is selective in the sense that groups are only delegated power to make decisions within clearly defined areas.

Even further towards the ideal model of strategy O we find the "collaborative strategy".[675] In this strategy, participation from all organizational levels – including top management – is essential. At the same time, top managers are not given a more important role in the groups discussing the change than "ordinary" employees. They are regarded as ordinary members of the groups, with the same right to air their views and to participate in collective decisions. Managers participate with the same rights, and obligations, as others. The groups are also delegated wide decisional powers in that limits for what the groups can discuss and decide are not clearly defined. Thus the room for local experimentation, without the sanction of top management, is great.

Something resembling a "pure" strategy O is found in what has been called an "educational strategy".[676] The starting point for this strategy is an assumption that all members of an organization want to change if they see the need for it and have the capacity to change. To be able to detect a need for change, members of the organization must be educated to see what needs to change. And to be able to change, they must be provided with skills and resources enabling them to actually change things. Any possible interest differences between employees and the organization are, within the framework of this strategy, erased. Developing people is equal to developing the organization. The higher the competence of the members of the organization to detect the need for change, to develop solutions, and to implement change themselves, the more decision-making power can delegated to the operative levels.

The seven strategies – the two "pure" and the five "hybrid" – can be placed physically on a scale where the pure types represent the extreme ends.

Most "recipes" for how to conduct successful change are based on a mixture of strategies E and O. At first glance, this may seem a very sensible way of acting, as it represents "the best of two worlds". Organize for broad participation, but be ready to intervene if resistance is detected. Elaborate a vision for the change, but be ready to use threats towards those not buying the vision. Give individual consideration to members of the organization, but be prepared to reward those who actively support the change while not giving anything to those who are lukewarm or negative towards the change.[677]

The logic of distinguishing the two strategies so clearly in this book is based on an assumption that the two strategies may represent opposites that are incommensurable, that they represent two different forms of logic that are not possible to reconcile. They may symbolize two different paradigms of

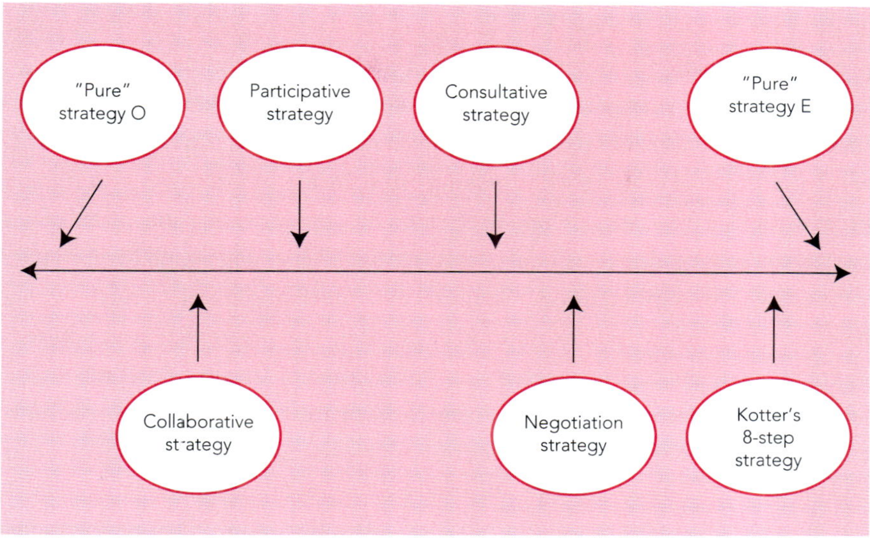

FIGURE 8.2: Change strategies placed on a scale varying between a "pure" strategy O and a "pure" strategy E

change.[678] If so, using elements of one strategy together with elements from another strategy might undermine the whole attempt to implement planned change. One example could illustrate this dilemma. "Participation", as a generally positive concept, is something that is integrated into almost any change strategy. In its pure form, as it was in the classic school of organization development (OD), participation was treated as real in the sense that it meant decisional influence for all participants. If participation is real in this sense, it must also be possible, within some limitations, to say "no" to a specific change. If participants experience several events where their voice is not given any weight, they are very likely to feel as though they are in a situation where participation is only symbolic, and may perhaps also feel like "hostages". Participation may thus be experienced as a kind of "pseudo-participation", which may again leads to change cynicism.[679]

Sequencing of change strategies

If it is problematic to combine change strategies, another question arises: Is it possible to use different strategies in different phases of the change process? That is, can they be used in their "pure" forms in the same organization and change process, but at different points in time?[680] Two options seem feasible.

The first is that change starts in a "hard" way by using strategy E. Top management makes the decisions to start the change, they enforce it through some structural or processual changes while making extensive use of incentives, threats, and promises. Once the first steps have been enforced, a more participative strategy has started to change culture to fit the new structure. The second possibility is to start with a "soft" strategy, focusing on cultural and informal elements, and designing processes with broad participation and delegation. This is a sort of "wait-and-see" strategy where the top managers await the outcome of the process. If results are produced, the process is allowed to go on. If the process stops for any reason, however, the top management intervenes by making changes in the formal elements and giving orders backed up by authority and the use of incentives.

One example can illustrate this mode of reasoning. Many Norwegian organizations find it challenging that a number of employees, especially women in the health and social sector, are working part time. Even if this is a voluntary and positive choice for the individual, it has negative consequences for wages, for the possibility of assuming leadership positions, and for pensions.[681] In the discussion about what to do with this problem, two different methods of sequencing are debated. The first, which has several similarities to strategy E, is based on Parliament making changes in national laws and regulations, laying down principles that at least public organizations are to employ people in full-time positions. This is clearly a top-down strategy with a strong emphasis on formal elements. After the regulations have been laid down, it is possible to envisage a more decentralized process with the intention of creating a "full-time culture" at the organizational level. An opposing strategy is to start working with norms and values concerning part-time and full-time work in the individual organization, with the aim of reducing part-time work. Once such cultures are established, eventual changes are made in the formal structure to fit with the new situation.

The main challenge associated with sequencing is associated with the phenomenon of path-dependency. Studies of decisions in organizations show clearly that decisions made at one point in time have decisive consequences for decisions made at a later point in time. Decisions are linked together in a temporal way, where previous decisions represent both possibilities and constraints for later decisions.[682]

Without having empirical evidence to point to, the following scenario at least seems plausible: using strategy E will always entail some kind of coercion to overcome resistance. Such processes are likely to create negative emotions in those involved. Such negative emotions will probably make it difficult to accept later invitations to participate and decide. How will employees react when first being subjected to coercion react when they are invited to participate by the same person or group that first forced them to do something they initially did not want to do? It is possible that people will interpret the invitation to participate as another way of manipulating them into doing something that is not good for them. In making sense of an invitation to participate, previous negative emotions connected to a change agent are activated, making it likely that the new initiative will also be interpreted negatively.

As a parallel, it may be difficult to move from a strategy O to a strategy E, but on somewhat different grounds. Strategy O is based on delegation of power to semi-autonomous groups who are enabled to make – at least limited – experiments, and thus to decide changes. This represents real delegation, and as such that the top management has given away some of its power to decide. Once groups have been delegated decision making and have been empowered, it may be difficult to recentralize decisions.[683]

Decoupling of strategies

Both the combination and the sequencing of change strategies may, as discussed above, be problematic. It is a potential danger that attempts to combine or sequence will be perceived and interpreted as "hypocrisy"[684] and "pseudo-participation",[685] which in turn produces resistance, resignation, and apathy.[686] The main reason for this is that there is a possibility that the process of change itself is perceived as unfair or as a way to manipulate people. Thus, resistance may not only be a consequence of the change content, but also of the way the change process is organized. Using strategy E may undermine the possibility of using strategy O, and vice versa. Change agents using threats, coercion, and fear will face serious problems of credibility once they change into actors inviting people to participate and decide. And change agents delegating power and encouraging participation may find it difficult to recentralize power at a later stage if necessary.

If the two strategies are difficult to combine, one should ask whether it is possible in any way to decouple them.[687] Decoupling can take at least three different forms.

A. DIFFERENT STRATEGIES USED IN DIFFERENT PARTS OF THE SAME ORGANIZATION

Such decoupling is, for rather obvious reasons, only possible in larger organizations. One example could be a divisionalized structure where one division is changed using an E-type strategy, while another undergoes a change implemented in an O-style strategy. Divisionalized structures are usually loosely coupled at the divisional level, making it possible to conduct different strategies in different divisions at the same time. Other large and relatively loosely coupled organizations – such as municipalities – should also have the possibility to utilize such spatial decoupling. What goes on in one part of the municipality is often met with little interest in other parts, as municipal sectors are rather loosely coupled. Thus it is possible for a larger municipality to use different strategies in different sectors, from relatively top-down strategies associated with outsourcing and partly privatizing and downsizing, to bottom-up processes in schools and the health sector.

B. DIFFERENT STRATEGIES COUPLED WITH DIFFERENT LEADERS

Another possibility is to link different change strategies with different people. The use of a specific change strategy will by many in the organization be often rather quickly linked to and associated with a specific person, most often a formal leader, especially if such a coupling is made explicit. In its most extreme form, one could think of two change agents splitting responsibility between themselves for different decisions and projects in the change process. One takes responsibility for the "hard" measures associated with strategy E, while the other is responsible for the softer measures. The technique is far from novel – everybody familiar with crime dramas will recognize the police trick of "good cop, bad cop" – but little explored in the realm of organizational change. This strategy requires, of course, that there are several individuals in charge of the change process.[688]

C. SYMBOLIC BREAKS WITH THE PAST

To break up the path dependency that will be present in all change processes, it is possible to try to decouple phases and events from each other temporarily. Sequencing of different strategies will often lead to situations where the present strategy is interpreted within the framework of experiences with previous phases in the change process. If this results in negative interpretations of the present, it may be wise to try and decouple the present from the past. One of the strongest breaks an organization can make with its past is to change leaders. Leaders are highly visible, and their removal will thus have a huge symbolic impact.[689] Changing a leader sends a clear signal to the organization that a specific period is over, and a new "era" is beginning. Thus, leader changes may prevent current events from being interpreted in the light of the past.

Ambidextrous organizations

This book is based on a general assumption that stability is the normal state of any organization, and that change is a deviation from that stability. "Organization" and "change" represent opposites, or at least phenomena that are in conflict with each other. Organization means setting focus on stability, predictability, and reduction of variance. Most studies of how organizations evolve over time indicate that, after a period of turbulence in the start-up phase, they move into a phase where the most important element is to refine the core activities and to produce predictability.[690] Organizations thus often regard change as a nuisance, something that disturbs their stability, and could thus be detrimental to efficiency and effectiveness. Still, organizations have to change to survive in the long run.

Traditional organization theory contains an implicit assumption that organizations must organize either for stability and efficiency, or for innovation and change. The first to acknowledge this distinction were two British researchers doing empirical research on firms in the early 1960s (Burns & Stalker 1961).[691] The backdrop for their studies was the strong economic growth experienced by the European countries in the aftermath of World War II, and the concurrent breakthroughs in technology and trade. Through many different studies they concluded that the then dominating organization form – bureaucratic and centralized – had problems in adapting to the swift and radical changes in technology and markets. They also detected new types of organizations that managed to adapt more easily to the new situation.

This finding triggered a major research project exploring the characteristics of the so-called "organization for change".[692] The researchers concluded that such organizations – called "organic" – were characterized by:[693]

1. No stable work function for individual employees; everybody should contribute to the common task of the organization and problems could not be pushed upwards, downwards, or sideways.
2. A strong feeling of belonging to the organization, weak distinctions between work and private life, and a strong commitment to the job (task and profession).
3. A decentralized structure based more on peer control than on hierarchical supervision and control.
4. A network structure of communication relying more on consultation than on order and command.
5. Extensive use of ad-hoc decisions, and thus constantly shifting decision arenas and participation.
6. High prestige of workers with close links to important professional and commercial external groups (partners, customers, etc.).

This type of organization was later labelled the adhocracy because so many decisions in the organization were made in a non-routine way.[694] The inverse organizational form was the mechanistic or bureaucratic structure with an emphasis on routines and hierarchy.

Moreover, in their studies Burns and Stalker detected two intriguing phenomena. One was that the more organic the organization, the better it was at innovating, both by being innovative itself, but also by acquiring innovations from others. The main explanation was that decentralization transferred decisional power to the operative core, and the operative core was more likely to detect the need for innovation than top management. In a mechanistic organization, suggestions for innovation from the operative core had to pass many layers of hierarchy, meeting resistance at each level from managers feeling threatened by innovation. The other phenomenon observed was that mechanistic organizations seemed to be more efficient at the production of goods and services. Efficient deployment of resources seemed to require a clear and stable structure of responsibilities, extensive routines and thus repetition of tasks and processes, and swift response to deviances from the routine processes. The findings by Burns and Stalker started a rush of studies on organizational innovation, and their main conclusions also seem to remain valid for today's organizations.[695]

Organic structure is a basic element in most, if not all, current theories of organizational innovation, whether they address the organization's "absorptive capacity"[696] or "dynamic capacity",[697] its ability to function as a "learning organization",[698] or its quality of being "designed for change".[699] In addition, these more novel theories have added important elements to describing organizations with a strong ability to innovate and change, for instance the role of staff knowledge, competence and research (absorptive capacity), culture (dynamic capabilities), system thinking (learning organizations), and core values (design for change). All these elements are discussed more in detail in this book's chapter on context for change.

Most studies on innovation and change, however, conclude that it seems to be very difficult for organizations to be good at both innovating and at producing efficiently at the same time. The reason is that the two process of innovation and efficient production seem to function best in two very different and probably conflicting contexts: an organic versus a mechanistic organization. This is one of the basic organizational paradoxes,[700] leading many researchers, theorists, and managers to pose the following question: Is it possible to design organizations that are equally good at innovating and changing – even radically – as they are at producing efficiently? Or are the two forms of learning – exploration and exploitation – mutually exclusive?

Tushman and O'Reilly (1996) claim that it is difficult, but not impossible. However, to be able to succeed in doing so, organizations must develop "dual competencies",[701] or become what they label "ambidextrous".[702] Originally, an ambidextrous person meant one who is able to write as well with the left hand as with the right. Transferred to an organization, it implies that it must be capable of doing two very different things concurrently. Thus it has to build into its structure, culture, and management an ability to constantly handle contradictions and paradoxes. On the one hand, it must have the ability to concentrate on some areas where it can compete with the best in the field. To obtain this, organizations must be able to limit focus, and constantly refine it to improve quality and lower costs. This can only be achieved by rigid demands on production, high stability, predictability, and incremental refinement. On the other hand, the organization must manage this without getting caught in its own success trap. Thus, ambidextrous organizations must be willing and able to "destroy" what they are best at when the need for innovation and change arises.[703]

This dual ability can only be obtained by designing organizations that host "multiple contradictory structures, processes, and cultures within the same firm".[704] This type of organization is characterized by:

1. Usually a dual structure, commonly physically separated, where one part focuses on production, economies of scope and scale, stability, and constant improvement of production processes (incremental innovation), and another part focuses on experimentation and innovation (radical innovation), but only marginally on efficiency and profits.
2. One part is clearly mechanistic, built with emphasis on rules, routines, and procedures, as well as a hierarchy to detect deviances in the production. The other part is organic in its form, often rather small, with ambiguous or no job descriptions, decentralized decision making, and extensive use of teamwork.
3. The two parts have both similar and dissimilar cultures. In the mechanistic part, values like process, quality, efficiency, and predictability have high status, while the organic part emphasizes values like risk, unpredictability, and lack of respect for rules and authorities. The common value is a commitment to the organization as a whole, that they are working towards the same goal, but with different means. Some personnel rotation between units exists to strengthen the feeling of belonging to the same organization.
4. The strategy, often formulated as a powerful vision, emphasizes what is common for the whole organization, what is the core activity, and what the organization's identity is. Those involved with production must understand that those working with innovation are important for them all in the long run, and those involved in innovation must accept that it is production that makes it possible for them to continue their work.
5. Leaders from all parts of the organization constitute the leader team, where the team's main challenge is to secure both continuity and change.[705] The leaders of the team must thus share the same visions and goals, but also offer differing views and perspectives. Heterogeneity in education, experience, gender, and age must be balanced against the need for some homogeneity. How long one team should exist should be balanced on the same grounds.

The theses of what an ambidextrous organization is, how ambidexterity is achieved, and the effect of being ambidextrous have been the object of numerous theoretical and empirical works during the past two decades.[706] A successful mix of the two types of learning – exploitation and exploration, or stability and change – can take on numerous forms. Three forms seem to be the most common: structural design (separate units with different structures), individual development (developing trust between members of the organization, as well as their ability to combine conflicting demands in their daily work), and design of management team (composing teams with people able to balance exploitation and exploration).

However, a growing number of studies point to the difficulties of existing with dual structures and cultures. Instead, they emphasize that ambidexterity should be treated as a sequencing of organizational forms.[707] Ambidexterity is thus obtained by moving between different configurations or archetypes. Operationalized in this fashion, the ability to obtain ambidexterity will depend on the organization's ability to successfully change between configurations, a type of change that we have termed radical as it changes the "deep structure" of the organization. Thus, the ability to reach ambidexterity will depend on the ability to implement planned change. This is exactly what this book has been about.

Epilogue

The tyranny of change?

The first edition of this book was written almost 15 years ago. During this relatively short period of time, the world has experienced great shocks and gone through significant changes. China has become an economic power player on the world market, lifting hundreds of millions of inhabitants out of poverty in just a couple of decades. The fear of, and the war against, terror has become ingrained in the daily lives of citizens all over the world after the attacks on the Twin Towers in New York at the beginning of the millennium. The Cold War between Russia and the West has almost returned. The Middle East and many of the Arab countries still live in a state of chaos with political turmoil, devastating wars, and unbelievable suffering among civilians. The USA elected its strangest president ever, and in France they managed to elect a president without support from any of the traditional political parties. Britain is on its way to leaving the EU, while the EU is shocked by streams of refugees, the growth of populist parties and movements, and members from the former "eastern bloc" moving in a non-democratic direction. Robotization and artificial intelligence lead to the obliteration of jobs, again creating high unemployment among specific population groups all over the world. There is little doubt that these changes are radical.

At the same time, an uneasy feeling sneaks in: How dramatic is the "rhythm of change" everybody is talking about? There is no doubt that our schools have gone through many reforms and changes over the last 50 years, but still I have no problem in recognizing a school when I accompany my children and grandchildren to school. Simple consumer products like bicycles, cars, and washing machines, perhaps with the exception of electric cars, are very similar to what I first bought 30 or 40 years ago. That streaming of film and music has replaced DVDs and CD, which in turn replaced LPs and videos, is clearly a radical change for many, probably mostly for the artists. However, the film and music industry is still dominated by a few old and large corporations, either directly or through indirect ownership. Today's most profitable – and most often used as examples of innovation – companies are beginning to age: Apple (established 1976), Google (established 1998), and Facebook (established 2004). The largest companies on the Norwegian Stock exchange in 2018 are not exactly youngsters, either: Statoil, now Equinor (established 1972), Telenor (established 1995, but dating back to 1855), DnB (established 2003, but with roots back to 1822), and Norsk Hydro (established 1905). Of course, these organizations have gone through major changes during their lifetimes, and some would even claim that they are not the same organizations as they were at birth. Still, it underlines how much stability there is. All the talk about how much and how quickly things are changing also has a tendency to cloud the stable elements that are still there.

And perhaps just as interesting: organizations may achieve success by refusing to change. The Swiss watch industry was unable to foresee the revolution created by digital quartz technology. Instead, they continued making mechanical watches. The whole industry went through a deep crisis in the 1970s and 80s, but many of them are still alive and thriving. Who wants a Rolex with quartz technology? During the 1960s and 70s there was strong pressure on the wine industry in Europe to replace their old clones of vines with new ones that would increase both the quantity and the quality of wines. Many winemakers gave in to the pressure and ripped out hundred-year-old vines to replace them with the new clones, only to experience that although the new clones were more productive and had good and consistent quality, they were also prone to new and unknown diseases. And even worse, the taste of the wine changed. Today, winemakers holding on to the old wines can charge an extra premium simply for not changing.

Moving on from anecdotic to more systematic evidence, there is an interesting study of 150 paper production firms over a period from 1970 to the early 2000s.[708] By examining the firms over time – through upturns and downturns – they were able to detect three strategies that firms met market downturns with. The first was the active strategy, characterized by firms that were the first to downsize and to sell equities and machinery to meet the downward cycle. On the opposite side the researchers found firms deploying a reluctant strategy, that is firms that did not take any special measures, at least not downsizing or selling out, to meet the downturn. And there was a middle category called inconsistent, where the researchers were not able to detect any specific strategy to meet the downturn in the market. Afterwards, the researchers estimated the return on capital (profits) for the firms during the whole period. The results are displayed in table E.1.

TABLE E.1: Mean return on capital split into different categories related to strategies of downsizing and selling assets

		STRATEGY FOR SELLING ASSETS		
		RELUCTANT	INCONSISTENT	ACTIVE
STRATEGY FOR DOWNSIZING	RELUCTANT	**8.85**	3.98	7.29
	INCONSISTENT	7.65	5.00	4.41
	ACTIVE	7.15	4.94	**3.33**

The absolutely highest return on capital is found in the group of firms that followed a reluctant strategy on both dimensions, while the lowest was found in the opposite corner of the table, among firms following an active strategy. Although this is just one study, using only one measure of change and change strategy, it still indicates that change – at least frequent change – is not always a beneficial thing for the organization.

Planned change, subjective driving forces, and "sellers of change"

The above argument deserves further reflection. The world is changing. Of course! But why do we so quickly assume that the whole world changes at the same tempo, in all sectors, and at the same time? Why do we end up screaming "The environments are turbulent!" so quickly?[709] And why do we take for granted that change is necessary, if not to say good? Most people will agree that changes within the field of information and communication technology (ICT) are taking place at a very high tempo, and that this has ramifications for most activities in most organizations. However, the effect of changes in ICT affects organizations in many different ways. Working at a university today is different from working there 10 or 20 years ago. For one thing, we are less dependent on physical proximity to libraries and colleagues. Still, it is difficult to say that my work has changed radically. The core activities remain pretty much the same, although the instruments we use have changed. Still, there are several actors claiming quite intensely that higher education should go through not only an incremental change, but a transformation.[710]

This leads to the next question: How much of what is said about the need for change is real, and how much is rhetoric? As has been emphasized throughout the book, it is evident that most driving forces are very seldom or never clear, unambiguous, and "objective". There is always "somebody" – change agents – perceiving a need for change, and initiating that change. And as long as none of us is able to know what is absolutely true or false, we have to rely on the opinions of others. Such a situation opens the door to a possibility that organizations can be "sold" a specific view of the world, again opening a space for "sellers" of change and change recipes.

If we accept that some or all of the talk about the necessity for change may be rhetoric and thus a form of sales activity, some new questions arise. One of them is: Who benefits from a general perception of change being necessary and good? The answer is obvious: those who sell change. One should never forget that selling recipes for how to "survive in an ever more rapidly changing world" is big business.[711] Previously in this book, we have on several occasions touched on change techniques that exist in the public space: Benchmarking, Total Business Reengineering, Balanced Scorecard, and several others. Behind these recipes we find authors who sell books by the millions, consultancy firms offering more or less standardized procedures to implement new techniques, and presenters demanding six-digit fees for short appearances at large conferences.

Nor should we forget the close links found between the more practically oriented and commercial consultancy firms and the academic and research-oriented institutions. Many of the new techniques associated with organizational change have been developed through research projects, more specifically projects aimed at finding out what makes some organizations better than others. In these studies, researchers reveal specific structures, processes, technologies, or cultures that are interpreted as the keys to success. These studies are then decontextualized and removed from their original limits in time and space, and are presented as general techniques that will work everywhere, always. As these techniques are developed by well-regarded researchers from some of the most prestigious research institutions, they are infused with strong legitimacy.

In the first chapter of this book we showed the great increase in research on organizational change from 1980 until today (figure 1.1). Some will surely claim that this increase in research output reflects the increased importance of the phenomenon of change. But the more research focuses on change and not stability, the more likely it is that research itself reinforces the impression that change is necessary. The author of this book is thus also part of the business that "sells" change. The more people perceive change as essential for today's organizations, the larger the market is for those of us selling change techniques and books.

We must also point out another important actor that is dependent on giving an impression of change – hopefully dramatic – every day: all types of mass media. The media industry – everything from magazines and newspapers, via film and TV, to the internet and social media – is one of today's fastest growing branches, reflecting the general increase in media consumption. Mass media are dependent on selling something as "new". The eternal hunt for news leads to ever-increasing dramatization of everyday events, giving an impression of dramatic, never-ending change. The impression that everything changes, and quickly – "don't miss our next news report" – must be upheld to keep old customers and generate new ones.

It is also possible to speculate on more subtle mechanisms at work. The fact that change is perceived as so essential by many people may be interpreted as though someone has succeeded in creating some kind of ideological hegemony. To say out loud that one is against change is almost the same as saying that one is against improvement and progress. So, who benefits from the ubiquity of such an impression? An interesting article, based on a neo-Marxist perspective, points out three general effects of a strong focus on organizational change.[712] First, change very often creates a sense of uncertainty in an organization's operative core – the workers or employees – as they are usually the ones who will have to change the most. Second, change often weakens or breaks down social relations at the operative level, weakening the unity of that group. And third, change creates a focus on organizational survival, again reinforcing an assumption that the organization is more important than the individuals constituting it. If the organization is not able to change, it will "die", and everyone will lose their jobs. Combined, the three elements work as a reinforcement of the importance of top management or owners of the organization. The more people accept that we live in a situation characterized by "turbulence", "hyper-competition", and "technological revolution", the higher the probability that owners will succeed in implementing changes that are first and foremost beneficial to themselves.

"To change or not to change, that is the question."

Throughout this book it has been emphasized that change is costly in economic and technological terms (new investments in machines and knowledge / skills), human terms (emotions, social relations, energy, stress), and time (that could have been used on alternative tasks). Change must be conducted while keeping up "business as usual". No matter how much one claims that change is the new normal, there will be a need for some stability to reap the benefits of changes that have been accomplished. Change is necessary, probably more so today than ever before. Still, that is not the same as saying that one should always strive for change.

Part of being a capable change agent is the ability to see when change is necessary, and when it is not. This capability is perhaps difficult to acquire, as not wanting to change may convey an impression that the agent is "slow", "old fashioned", or "non-progressive". Standing up to the pressure demands courageous change agents. Such agents are, according to Pfeffer and Sutton (2006) able to pose and answer eight questions before engaging in organizational change.

Question 1: Is the new practice better than what you are doing right now?
The first question a capable change agent should ask is whether the change initiative really represents an improvement. Is it possible that the organization has already implemented something similar? Just as important is asking for proof that the proposed change will lead to an improvement. Has any research been conducted in organizations similar to ours? Is it possible to identify anyone other than those interested in selling the proposition who supports the idea? If the answers to these questions are not clear – and they rarely are! – it is wise to test out the idea in a very limited form, for instance in only one department.

Question 2: Is the change worth it?
An economist will always ask: Are the benefits greater that the costs? The change may represent an improvement, but this improvement must outweigh – in positive

terms – the costs associated with the change (investments, stress, dissatisfaction, etc.). At the same time, one should reflect on the longevity of the effects of the change. If new change must be implemented rather quickly, the cost will increase, and the gain of the change must be even higher.

Question 3: Are symbolic changes sufficient?

Are unsure whether this change will represent an improvement or not, but influential actors outside the organization are pushing for change? This could apply to owners or politicians claiming that a specific change is essential, but you, as responsible for the change, fear that it may be superfluous or even detrimental to the organization. In situations like that, it is legitimate to ask whether symbolic changes will be sufficient. A symbolic change is where something only seemingly changes, while daily activities continue as before. Decoupling may be an efficient strategy in such instances.

Question 4: Who benefits from the change?

Organizations are – at any given point in time – rather stable distributions of power, prestige, and rewards. Changes will usually redistribute these resources, so somebody wins and others lose. A rule of thumb for continuing with a change is that the whole organization will benefit from it, not only a few groups. This is not to say that everybody benefits equally (Pareto optimality), but that the organization in sum is better off than before the change. Some of the most spectacular bankruptcies in recent times, for instance the gas company Enron's bankruptcy in 2001 or the Icelandic bank Kaupthing's bankruptcy in association with the financial crisis in 2008, are indices about changes being implemented that only benefit a few groups – mostly top managers – while making the whole organization suffer.

Question 5: Do you have enough power?

As discussed thoroughly in this book, change will almost always trigger resistance. No matter how capable the change agent is in creating support for the change, there will be groups activating resources to oppose and try to stop the proposed change. If the change agents are too weak to meet such resistance at critical phases in the change process, the result may be long, antagonistic battles that may end up detrimental for the whole organization. In a worst-case scenario, equally strong groups will engage in a long-term war that nobody is strong enough to win. In such situations, change should not be initiated.

Question 6: Are people tired of change?
Organizations are changing all the time, and not all change projects are equally well coordinated. New change initiatives may come before other change processes have been ended, resulting in a "pile-up" of change processes. If a new change comes on top of several other change processes, it will demand great resources and increase stress, and may produce negative emotions. If this is the case, the change is probably not going to be a success.

Question 7: Is the change initiative flexible enough?
Change is, as noted, an uncertain project where many unpredicted events, not all of them positive, are going to happen. This demands at least some flexibility, so that the process can be revised and adapted to new contingencies, and it must be possible to add some elements to the initial plan and subtract others. Change initiatives without such possibilities, for example a system that someone claims must be implemented fully or not at all, should be met with scepticism. Each organization is unique, and if someone argues that a change will fit all organizations, they are probably wrong.

Question 8: Can you pull the plug?
Uncertainty also means that an initiated change process may turn out to be a failure, or at least does not produce the results it was expected to. The probability that this will be the case is not negligible. Thus one should ask whether one is able to stop the process if it proves to be a failure. For many, stopping a change initiative will mean a loss of prestige. It also requires a constant follow-up of the process, and a continuous evaluation of how it is working out. This will take quite some time and resources. Are you willing to spend these resources, and risk the loss of prestige? If not, the change should probably not be initiated.

Several other questions could have been posed, but they convey the main point: be critical about whether you should engage in a change process or not. Change is demanding, and the more radical and large-scale it is, the more demanding it is. Good leadership is not only starting and implementing change, but also knowing when one should resist change and focus on predictability and stability.

Literature

Abernathy, W.J. (1978): *The Productivity Dilemma*. Baltimore, Johns Hopkins University Press.

Abernathy, W.J. & Clark, K. (1985): Mapping the Winds of Creative Destruction. *Research Policy*, vol. 14:3–22.

Abrahamson, E (1996): Technical and Aesthetic Fashion. In Czarniawska, B. & Sevon, G. (Eds.), *Translating Organizational Change*. Berlin, de Gruyter.

Albert, S. (1995): Towards a Theory of Timing: An Archival Study of Timing Decisions in the Persian Gulf War. *Research in Organization Behavior*, vol. 17:1–70.

Allison, G.T. (1971): *Essence of Decision: Explaining the Cuban Missile Crisis*. Boston, Little & Brown.

Allison, G.T. (1983): Public and Private Management: Are They Fundamentally Alike in All Unimportant Respects? In Perry, J.L. & Kraemer, K.L. (Eds.), *Public Management. Public and Private Perspectives*. Palo Alto, Mayfield Publishing.

Alvesson, M. (1992): Leadership as Social Integrative Action: A Study of a Computer Consultancy Company. *Organization Studies*, vol. 13:185–209.

Amankwah-Amoah, J., Ottosson, J. & Sjögren, H. (2017): United We Stand, Divided We Fall: Historical Trajectory of Strategic Renewal Activities at the Scandinavian Airlines System, 1946–2012. *Business History*, vol. 59(4):572–606.

Amburgey, T.L., Kelly, D. & Barnett, W.P. (1993): Resetting the Clock. The Dynamics of Organizational Change and Failure. *Administrative Science Quarterly*, vol. 38:51–73.

Amundsen, O. & Kongsvik, T. (2008): *Endringskynisme. Organisasjonsendringers møte med praksis.* Oslo, Gyldendal Akademisk.

Anderson, P. & Tushman, M.L. (1990): Technological Discontinuities and Dominant Designs: A Cyclical Model of Technological Change. *Administrative Science Quarterly*, vol. 35:604–633.

Andrews, K.R. (1965): *The Concept of Corporate Strategy*. New York, Irwin.

Andriopolous, C. & Lewis, M.W. (2009): Exploitation-Exploration Tensions and Organizational Ambidexterity: Managing Paradoxes of Innovation. *Organization Science*, vol. 20(4): 696–717.

Antonakis, J., Fenley, M. & Liechti, S. (2011): Can Charisma be Taught? Tests of Two Interventions. *Academy of Management Learning & Education*, vol. 10(3):374–396.

Antonsen, M. & Beck Jørgensen, T. (2000a): Institutionel forandring. In Antonsen, M. & Beck Jørgensen, T. (Eds.), *Forandringer i teori og praksis – skiftende billeder fra den offentlige sektor*. Copenhagen, Jurist- og Økonomforbundets Forlag.

Antonsen, M. & Beck Jørgensen, T. (2000b) (Eds.): *Forandringer i teori og praksis – skiftende billeder fra den offentlige sektor.* Copenhagen, Jurist- og Økonomforbundets Forlag.

Antonsen, M., Greve, C. & Beck Jørgensen, T. (2000): Teorier om forandring i den offentlige sektor. In Antonsen, M. & Beck Jørgensen, T. (Eds.), *Forandringer i teori og praksis – skiftende billeder fra den offentlige sektor.* Copenhagen, Jurist- og Økonomforbundets Forlag.

Argyris, C. (1962): *Interpersonal Competence and Organizational Effectiveness*. Homewood, IL, Irwin.

Argyris, C. (1973): Some Limits of Rational Man Organization Theory. *Public Administration Review*, vol. 33:263–267.

Argyris, C. (1982): *Reasoning, Learning and Action: Individual and Organizational*. San Francisco, Jossey-Bass.

Argyris, C. (1990): *Overcoming Organizational Defences. Facilitating Organizational Learning*. Boston, Allyn & Bacon.

Argyris, C. (2000): The Relevance of Actionable Knowledge for Breaking the Code. In Beer, M. & Nohria, N. (Eds.), *Breaking the Code of Change*. Boston, Harvard Business School.

Argyris, C. & Schön, D.A. (1974): *Theory in Practice. Increasing Professional Effectiveness*. San Francisco, Jossey-Bass.

Armenakis, A.A. & Bedeian, A.G. (1999): Organizational Change: A Review of Theory and Research in the 1990s. *Journal of Management*, vol. 25:293–315.

Armenakis, A.A. & Harris, S. (2009): Reflections: Our Journey in Organizational Change Research and Practice. *Journal of Change Management*, vol. 9(2):127–142.

Armenakis, A.A., Harris, S. & Feild, H. (1999): Paradigms in Organizational Change: Change Agent and Change Target Perspective. In Golembiewski, R. (Eds.), *Handbook of Organizational Behaviour*. New York, Marcel Dekker.

Armenakis, A.A., Harris, S. & Mossholder, K. (1993): Creating Readiness for Organizational Change. *Human Relations*, vol. 46:681–703.

Autor, D.H. (2015): Why Are There Still So Many Jobs? The History and Future of Workplace Automation. *Journal of Economic Perspectives*, vol. 29(3): 3–30.

Axson, D.A.J. (2010): *The Management Mythbuster*. Hoboken, NJ, Wiley.

Bakari, H., Hunjra, A.I. & Niazi, G.S.K. (2017): How Does Authentic Leadership Influence Planned Organizational Change? The Role of Employees' Perceptions: Integration of Theory of Planned Behavior and Lewin's Three Step Model. *Journal of Change Management*, vol. 17(2): 155–187.

Bakken, T. & Hernes, T. (2006): Organizing is Both a Verb and a Noun. *Organization Studies*, vol. 27:1599–1616.

Barker, V.L. & Duhaime, I.M. (1997): Strategic Change in the Turnaround Process: Theory and Empirical Evidence. *Strategic Management Journal*, vol. 18:13–38.

Barnett. W.P. (1997): The Dynamics of Competitive Intensity. *Administrative Science Quarterly*, vol. 42:128–160.

Barnett, W.P. & Freeman, J. (2001): Too Much of a Good Thing? Product Proliferation and Organizational Failure. *Organization Science*, vol. 12:539–558.

Baron, J.N. & Hannan, M.T. (2002): Organizational Blueprints for Success in High-Tech Start-Ups: Lessons from the Stanford Project on Emerging Companies. *California Management Review*, vol. 44:8–36.

Bartlett, C.A. & Ghosal, S. (1993): Beyond the M-Form: Toward a Managerial Theory of the Firm. *Strategic Management Journal*, vol. 14:23–46.

Barton, L. (1993): *Crisis in Organizations: Managing in the Heat of Chaos*. Cincinatti, OH, College Divisions South-Western.

Bartunek, J.M., Balogun, J. & Do, B. (2011): Considering Planned Change Anew: Stretching Large Group Interventions Strategically, Emotionally, and Meaningfully. *Academy of Management Annals*, vol. 5(1): 1–52.

Bass, B.M. (1985): *Leadership and Performance Beyond Expectations*. New York, Free Press.

Bass, B.M. (1990a): From Transactional to Transformative Leadership: Learning to Share the Vision. *Organizational Dynamics*, vol. 18:19–31.

Bass, B.M. (1990b): *Bass' and Stogdill's Handbook of leadership. Theory, Research and Applications* (3rd ed.) (chapter 12). New York, Free Press.

Bass, B.M. (1998): *Transformational Leadership: Industrial, Military and Educational Impact*. Mahwah, Lawrence Erlbaum.

Bass, B.M. (1999): Two Decades of Research and Development in Transformational Leadership. *European Journal of Work and Organizational Psychology*, vol. 8:9–32.

Bass, B.M. & Avolio, B.J. (1993): Transformational Leadership and Organizational Culture. *Public Administration Quarterly*, Spring:112–121.

Battilana, J. & Casciaro, T. (2012): Change Agents, Networks, and Institutions: A Contingency Theory of Organizational Change. *Academy of Management Journal*, vol. 55(2):381–398.

Beatty, R.W. & Ulrich, D.O. (1991): Re-Energizing the Mature Organization. *Organizational Dynamics*, vol. 20:16–30.

Beck, N., Brüderl, J. & Woywode, M. (2008): Momentum or Deceleration? Theoretical and Methodological Reflections on the Analysis of Organizational Change. *Academy of Management Journal*, vol. 51(3):413–435.

Beck Jørgensen, T. (2000): Forandringernes mangfoldighed: Empiriske og teoretiske konklusjoner. In Antonsen, M. & Beck Jørgensen, T. (Eds.), *Forandringer i teori og praksis – skiftende billeder fra den offentlige sektor*. Copenhagen, Jurist- og Økonomforbundets Forlag.

Beer, M. (1987): Revitalizing Organizations: Change Process and Emergent Models. *Academy of Management Executive*, vol. 1:51–55.

Beer, M. & Nohria, N. (2000a): Resolving the Tension Between Theories E and O of Change. In Beer, M. & Nohria, N.(Eds.), *Breaking the Code of Change*. Boston, Harvard Business School.

Beer, M. & Nohria, N. (2000b) (Eds.): *Breaking the Code of Change*. Boston, Harvard Business School.

Beer, M., Eisenstadt, R.A. & Spector, B (1990): *The Critical Path to Corporate Renewal*. Cambridge, MA, Harvard Business School Press.

Benner, M.J. & Tushman, M.L. (2003): Exploitation, Exploration and Process Management: The Productivity Dilemma Revisited. *Academy of Management Review*, vol. 28:238–256.

Benner, M.J., & Tushman, M.L. (2015): Reflections on the 2013 Decade Award – "Exploitation, Exploration, and Process Management: The Productivity Dilemma Revisited" Ten Years Later. *Academy of Management Review*, vol. 40(4):497–514.

Bennis, W. (1969): *Organization Development: Its Nature, Origins and Prospects*. Reading, MA, Addison-Wesley.

Bennis, W. (2000): Leadership of Change. In Beer, M. & Nohria, N. (Eds.), *Breaking the Code of Change*. Boston, Harvard Business School.

Benson, J.K. (1975): The Interorganizational Network as Political Economy. *Administrative Science Quarterly*, vol. 20:229–249.

Berg, M.E. (1995): *Organisasjonsutvikling: Metoder og teknikker*. Oslo, Cappelen.

Berger, P.L. & Luckman, T. (1967): *The Social Construction of Reality*. New York, Anchor Books.

Beyer, J.M. (1999): Taming and Promoting Charisma to Change Organizations. *Leadership Quarterly*, vol. 10:307–330.

Bies, R.J. & Tyler, T.R. (1993): The Litigation Mentality in Organizations: A Test of Alternative Psychological Explanations. *Organization Science*, vol. 4:352–366.

Blair, R. & Haynes, J. (2011): The Efficiencies Defense in the 2010 Horizontal Merger Guidelines. *Review of Industrial Organization*, vol. 39(1 / 2):57–68.

Blau, P.M. & Scott, W.R. (1963): *Formal Organizations*. San Francisco, Chandler.

Bluedorn, A.C. & Denhardt, R.B. (1988): Time and Organizations. *Journal of Management*, vol. 14:299–320.

Boeker, W. (1997): Executive Migration and Strategic Change: The Effect of Top Manager Movement on Product-Market Entry. *Administrative Science Quarterly*, vol. 42:213–236.

Bolman, L.G. & Deal, T.E. (1991): *Reframing Organizations. Artistry, Choice and Leadership.* San Francisco, Jossey-Bass.

Boonstra, J.J. & Gravenhorst, K.M.B. (1998): Power Dynamics and Organizational Change: A Comparison of Perspectives. *European Journal of Work and Organizational Psychology*, vol. 7:97–120.

Boonstra, J.J. & Vink, M.J. (1996): Technological and Organization Innovation: A Dilemma of Fundamental Change and Development. *European Journal of Work and Organizational Psychology*, vol. 5:351–376.

Borum, F. (1976): *Organisation, magt og forandring*. Copenhagen, Handelshøjskolen i København / Nyt Nordisk Forlag.

Borum, F. (1980): A Power Strategy Alternative to Organization Development. *Organization Studies*, vol. 2:123–146.

Borum, F. (1993): Strategier for ændring av organisationer. *Ledelse & Erhverv*, vol. 3:133–147.

Borum, F. (1995): *Strategier for organisationsændring*. Copenhagen, Handelshøjskolens Forlag.

Borum, F. (1999): Perspektiver på forandringsprocesser i sundheds- og sykehusfeltet. In Bentsen, E.Z., Borum, F., Erlingsdottir, G. & Sahlin-Andersson, K. (Eds.), *Når styringsambitioner møder praksis*. Copenhagen, Handelshøjskolens Forlag.

Bostrom, N. (2014): *Superintelligence. Paths, Dangers, Strategies.* Oxford: Oxford University Press.

Bourgeois, L.J. & Brodwin, D.R. (1984): Strategic Implementation: Five Approaches to an Elusive Phenomenon. *Strategic Management Journal*, vol. 5:241–264.

Bouwen, R. (1995): The Reconstruction of Power Relationships: Four Approaches Dealing With the New Logic and the Dominant Logic in Organizational Innovation. In Boonstra, J.J. (Eds.), *Power Dynamics and Organizational Change: Symposium Conducted at the Seventh European Congress on Work and Organizational Psychology*. Leuwen, Belgium, EAWOP.

Bowman, E.H. & Hurry, D. (1993): Strategy Though the Option Lens: An Integrated View of Resource Investments and the Incremental-Choice process. *Academy of Management Review*, vol. 18:760–782

Bozeman (1987): *All Organizations are Public*. San Francico, Jossey-Bass.

Braddon, D. (2000): *Exploding the Myth? The Peace Dividend, Regions and Market Adjustment*. Amsterdam, Harwood Academic Publishers.

Brandi, S., Hildebrandt, S. & Nordhaug, O. (2001): Kompetansegullets tidsalder. In Brandi, S., Hildebrandt, S. & Nordhaug, O., *Kompetansegullet @ det nye arbeidsliv*. Oslo, Cappelen Akademisk Forlag.

Brock, D., Powell, M. & Hinings, C.R. (1999) (Eds.): *Restructuring the Professional Organization. Accounting, Health Care and Law.* London, Routledge.

Brown, A.D., Gabriel, Y. & Gherardi, S. (2009): Storytelling and Change: An Unfolding Story. *Organization*, vol. 16(3):323–333.

Brunsson, N. (1989): *The Organization of Hypocrisy. Talk, Decisions and Actions in Organizations.* Chichester, John Wiley.

Brunsson, N. (2003): Organized Hypocrisy. In Czarniawska, B. & Sevon, G. (Eds.), *The Northern Lights – Organization Theory in Scandinavia.* Malmö, Liber / Oslo, Abstrakt / Copenhagen, Copenhagen Business School Press.

Brunsson, N. (2007): *The Consequences of Decision-Making.* Oxford, Oxford University Press.

Brunsson, N. (2009): *Reform as Routine. Organizational Change and Stability in the Modern World.* Oxford, Oxford University Press.

Brunsson, N., Forsell, A. & Winberg, H (1989): *Reform som tradition – Administrative reformer i Statens Järnvegar.* Stockholm, EFI.

Brunsson, N. & Olsen, J.P. (1997): *The Reforming Organization.* Bergen, Fagbokforlaget.

Brusoni, S., Prencipe, A. & Pavitt, K. (2001): Knowledge Specialization, Organizational Coupling, and the Boundaries of the Firm. *Administrative Science Quarterly*, vol. 46:597–622.

Bryman, A. (1992): *Charisma and Leadership in Organizations.* London, Sage.

Bryson, A., Barth, E. & Dale-Olsen, H. (2013): The Effects of Organizational Change on Worker Well-Being and the Moderating Role of Trade Unions. *ILR Review*, vol. 66(4): 989–1011.

Buono, A.F. & Kerber, K.W. (2010): Creating a Sustainable Approach to Change: Building Organizational Change Capacity. *SAM Advanced Management Journal*, vol. 75(2):4–21.

Burke, W.W. (2002): *Organization Change. Theory and Practice.* Thousand Oaks, Sage.

Burke, W.W. & Litwin, G.H. (1992): A Causal Model of Organizational Performance and Change. *Journal of Management*, vol. 18:523–545.

Burke, W.W. & Trahant, B. (2000): *Business Climate Shifts: Profiles of Change Makers.* Boston, Butterworth Heineman.

Burnes, B. (1992): *Managing Change.* London, Pitman.

Burnes, B. (2011): Introduction: Why Does Change Fail, and What Can We Do About It? *Journal of Change Management*, vol. 11(4):445–450.

Burnes, B. & Bargal, D. (2017): Kurt Lewin: 70 Years on. *Journal of Change Management*, vol. 17(2): 91–100. doi:10.1080/14697017.2017.1299371

Burns, J.M. (1978): *Leadership.* New York, Harper & Row.

Burns, T. (1977): *The BBC.* London, Macmillan.

Burns, T. & Stalker, G.M. (1961): *The Management of Innovation.* London, Tavistock.

Burrell, G. & Morgan, G. (1979): *Sociological Paradigms and Organisational Analysis.* London, Ashgate.

Busch, T. (1990): Kognitiv og sosial læringsteori. In Nordahug, O. (Eds.), *Læring i organisasjoner. Utvikling av menneskelige ressurser.* Oslo, Tano.

Busch, T. (2011): Organizational Adaptation to Disruptions in the Natural Environment: The Case of Climate Change. *Scandinavian Journal of Management*, vol. 27(4):389–404.

By, R.T. (2005): Organisational Change Management: A Critical Review. *Journal of Change Management*, vol. 5(4):369–380.

By, R.T. (2007): Ready or Not… *Journal of Change Management*, vol. 7(1):3–11.

By, R.T., Hughes, M. & Ford, J. (2016): Change Leadership: Oxymoron and Myths. *Journal of Change Management*, vol. 16(1):8–17. doi:10.1080/14697017.2016.1137425

Byrkjeflot, H. (2011): Offentlig eller privat – spiller det noen rolle for ledelse? In Askvik, S., Espedal, B. & Gammelsæter, H. (Eds.), *Kunnskap om ledelse – festskrift til Torodd Strand*. Bergen, Fagbokforlaget.

Campbell, J.L. (2007): Why Would Corporations Behave in Socially Responsible Ways? An Institutional Theory of Corporate Social Responsibility. *Academy of Management Review*, vol. 32(3): 946–967. doi:10.5465/AMR.2007.25275684

Carlos, W.C., & Lewis, B.W. (2018): Strategic Silence: Withholding Certification Status as a Hypocrisy Avoidance Tactic. *Administrative Science Quarterly*, vol. 63(1):130–169.

Carlzon, J. (1985): *Riv Pyramidene!* Oslo, Gyldendal Norsk Forlag.

Carroll, J.S. & Hatakenata, S. (2001): Driving Organizational Change in the Midst of Crisis. *MIT Sloan Management Review*, Spring:70–79.

Cartwright, S. & Schoenberg, R. (2006): Thirty Years of Mergers and Acquisitions Research: Recent Advances and Future Opportunities. *British Journal of Management*, vol. 17:1–5.

Chatman, J.A., Caldwell, D.F., O'Reilly, C.A. & Doerr, B. (2014): Parsing Organizational Culture: How the Norm for Adaptability Influences the Relationship between Culture Consensus and Financial Performance in High-Technology Firms. *Journal of Organizational Behavior*, vol. 35(6): 785–808.

Chatman, J.A. & O'Reilly, C.A. (2016): Paradigm Lost: Reinvigorating the Study of Organizational Culture. *Research in Organizational Behavior*, vol. 36:199–224.

Chin, R. & Benne, K.D. (1994): General Strategies for Effecting Changes in Human Systems. In French, W.L., Bell, C.H. & Zawacki, R.A. (Eds.), *Organization Development and Transformation: Managing Effective Change* (4th ed.). Boston, Irwin.

Christensen, C.M. (1998): *The Innovator's Dilemma: When New Technologies Cause Great Firms to Fail.* Boston, Harvard University Press.

Christensen, C.M. (2002): The Rules of Innovation. *MIT Technology Review*, vol. 105(5):32–38.

Christensen, C.M. (2006): The Ongoing Process of Building a Theory of Disruption. *Journal of Product Innovation Management*, vol. 23(1):39–55.

Clegg, S.R. (1989): *Frameworks of Power*. London, Sage.

Clegg, S.R. & Hardy, C. (1996): Organizations, Organizatrions and Organizing. In Clegg, S.R., Hardy, C. & Nord, W.R. (Eds.), *Handbook of organization studies*. London, Sage.

Clugston, M., Howell, J.P. & Dorfman, P.W. (2000): Does Cultural Socialization Predict Multiple Bases and Foci of Commitment? *Journal of Management*, vol. 26:5–30.

Cobb, A.T. (1986): Political Diagnosis: Applications in Organizational Development. *Academy of Management Review*, vol. 11:482–496.

Coch, L. & French, J. (1948): Overcoming Resistance to Change. *Human Relations*, vol. 1:512–532.

Coetsee, L. (1999): From Resistance to Commitment. *Public Administration Quarterly*, vol. 23: 204–223.

Cohen, M.D., March, J.G. & Olsen, J.P. (1972): A Garbage Can Model of Organizational Choice. *Administrative Science Quarterly*, vol. 17:1–25.

Cohen, W.M. & Levinthal, D.A. (1990): Absorptive Capacity: A New Perspective on Learning and Innovation. *Administrative Science Quarterly*, vol. 35:128–152.

Cole, R.E. & Scott, W.R. (2000) (Eds.): *The Quality Movement & Organization Theory*. Thousand Oaks, Sage.

Colman, H.L., Stensaker, I. & Tharaldsen, J.E. (2011) (Eds.), *A Merger of Equals?: The Integration of Statoil and Hydro's Oil and Gas Activities*. Bergen, Fagbokforlaget.

Coleman, J.S. (1986): Social Theory, Social Research and a Theory of Action. *American Journal of Sociology*, vol. 16:1309–1335.

Collins, J. (2001a): *From Good to Great: Why Some Companies Make the Leap and Others Don't*. New York, HarperCollins.

Collins, J. (2001b): *How the Mighty Fall and Why Some Companies Never Give In*. New York, HarperCollins.

Collins, J. & Porras, J.I. (1994): *Built to Last: Successful Habits of Visionary Companies*. New York, Harper Business.

Colombo, M.G. & Delmastro, M. (2002): The Determinants of Organizational Change and Structural Inertia: Technological and Organizational Factors. *Journal of Economics & Strategy*, vol. 11:595–635.

Conger, J.A. (2000): Effective Change Begins at the Top. In Beer, M. & Nohria, N. (Eds.), *Breaking the Code of Change*. Boston, Harvard Business School.

Craft, J.A. (1991): Unions, Bureaucracy and Change: Old Dogs Learn New Tricks Very Slowly. *Journal of Labor Research*, vol. 12:393–405.

Crozier, M. (1964): *The Bureaucratic Phenomenon*. Chicago, University of Chicago Press.

Crozier, M. & Friedberg, E. (1977): *L'Acteur et le Systeme*. Paris, Editions de seuil.

Cullen, S., Lacity, M. & Willcocks, L.P. (2014): *Outsourcing – All You Need to Know*. London, White Plume Publishing.

Cummings, T.G. & Worley, C.G. (2001): *Organization Development and Change*. (7th ed.). Cincinatti, South-Western College Publishing.

Cunningham, G.B. (2006): The Relationships among Commitment to Change, Coping with Change, and Turnover Intensions. *European Journal of Work and Organizational Psychology*, vol. 15(1):29–45.

Cyert, R.M. & March, J.G. (1963/1992): *A Behavioral Theory of the Firm*. Englewood Cliffs, Prentice Hall.

Dacin, M.-T., Goodstein, J. & Scott, W.R. (2002): Institutional Theory and Institutional Change: Introduction to the Special Research Forum. *Academy of Management Journal*, vol. 45:45–58.

Daft, R.L. (1983): Symbols in Organizations: A Dual Content Framework of Analysis. In Pondy, R.L., Frost, P.J., Morgan, G. & Dandrigde, T.C. (Eds.), *Organizational Symbolism*. Greenwich, JAI Press.

Daft, R.L. & Lengel, R.H. (1986): Organizational Information Requirements, Media Richness and Structural Design. *Management Science*, vol. 32(5): 554–571.

Damanpour, F. (1991): Organizational Innovation: A Meta-Analysis of Effects of Determinants and Moderators. *The Academy of Management Journal*, vol. 34(3): 555–590.

Danneels, E. (2003): Tight-Loose Coupling with Customers: The Enactment of Customer Orientation. *Strategic Management Journal*, vol. 24(6):559–576.

D'Aunno, T., Succi, M. & Alexander, J.A. (2000): The Role of Institutional and Market Forces in Divergent Organizational Change. *Administrative Science Quarterly*, vol. 45:679–703.

D'Aunno, T., Sutton, R.I. & Price, R.H. (1991): Isomorphism and External Support in Conflicting Institutional Environments: A Study of Drug Abuse Treatment Units. *Academy of Management Journal*, vol. 34:636–661.

D'Aveni, R.A. & Gunther, R.E. (1994): *Hypercompetition: Managing the Dynamics of Strategic Maneuvering*. New York, The Free Press.

Davidson, J. (2002): Overcoming Resistance to Change. *Public Management*, vol. 84:20–24.

Dawson, P. (2014): Reflections: On Time, Temporality and Change in Organizations. *Journal of Change Management*, vol. 14(3): 285–308.

Deal, T.E. & Kennedy, A.A. (1982): *Corporate Cultures. The Rites and Rituals of Corporate Life*. Reading, MA, Addison Wesley.

Deal, T.E. & Kennedy, A.A. (1999): *The New Corporate Cultures. Revitalizing the Workplace after Downsizing, Mergers and Reengineering*. Cambridge, MA, Perseus Publishing.

Denis, J.-L., Lamothe, L. & Langley, A. (2001): The Dynamics of Collective Leadership and Strategic Change in Pluralistic Organizations. *Academy of Management Journal*, vol. 44:809–837.

Diamond, M.A. (1986): Resistance to Change: A Psychoanalytical Critique of Argyris and Schon's Contributions to Organization Theory and Intervention. *Journal of Management Studies*, vol. 23:543–562.

Dixit, A. & Pyndick, R. (1994): *Investment under Uncertainty*. Princeton, Princeton University Press.

Donaldson, L. (1996): The Normal Science of Structural Contingency Theory. In Clegg, S.R., Hardy, C. & Nord, W.R (Eds.), *Handbook of Organization Studies*. London, Sage.

Donaldson, L. (1999) *Performance-driven Organizational Change: The Organizational Portfolio*. Thousand Oaks, Sage.

Donaldson, L. (2000): Organizational Portfolio Theory: Performance-Driven Organizational Change. *Contemporary Economic Policy*, vol. 18:386–296.

Donaldson, L. (2001) *The Contingency Theory of Organizations*. Thousand Oaks, Sage.

Doz, Y.L. & Pralahad, C.K. (1987): A Process Model of Strategic Redirection in Large Complex Firms: The Case of Multinational Corporations. In Pettigrew, A. (Eds.), *The Management of Strategic Change*. Oxford, Blackwell.

du Gay, P. & Vikkelsø, S. (2012): Reflections: On the Lost Specification of 'Change'. *Journal of Change Management*, vol. 12(2):121–143.

Dunphy, D. (2000): Embracing Paradox. Top-Down versus Participative Management of Organizational Change. In Beer, M. & Nohria, N. (Eds.), *Breaking the Code of Change*. Boston, Harvard Business School.

Dunphy, D.C. & Stace, D.A. (1988): Transformational and Coercive Strategies for Planned Organizational Change: Beyond the O.D. Model. *Organization Studies*, vol. 8:317–334.

Dunsing, D. & Matejka, K. (1994): Overcoming the BOHICA Effect. *Business Horizons*, July–Agust:40–42.

Dykman, C.A. & Davis, C.K. (2012): Addressing Resistance to Workflow Automation. *Journal of Leadership, Accountability & Ethics*, vol. 9(3):115–123.

Døving, E. & Nordhaug, O. (2006): Turnover, Change and Learning in Organizations. In Lines, R., Stensaker, I.G. & Langley, A. (Eds.), *New Perspectives on Organizational Change and Learning*. Bergen, Fagbokforlaget.

Egeberg, M. (1984): *Organisasjonsutforming i offentlig virksomhet*. Oslo, Aschehoug / Tanum Norli.

Egeberg, M. (2012): How Bureaucratic Structure Matters: An Organizational Perspective. In Peters, B.G. & Pierre, J. (Eds.), *The SAGE Handbook of Public Administration*. Thousand Oaks, Sage Publications.

Eisenberg, E.M. (2006): Karl Weick and the Aesthetics of Contingency. *Organization Studies*, vol. 27(11):1693–1707.

Ekman, G. (2004): *Fra prat til resultat. Om lederskap i hverdagen*. Oslo, Abstrakt forlag.

Elrod II, P.D. & Tippett, D.D. (2002): The "Death Valley" of Change. *Journal of Organizational Change Management*, vol. 15(3):273–291.

Emans, B.J.M., Munduate, L., Klaver, E. & Van de Vliert, E. (2003): Constructive Consequences of Leaders' Forcing Influence Styles. *Applied Psychology: An International Review*, vol. 52:36–54.

Espedal, B. (2006): The Dynamics of Organizational Routines. In Lines, R., Stensaker, I.G. & Langley, A. (Eds.), *New Perspectives on Organizational Change and Learning*. Bergen, Fagbokforlaget.

Espedal, B. (2009): Maneuvering Space for Leadership. *Journal of Leadership & Organizational Studies*, vol. 16(2):197–212.

Etzioni, A. (1982): *Moderne organisasjoner*. Oslo, Tanum.

Falbe, C.M. & Yukl, G. (1992): Consequences for Managers of Using Single Influence Tactics and Combination of Tactics. *Academy of Management Journal*, vol. 35:638–652.

Feldman, M.S. & Pentland, B.T. (2003): Reconceptualizing Organizational Routines as a Source of Flexibility and Change. *Administrative Science Quarterly*, vol. 48:94–118.

Fiedler, F.E. (1967): *A Theory of Leadership Effectiveness*. New York, McGraw Hill.

Fiol, C.M., Harris, D. & House, R. (1999): Charismatic Leadership: Strategies for Effecting Social Change. *Leadership Quarterly*, vol. 10:449–482.

Ford, J.D., Ford, L.W. & D'Amelio, A. (2008): Resistance to Change: The Rest of the Story. *Academy of Management Review*, vol. 33(2):362–377.

Ford, L.W., & Ford, J.D. (2012): The Leadership of Organization Change: A View from Recent Empirical Evidence. *Research in Organizational Change and Development*, vol. 20:1–36. Bingley, Emerald Group Publishing Limited.

Foster, R.D.(2010): Resistance, Justice, and Commitment to Change. *Human Resource Development Quarterly*, vol. 21(1):3–39.

French, J.R.P. & Raven, B. (1959): The Bases of Social Power. In Cartwright, D. (Eds.), *Studies of Social Power*. Ann Arbor, University of Michigan.

French, W.L. & Bell Jr., C.H. (1995): *Organization Development: Behavioural Science Interventions for Organizational Improvement* (5th ed.). Englewood Cliffs, Prentice Hall.

Fritz, R. (1990): *Creativity*. New York, Ballantine.

Fry, J.N. & Killing, J.P. (1989): *Strategic Analysis and Action*. Englewood Cliffs, Prentice Hall.

Gagliardi, P. (1990): Artifacts as Pathways and Remains of Organizational Life. In Gagliardi, P. (Eds.), *Symbols and Artifacts. Views of the Corporate Landscape*. Berlin, de Gruyter.

Galbraith, J.R. (1977): *Organization Design*. Reading, MA, Addison Wesley.

Galbraith, J.R. (2000): The Role of Formal Structures and Processes. In Beer, M. & Nohria, N. (Eds.), *Breaking the Code of Change*. Boston, Harvard Business School.

Galpin, T. (1996) *The Human Side of Change: A Practical Guide to Organization Redesign*. San Francisco, Jossey-Bass.

Gardner, H. (1995): *Leading Minds: The Anatomy of Leadership*. New York, Basic Books.

Gersick, C.J.G. (1991): Revolutionary Change Models: A Multilevel Exploration of the Punctuated Equilibrium Paradigm. *Academy of Management Review*, vol. 16:10–36.

Ghemawat, P. (1991): *Commitment: The Dynamic of Strategy*. New York, The Free Press.

Ghemawat, P. & Costa, J. (1993): The Organizational Tension Between Static and Dynamic Efficiency. *Strategic Management Journal*, vol. 14:59–73.

Ghoshal, S. (2003): Miles and Snow: Enduring Insights for Managers. *Academy of Management Executive*, vol. 17:109–114.

Ghoshal, S. & Bartlett, C.A. (2000): Rebuilding Behavioral Context: A Blueprint for Corporate Renewal. In Beer, M. & Nohria, N. (Eds.), *Breaking the Code of Change*. Boston, Harvard Business School.

Giddens, A. (1979): *Central Problems in Social Theory*. Berkeley, University of California Press.

Giddens, A. (1985): *The Constitution of Society*. Berkeley, University of California Press.

Gilbert, C.G. (2005): Unbundling the Structure of Inertia: Resource Versus Routine Rigidity. *Academy of Management Journal*, vol. 48:741–763.

Ginsberg, A. & Abrahamson, E. (1991): Champions of Change and Strategic Shifts: The Role of Internal and External Change Advocates. *Journal of Management Studies*, vol. 28:173–190.

Gioia D.A. & Chittipeddi, K. (1991): Sensemaking and Sensegiving in Strategic Change Initiation. *Strategic Management Journal*, vol. 12(6):433–448.

Gjerde, S. (2003): *Coaching. Hva, hvorfor, hvordan*. Bergen, Fagbokforlaget.

Golembiewski, R.T. (1972): *Renewing Organizations: The Laboratory Approach to Planned Change*. Itasca, IL., Peacock Publishers.

Golembiewski, R.T. (1991): Organizational Development in the Third World: Values, Closeness of Fit and Culture Boundedness. *International Journal of Human Resource Management*, vol. 2:39–53.

Gordon, S.S., Stewart, W.H. Jr., Sweo, R. & Luker, W.A. (2000): Convergence Versus Strategic Reorientation: The Antecendents of Fast-paced Organizational Change. *Journal of Management*, vol. 26:911–945.

Graham, D.W. (1997): Heraclitus' Criticism of Ionian Philosophy. *Oxford Studies in Ancient Philosophy*, vol. 15:1–50.

Granovetter, M. (1973): The Strength of Weak Ties. *American Journal of Sociology*, vol. 78:1360–1380.

Grant, R.M. (2010): *Contemporary Strategy Analysis* (7th ed.). Chichester, John Wiley.

Gratton, L. (2011): The End of the Middle Manager. *Harvard Business Review*, vol. 89(1–2):36–36.

Gravenhorst, K.M.B., Werkman, R.A. & Boonstra, J.J. (2003): The Change Capacity of Organizations: General Assessment of Five Configurations. *Applied Psychology: An International Review*, vol. 52:83–105.

Greenwood, R. & Hinings, C.R. (1987): Editorial Introduction: Organizational Transformation. *Journal of Management Studies*, vol. 24:561–564.

Greenwood, R. & Hinings, C.R. (1988): Organizational Design Types, Tracks and the Dynamics of Strategic Change. *Organization Studies*, vol. 9:293–316.

Greenwood, R. & Hinings, C.R. (1993): Understanding Strategic Change: The Contribution of Archetypes. *Academy of Management Journal*, vol. 36:1052–1081.

Greenwood, R. & Hinings, C.R. (1996): Understanding Radical Organizational Change: Bringing Together the Old and New Institutionalism. *Academy of Management Review*, vol. 21:1022–1054.

Greenwood, R., Suddaby, R. & Hinings, C.R. (2002): Theorizing Change: The Role of Professional Associations in the Transformation of Institutionalized Fields. *Academy of Management Journal*, vol. 45:56–80.

Greiner, L.E. (1988): Evolution and Revolution as Organizations Grow. *Harvard Business Review*, May–June:55–67 (originally published in 1972).

Greiner, L.E. & Schein, V.E. (1988): *Power and Organization Development: Mobilizing Power to Implement Change* Reading, MA, Addison-Wesley.

Grobman, G.M. (2005): Complexity Theory: A New Way to Look at Organizational Change. *Public Administration Quarterly*, vol. 29(3/4):351–384.

Groth, L. (1999): *Future Organizational Design. The Scope for the IT-Based Enterprise*. Chichester, Wiley.

Grugulis, I. & Wilkinson, A. (2002): Managing Culture at British Airways: Hype, Hope and Reality. *Long Range Planning*, vol. 35:179–194.

Gustavsen, B. (1990): *Strategier for utvikling i arbeidslivet*. Oslo, Tano.

Hagedorn-Rasmussen, P. (2003): *Forandring som vare. Ledelseskoncepter, konsulenter og forandringer i arbejdslivet*. Fredriksberg, Forlaget Sociologi.

Hall, R.H. (1972): *Organizations, Structure and Processes*. Englewood Cliffs, NJ, Prentice Hall.

Hambrick, D., Cho, T. & Chen, M. (1996): The Influence of Top Management Team Heterogeneity on Firms' Competitive Moves. *Administrative Science Quarterly*, vol. 41:659–684.

Hambrick, D., Geletkanycz, M. & Fredrickson, J. (1993): Top Executive Commitment to Status Quo: A Test of Some of Its Determinants. *Strategic Management Journal*, vol. 14:410–418.

Hamel, G. & Pralahad, C.K. (1989): Strategic Intent. *Harvard Business Review*, vol. 67:63–76.

Hammer, M. (1990): Reengineering Work: Don't Automate, Obliterate. *Harvard Business Review*, vol. 68:104–112.

Hammer, M. & Champy, J. (1993): *Reengineering the Corporation – A Manifesto for Business Revolution*. London, Nicholas Brealey.

Hannan, M.T. & Freeman, J. (1989): *Organizational Ecology*. Cambridge, MA, Harvard University Press.

Hargrave, T.J. & Van De Ven, A.H. (2006): A Collective Action Model of Institutional Innovation. *Academy of Management Review*, vol. 31(4):864–888.

Harrison, M.I. (1991): The Politics of Consulting for Organizational Change. *Knowledge & Policy*, vol. 4(3):92–107.

Hatch, M.J. (1993): The Dynamics of Organizational Culture. *Academy of Management Review*, vol. 18:657–693.

Heese, J., Krishnan, R. & Moers, F. (2016): Selective Regulator Decoupling and Organizations' Strategic Responses. *Academy of Management Journal*, vol. 59(6):2178–2204. doi:10.5465/amj.2015.0446

Heldal, F. (2015): Managerial Control versus Professional Autonomy in Organizational Change: Tearing Down the Walls and Fighting Fire with Fire. *Journal of Change Management*, vol. 15(3):188–209. doi:10.1080/14697017.2015.1028573

Helliwell, J. & Fowler, A. (1994): Introducing IT into a Mature Production Related Work Environment: The Human Resource Factor. *Journal of Information Technology*, vol. 9:39–50.

Henderson, R.M. & Clark, K.B. (1990): Architectural Innovation: The Reconfiguration of Existing Product Technologies and the Failure of Established Firms. *Administrative Science Quarterly*, vol. 35:9–30

Hernes, G. (1975): *Makt og avmakt*. Oslo, Universitetsforlaget.

Hernes, G. (1976): Structural Change in Social Processes. *American Journal of Sociology*, vol. 82:513–545.

Hernes, T. (2014) *A Process Theory of Organizations*. Oxford, Oxford University Press.

Hernes, T., Hendrup, E. & Schäffner, B. (2015): Sensing the Momentum: A Process View of Change in a Multinational Corporation. *Journal of Change Management*, vol. 15(2):117–141.

Herscovitch, L. & Meyer, J.P. (2002): Commitment to Organizational Change: Extension of the Three-Component Model. *Journal of Applied Psychology*, vol. 87:474–487.

Hersey, P. & Blanchard, K.H. (1988): *Management of Organizational Behaviour: Utilizing Human Resources*. Englewood Cliffs, Prentice Hall.

Higgs, M. & Rowland, D. (2010): Emperors With Clothes On: The Role of Self-awareness in Developing Effective Change Leadership. *Journal of Change Management*, vol. 10(4):369–385. doi:10.1080/14697017.2010.516483

Hinings, C.R. & Greenwood, R. (1988a): The Normative Prescription of Organizations. In Zucker, L.G. (Eds.), *Institutional Patterns and Organizations*. Chicago, Ballinger.

Hinings, C.R. & Greenwood, R. (1988b): *The Dynamics of Strategic Change*. Oxford, Basil Blackwell.

Hirschhorn, L. (1997): *Reworking Authority: Leading and Following in the Post-Modern Organization*. Cambridge, MA, MIT Press.

Hirschhorn, L. (2002): Campaigning for Change. *Harvard Business Review*, July:98–104.

Hirschman, A.O. (1970): *Exit, Voice and Loyalty. Responses to Decline in Firms, Organizations and States*. Cambridge, Harvard University Press.

Hofstede, G. (1997): *Cultures and Organizations. Software of the Mind. Intercultural Cooperation and its Importance for Survival*. New York, McGraw Hill.

Hofstede, G. (2001): *Cultures' Consequences: Comparing Values, Behaviors, Institutions and Organizations Across Nations*. Thousand Oaks, Sage.

Hofstede, G. & Bond, M. (1988): The Confucius Connection: From Cultural Roots to Economic Growth. *Organizational Dynamics*, vol. 16:4–21.

Hofstede, G., Hofstede, G.J. & Minkov, M. (2010): *Cultures and Organizations. Software of the Mind. Intercultural Cooperation and its Importance for Survival* (3rd ed.). New York, McGraw Hill.

Hofstede, G., Neuijen, B., Ohayv, D.O. & Sanders, G. (1990): Measuring Organizational Cultures. *Administrative Science Quarterly*, vol. 35:286–316.

Holt, D.T., Armenakis, A.A., Field, H.S. & Harris, S.G. (2007): Readiness for Organizational Change. *Journal of Applied Behavioral Science*, vol. 43(2):232–255.

House, R. (1996): Path-Goal Theory of Leadership: Lessons, Legacy and a Reformulated Theory. *Leadership Quarterly*, vol. 7:323–352.

Huber, G.P. (1996): Organizational Learning: The Contributing Processes and the Literature. In Cohen, M.D. & Sproull, L.S. (Eds.), *Organizational Learning*. Thousand Oaks, Sage.

Hughes, M. (2011): Do 70 Per Cent of All Organizational Change Initiatives Really Fail? *Journal of Change Management*, vol. 11(4):451–464.

Huy, Q.N. (2001): Time, Temporal Capability and Planned Change. *Academy of Management Review*, vol. 26:601–623.

Håkansson, H. & Waluszewski, A. (2002): Path Dependence: Restricting or Facilitating Technical Development? *Journal of Business Research*, vol. 55:561–570.

Ivanova, O. & Persson, S. (2017): Transition as a Ubiquitous and a Continuous Process: Overcoming the Western View. *Journal of Change Management*, vol. 17(1):31–46.

Iversen, R.D. (1996): Employee Acceptance of Organizational Change: The Role of Organizational Commitment. *The International Journal of Human Resource Management*, vol. 7:122–149.

Jacobsen, D.I. (1989): Effekter av forvaltningens fysiske struktur på beslutningsatferden. In Egeberg, M. (Eds.), *Institusjonspolitikk og forvaltningsutvikling*. Oslo, Tano.

Jacobsen, D.I. (1992): *Struktur, individer, makt og kaos, eller "Forsøk på å forstå hva som skjer i en organisasjonsendringsprosess"*. Kristiansand, ADH-serien, rapport nr. 37.

Jacobsen, D.I. (1995): Et kritisk blikk på produktivitet og effektivitet i offentlig sektor. In Jacobsen, D.I., Johnsen, Å. & Robertsen, K. (Eds.), *Resultatvurdering i offentlig sektor*. Oslo, Kommuneforlaget.

Jacobsen, D.I. (2001a): Higher Education as an Arena for Political Socialisation: Myth or Reality? *Scandinavian Political Studies*, vol. 24:351–368.

Jacobsen, D.I. (2001b): Profesjonelle verdier – hvor skapes de? *Nordiske Organisasjonsstudier*, vol. 3:24–42.

Jacobsen, D.I. (2003): *"Vi har det så greit ..." En studie av forholdet mellom politikk og administrasjon i 30 norske kommuner*. Oslo, maktutredningen, rapport nr. 66.

Jacobsen, D.I. (2004): Sand in the machinery? Comparing bureaucrats' and politicians' attitudes toward public sector reform. *European Journal of Political Studies*, vol. 44(6):767–799.

Jacobsen, D.I. (2006): Fenomenologi og kvantitativ metode – som ild og vann eller gin og tonic? In Nyeng, F. & Wennes, G. (Eds.), *Tall, tolkning og tvil bak metodevalg i økonomi, ledelse og markedsføring*. Oslo, Cappelen Akademisk forlag.

Jacobsen, D.I (2010): Deltakelse som virkemiddel i organisatoriske endringsprosesser – et tveegget sverd? In Knudsen, H., Falkenberg, J., Grønhaug, K. & Garnes, Å. (Eds.), *Mysterion, Strategike og Kainotomia*. Oslo, Novus forlag.

Jacobsen, D.I. (2016a): Adopting and Refining e-services – the Role of Organization Size. *Public Organization Review*, vol. 18(1):111–123.

Jacobsen, D.I. (2016b): *Engangsorganisasjonen*. Bergen: Fagbokforlaget.

Jacobsen, D.I. (2017): Publicness as an Antecedent of Transformational Leadership: The Case of Norway. *International Review of Administrative Sciences*, vol. 83(1):23–42.

Jacobsen, D.I., Hillestad, T., Hildrum, J. & Yttri, B. (2018): *Alternative Routes to Innovation – The Effects Of Cultural And Structural Fit*. Forthcoming.

Jacobsen, D.I. & Thorsvik, J. (2013): *Hvordan organisasjoner fungerer*. Bergen, Fagbokforlaget.

Janis, I.L. (1982): *Groupthink: Psychological Studies of Policy Decisions and Fiascoes* (2nd ed.). Boston, Houghton Mifflin.

Jansen, K.J. (1996): Characteristic Level of Change: An Inherent Constraint to Organizational Action. *The International Journal of Organizational Analysis*, vol. 4:285–298.

Jaques, E. (1951): *The Changing Culture of a Factory*. London, Tavistock.

Jaros, S.(2010): Commitment to Organizational Change: A Critical Review. *Journal of Change Management*, vol. 10(1):79–108.

Jensen, M.C. (2000): Value Maximization and the Corporate Objective Function. In Beer, M. & Nohria, N. (Eds.), *Breaking the Code of Change*. Boston, Harvard Business School.

Jensen, M.C. (2001): Value Maximisation, Stakeholder Theory, and the Corporate Objective Function. *European Financial Management*, vol. 7:297–317.

Jermier, J.M. & Kerr, S. (1997): Substitutes for Leadership: Their Meaning and Measurement – Contextual Recollections and Current Observations. *Leadership Quarterly*, vol. 8:95–102.

Jespersen, P.K. (1999): New Public Management reformers betydning for den administrative og lægefaglige profession i sygehusorganisationen. In Bentsen, E.-V., Borum, F., Erlingsdottir, G. &

Sahlin-Anderson, K. (Eds.), *Når styringsambitioner møter praksis – den svære omstilling af sygehus- og sundhetsvæsenet i Danmark og Sverige*. Copenhagen, Handelshøjskolens Forlag.

Johannessen, S.O. (2003): *Myter og erfaringer om ledelse. Ledelse fra et kompleksitetsperspektiv*. Oslo, Gyldendal Akademisk.

Johns, G. (2006): The Essential Impact of Context on Organizational Behavior. *Academy of Management Review*, vol. 31(2):386–408.

Johns, G. (2017): Reflections on the 2016 Decade Award: Incorporating Context in Organizational Research. *Academy of Management Review*, vol. 42(4):577–595.

Johnsen, Å. (2007): *Resultatstyring i offentlig sektor.* Bergen: Fagbokforlaget.

Johnson, J.R. (1998): Embracing Change: A Leadership Model for the Learning Organization. *International Journal of Training and Development*, vol. 2:141–150.

Josefy, M., Kuban, S., Ireland, R.D. & Hitt, M.A. (2015): All Things Great and Small: Organizational Size, Boundaries of the Firm, and a Changing Environment. *Academy of Management Annals*, vol. 9(1):715–802.

Judson, A. (1991): *Changing Behaviour in Organizations: Minimizing Resistance to Change*. Cambridge, MA, Basil Blackwell.

Kanter, R. (1983): *The Change Masters*. New York, Simon & Schuster.

Kee-Young, K. & Hyunchul, A. (2010): Moderating Effects of Localization Differences on ERP Use: A Socio-Technical Systems Perspective. *Computers in Human Behavior*, vol. 26(2):186–198.

Kelman, H. (1961): Processes of Opinion Change. *Public Opinion Quarterly*, vol. 25:57–78.

Kieser, A. (1994): Why Organization Theory Needs Historical Analysis and How This Should Be Performed. *Organization Science*, vol. 5:608–620.

Kiesler, S. & Sproull, L. (1982): Managerial Response to Changing Environments: Perspectives on Problem Sensing from Social Cognition. *Administrative Science Quarterly*, vol. 27:548–570.

Kikulis, L.M., Slack, T. & Hinings, C.R. (1995): Sector-Specific Patterns of Organizational Design Change. *Journal of Management Studies*, vol. 32:67–100.

Koch, C. (2000): Building Coalitions in an Era of Technological Change. Virtual Manufacturing and the Role of Unions, Employees and Management. *Journal of Organizational Change Management*, vol. 13:275–288.

Kotter, J.P. (1995): Leading Change: Why Transformation Efforts Fail. *Harvard Business Review*, March–April:59–67.

Kotter, J.P. (2008): *A Sense of Urgency*. Boston, Harvard Business School Press.

Kotter, J.P. (2012): *Leading Change*. Boston, Harvard Business School Press.

Kotter, J.P. & Heskett, J.L. (1992): *Corporate Culture and Performance*. New York, The Free Press.

Kouzes, J.M. & Posner, B.Z. (1987): *The Leadership Challenge*. San Francisco, Jossey-Bass.

Kraatz, M.S. & Zajac, E.J. (2001): How Organizational Resources Affect Strategic Change and Performance in Turbulent Environments: Theory and Evidence. *Organization Science*, vol. 12:632–657.

Krause, D.E., Gebert, D. & Kearney, E. (2007): Implementing Process Innovations: The Benefits of Combining Delegative-Participative With Consultative-Advisory Leadership. *Journal of Leadership & Organizational Studies*, vol. 14(1):16–25.

Kunisch, S., Bartunek, J.M., Mueller, J. & Huy, Q.N. (2017): Time in Strategic Change Research. *Academy of Management Annals*, vol. 11(2):1005–1064.

Kuvaas, B. (2008): HR-strategi og internt konsistent HR. In Kuvaas, B. (Eds.), *Lønnsomhet gjennom menneskelige ressurser. Evidensbasert HRM*. Bergen, Fagbokforlaget.

Ladegård, G. & Vabo, S.I. (2010): Ledelse og styring – teoretisk rammeverk. In Ladegård, G. & Vabo, S.I. (Eds.), *Ledelse og styring*. Bergen, Fagbokforlaget.

Laine, P. & Kuoppakangas, P. (2015): A Reconceptualization of Change Strategy – One Application of Dilemma Theory. *Journal of Change Management*, vol. 15(4):332–352.

Langley, A. & Denis, J.-L. (2006): Neglected Dimensions of Organizational Change. In Lines, R., Stensaker, I.G. & Langley, A. (Eds.), *New perspectives on Organizational Change and Learning*. Bergen, Fagbokforlaget.

Langslet, G.J. (1999): *LØFT: løsningsfokusert tilnærming til organisasjonsutvikling, ledelsesutvikling og konfliktløsning*. Oslo, Ad Notam Gyldendal.

Langslet, G.J. (2002): *LØFT for ledere: løsningsfokusert tilnærming til typiske ledelsesutfordringer*. Oslo, Gyldendal akademisk.

Lant, T.K., Milliken, F.J. & Batra, B. (1992): The Role of Managerial Learning and Interpretation in Strategic Persistence and Reorientation: An Empirical Exploration. *Strategic Management Journal*, vol. 13:585–608.

Lau, C.-M. & Ngo, H.-Y. (2001): Organization Development and Firm Performance: A Comparison of Multinational and Local Firms. *Journal of International Business Studies*, vol. 32:95–115.

Laudal, T., Bjaalid, G. & Mikkelsen, A. (2017): Hairy Goals and Organizational Fit: A Case of Implementing ICT-Supported Task Planning in a Large Hospital Region. *Journal of Change Management*, vol. 17(1):9–30.

Lavie, D., Stettner, U. & Tushman, M.L. (2010): Exploration and Exploitation Within and Across Organizations. *Academy of Management Annals*, vol. 4(1):109–155.

Lawler, E. (1987): The Design of Effective Reward Systems. In Lorsch, J.W. (Eds.), *Handbook of Organizational Behavior*. Englewood Cliffs, Prentice Hall.

Lawler, E. & Worley, C.G. (2005): *Built to Change. How to Achieve Organizational Effectiveness*. San Francisco, Jossey-Bass.

Ledford, G.E. & Heneman, R.L. (2000): Compensation. A Troublesome Lead System in Organizational Change. In Beer, M. & Nohria, N. (Eds.), *Breaking the Code of Change*. Boston, Harvard Business School.

Lee, K. & Pennings, J.M. (2002): Mimicry and the Market: Adoption of New Organizational Forms. *Academy of Management Journal*, vol. 45:144–162.

Lehman, D.W., Hahn, J., Ramanujam, R. & Alge, B.J. (2011): The Dynamics of the Performance-Risk Relationship Within a Performance Period: The Moderating Role of Deadline Proximity. *Organization Science*, vol. 22(6):1613–1630.

Leigh, A. (1988): *Effective Change: Twenty Ways to Make It Happen*. London, Institute of Personnel Management.

Leitko, T.A. & Szczerbacki, D. (1987): Why Traditional OD Strategies Fail in Professional Bureaucracies. *Organizational Dynamics*, vol. 15:52–65.

Leitner, K.-H. & Güldenberg, S. (2010): Generic Strategies and Firm Performance in SMEs: A Longitudinal Study of Austrian SMEs. *Small Business Economics*, vol. 35(2):169–189.

Levin, M. & Klev, R. (2002): *Forandring som praksis: læring og utvikling i organisasjoner*. Bergen: Fagbokforlaget.

Levinthal, D.A. & March, J.G. (1993): The Myopia of Learning. *Strategic Management Journal*, vol. 14:95–112.

Levitt, B. & March, J.G. (1988): Organizational Learning. *Annual Review of Sociology*, vol. 14:319–340.

Lewicki, R.J. & Litterer, J.A. (1985): *Negotiation*. Homewood, IL, Irwin.

Lewin, K. (1997): *Resolving Social Conflict & Field Theory in Social Science*. Washington, DC, American Psychological Association.

Liker, J. & Franz, J.K. (2011): *The Toyota Way to Continuous Improvement: Linking Strategy and Operational Excellence to Achieve Superior Performance*. New York, McGraw Hill.

Lincoln, J.R. & Kalleberg, A.L. (1990): *Culture, Control and Commitment. A Study of Work Organization and Work Attitudes in the United States and Japan*. Cambridge, Cambridge University Press.

Lincoln, Y. & Guba, E. (1985): *Naturalistic Inquiry*. Beverly Hills, Sage.

Lindblom, C.E. (1959): The Science of Muddling Through. *Public Administration Review*, vol. 19:79–88.

Lindblom, C.E. (1968): *The Policy-Making Process*. Englewood Cliffs, Prentice Hall.

Lines, R., Sáenz, J. & Aramburu, N. (2011): Organizational Learning As a Byproduct of Justifications for Change. *Journal of Change Management*, vol. 11(2):163–184.

Locke, E.A. & Latham, G.P. (2002): Building a Practically Useful Theory of Goal Setting and Task Motivation. *American Psychologist*, vol. 57:705–717.

Lowe, K.B. & Galen Kroeck, K. (1996): Effectiveness Correlates of Transformational and Transactional Leadership: A Meta-Analytic Review of the MLQ Litterature. *Leadership Quarterly*, vol. 7:3–35.

Lukes, S. (1974): *Power. A Radical View*. London, Macmillan.

Lyngdal, L.E. (1992): *Organisasjonsutvikling i teori og praksis*. Oslo, Tano.

Löfström, C. (2003): *Ingenting har hänt. Om att se det man förvänter seg att se vid reformer*. Paper presented at 17th Conference on Business Studies, 14–16 August, Reykjavik, Iceland, Track 11: Public Management and Public Sector Reforms.

Mahoney, J. (2000): Path Dependence in Historical Sociology. *Theory and Society*, vol. 29:507–548.

Maitlis, S. (2005): The Social Processes of Organizational Sensemaking. *Academy of Management Journal*, vol. 48(1):21–49.

Maitlis, S. & Christianson, M. (2014): Sensemaking in Organizations: Taking Stock and Moving Forward. *Academy of Management Annals*, vol. 8(1):57–125.

Maitlis, S. & Morance, T.B. (2007): Triggers and Enablers of Sensegiving in Organizations. *Academy of Management Journal*, vol. 50(1):57–84.

March, J.G. (1981): Footnotes to Organizational Change. *Administrative Science Quarterly*, vol. 26:563–577.

March, J.G. (1988): The Technology of Foolishness. In March, J.G., *Decisions and Organizations*. Cambridge, MA, Basil Blackwell.

March, J.G. (1991): Exploration and Exploitation in Organizational Learning. *Organization Science*, vol. 2:71–87.

March, J.G. & Olsen, J.P. (1976): *Ambiguity and Choice in Organizations*. Bergen, Universitetsforlaget.

March, J.G. & Olsen, J.P. (1989): *Rediscovering Institutions*. New York, The Free Press.

Martin, J. (1992): *Cultures in Organizations: Three Perspectives*. New York, Oxford University Press.

Martinsons, M.G. (1996): Cultural Constraints on Radical Re-engineering: Hammer and Lewin Meet Confucius. *Journal of Applied Management Studies*, vol. 5:85–97.

Masuch, M. (1985): Vicious Circles in Organizations. *Administrative Science Quarterly*, vol. 30:14–33.
McClellan, J.G. (2014): Announcing Change: Discourse, Uncertainty, and Organizational Control. *Journal of Change Management*, vol. 14(2):192–209.
McHugh, M. (1997): The Stress Factor: Another Item for the Change Management Agenda? *Journal of Organizational Change Management*, vol. 10:345–362.
McKendall, M. (1993): The Tyranny of Change: Organization Development Revisited. *Journal of Business Ethics*, vol. 12:93–104.
Meaney, M., & Pung, C. (2008): McKinsey Global Results: Creating Organizational Transformation. *McKinsey Quarterly,* August:1–7.
Meyer, C.B. & Stensaker, I.G (2009): Making radical change happen through selective inclusion and exclusion of stakeholders. *British Journal of Management*, vol. 20:219–237.
Meyer, C.B. & Stensaker, I.G. (2011): *Endringskapasitet*. Bergen, Fagbokforlaget.
Meyer, J.P., Srinivas, E.S., Lal, J.B. & Topolnytsky, L. (2007): Employee Commitments and Support for Organizational Change: Test of the Three-Component Model in Two Cultures. *Journal of Applied Psychology*, vol. 80:185–211.
Meyer, J.W. (1996): Otherhood: The Promulgation and Transmission of Ideas in the Modern Organizational Environment. In Czarniawska, B. & Sevon, G. (Eds.), *Translating Organizational Change*. Berlin, de Gruyter.
Meyer, J.W. & Rowan, B. (1977): Institutionalized Organizations: Formal Structures as Myth and Ceremony. *American Journal of Sociology*, vol. 83:340–363.
Meyer, J.W. & Scott, W.R. (1992): *Organizational Environments. Ritual and Rationality*. London, Sage.
Meyer, M.W. & Zucker, L.G. (1989): *Permanently Failing Organizations*. Thousand Oaks, Sage.
Meyerson, D. & Martin, J. (1987): Cultural Change. *Journal of Management Studies*, vol. 24:623–647.
Miles, R.E. & Snow, C.C. (1978): *Organization Strategy, Structure and Process*. New York, McGraw Hill.
Miles, R.H. (1997): *Leading Corporate Transformation*. San Francisco, Jossey-Bass.
Miller, D. & Friesen, P.H. (1984): *Organizations: A Quantum View*. Englewood Cliffs, Prentice-Hall.
Milliken, F.J. & Lant, T.K. (1991): The Effect of an Organization's Recent Performance History on Strategic Persistence and Change: The Role of Managerial Interpretations. In Dutton, J., Huff, A. & Shrivastava, P. (Eds.), *Advances in Strategic Management*. Greenwich, JAI Press.
Miner, A. (1987): Ideosyncratic Jobs in Formalized Organizations. *Administrative Science Quarterly*, vol. 32:327–351.
Miner, A. (1990): Structural Evolution Through Ideosyncratic Jobs: The Potential for Unplanned Learning. *Organization Science*, vol. 1:195–210.
Miner, A.S. & Akinsanmi, O. (2016): Idiosyncratic Jobs, Organizational Transformation, and Career Mobility. *Research in the Sociology of Organizations*, vol. 47:61–101.
Mintzberg, H. (1973): *The Nature of Managerial Work*. New York, Harper & Row.
Mintzberg, H. (1979): *The Structuring of Organizations*. Englewood Cliffs, Prentice Hall.
Mintzberg, H. (1983): *Power In and Around Organizations*. Englewood Cliffs, Prentice Hall.
Mintzberg, H. (1994): *The Rise and Fall of Strategic Planning*. New York, The Free Press.
Mintzberg, H. (1996): Musings on Management. *Harvard Business Review*, vol. 74(4):61–67.
Mintzberg, H. (2007): *Tracking Strategies. Toward a General Theory*. New York, Oxford.
Mintzberg, H., Quinn, J.B. & James, R.M. (1988): *The Strategy Process. Concepts, Contexts and Cases*. Englewood Cliffs, Prentice Hall.

Mintzberg, H. & Westley, F. (1992): Cycles of Organizational Change. *Strategic Management Journal*, vol. 13:39–59.

Miron-Spektor, E., Paletz, S.B.F. & Lin, C.-C. (2015): To Create Without Losing Face: The Effects of Face Cultural Logic and Social-Image Affirmation on Creativity. *Journal of Organizational Behavior*, vol. 36(7):919–943.

Monnot, M.J. (2017): Organizational Change Agent Influence: A Conditional Process Model of Key Individual Psychological Resources. *Journal of Change Management*, vol. 17(3):268–295.

Morris, J., Blyton, P., Bacon, N. & Franz, H.-W. (1992): Beyond Survival: The Implementation of New Forms of Work Organization in the UK and German Steel Industries. *The International Journal of Human Resource Management*, vol. 3:307–329.

Mueller, D.C. (1989): *Public Choice II*. Cambridge, Cambridge University Press.

Nadler, D.A. (1987): The Effective Management of Organizational Change. In Lorsch, J.W. (Eds.), *Handbook of Organizational Behaviour*. Englewood Cliffs, Prentice Hall.

Nadler, D.A. & Lawler, E.E. (1995): Motivation: A Diagnostic Approach. In Staw, B.M. (Eds.), *Psychological Dimensions of Organizational Behavior*. Englewood Cliffs, Prentice Hall.

Nadler, D.A. & Tushman, M.L. (1990): Beyond the Charismatic Leader: Leadership and Organizational Change. *California Management Review*, Winter:77–97.

Nelson, R.R. & Winter, S.G. (1982): *An Evolutionary Theory of Economic Change*. Cambridge, MA, Belknap.

Nielsen, J.F. & Riiskjær, E. (2013): From Patient Surveys to Organizational Change: Rational Change Processes and Institutional Forces. *Journal of Change Management*, vol. 13(2):179–205.

Nonaka, I. (1994): A Dynamic Theory of Organizational Knowledge Creation. *Organization Science*, vol. 5:14–37.

Nonaka, I., Hirose, A. & Takeda, Y. (2016): "Meso"-Foundations of Dynamic Capabilities: Team-Level Synthesis and Distributed Leadership as the Source of Dynamic Creativity. *Global Strategy Journal*, vol. 6(3):168–182. doi:10.1002/gsj.1125

Nonaka, I., Kodama, M., Hirose, A. & Kohlbacher, F. (2014): Dynamic Fractal Organizations for Promoting Knowledge-Based Transformation – A New Paradigm for Organizational Theory. *European Management Journal*, vol. 32(1):137–146.

Nonaka, I. & Takeuchi, H. (1995): *The Knowledge-Creating Company: How Japanese Companies Foster Creativity and Innovation for Competitive Advantage*. New York, Oxford University Press.

Nonaka, I., Takeuchi, H. & Umemoto, K. (1996): A Theory of Organizational Knowledge Creation. *IJTM*, vol. 11:833–845.

Nonaka, I., Toyama, R. & Konno, N. (2000): SECI, Ba and Leadership: A Unified Model of Dynamic Knowledge Creation. *Long Range Planning*, vol. 33:5–34.

Nordström, K.A. & Ridderstråle, J. (1999): *Funky Business*. Stockholm, BookHouse Publishing.

Norris, G. (2000) *E-business and ERP: Transforming the Enterprise*. New York, Wiley.

North, D.C. (1990): *Institutions, Institutional Change and Economic Performance*. Cambridge, MA, Cambridge University Press.

NOU 2016:1 (2016.): *Arbeidstidsutvalget – Regulering av arbeidstid – vern og fleksibilitet*. Oslo, Arbeids- og sosialdepartementet.

Ocasio, W. (1995): The Enactment of Economic Diversity: A Reconciliation of Theories of Failure-Induced Change and Threat-Rigidity. In Staw, B.M. & Cummings, L.L. (Eds.), *Research in Organizational Behavior*, vol. 17. Greenwich, JAI Press.

Ocasio, W., Laamanen, T. & Vaara, E. (2018): Communication and Attention Dynamics: An Attention-Based View of Strategic Change. *Strategic Management Journal*, vol. 39(1):155–167. doi:10.1002/smj.2702

Oliver, C. (1992): The Antecedents of Deinstitutionalization. *Organization Studies*, vol. 13:563–588.

Oliver, T. (1986): *The Real Coke, The Real Story*. New York, Random House.

Olsen, J.P. (1996): Norway: Slow Learner – or Another Triumph of the Tortoise? In Olsen, J.P. & Peters, G.B. (Eds.), *Lessons From Experience. Experiential Learning in Administrative Reforms in Eight Democracies*. Oslo, Scandinavian University Press.

Olsen, J.P. & Peters, G.B. (1996): Learning from Experience? In Olsen, J.P. & Peters, G.B. (Eds.), *Lessons From Experience. Experiential Learning in Administrative Reforms in Eight Democracies*. Oslo, Scandinavian University Press.

Olsen, T.H. & Stensaker, I. (2014): A Change-Recipient Perspective on Training During Organizational Change. *International Journal of Training & Development*, vol. 18(1):22–36.

Oreg, S., Bartunek, J.M., Lee, G. & Do, B. (2018): An Affect-Based Model of Recipients' Responses to Organizational Change Events. *Academy of Management Review*, vol. 43(1):65–86.

Oreg, S., Vakola, M. & Armenakis, A. (2011): Change Recipients' Reactions to Organizational Change: A 60-Year Review of Quantitative Studies. *The Journal of Applied Behavioral Science*, vol. 47(4):461–524.

O'Reilly, C. & Chatman, J.A. (1996): Culture as Social Control: Corporations, Cults, and Commitment. *Research in Organizational Behavior*, vol. 18:157–201

O'Reilly, C. & Tushman, M.L. (2008): Ambidexterity as a Dynamic Capability: Resolving the Innovator's Dilemma. *Research in Organizational Behavior*, vol. 28:185–206.

Orton, J.D. & Weick, K.E. (1990): Loosely Coupled Systems: A Reconceptualization. *Academy of Management Review*, vol. 15:203–223.

O'Toole, J. (1999): *Leadership A to Z: A Guide for the Appropriately Ambitious*. San Francisco, Jossey-Bass.

Parnell, J.A. & Hershey, L. (2005): The Strategy-Performance Relationship Revisited: The Blessing and Curse of the Combination Strategy. *International Journal of Commerce and Management*, vol. 15(1):17–33.

Pascale, R.T., Millemann, M. & Gioja, L. (2000): *Surfing the Edge of Chaos: The Laws of Nature and the New Laws of Business*. New York, Crown Business.

Pennings, J.M. (1992): Structural Contingency Theory: A Reappraisal. Research in *Organizational Behavior*, vol. 14:267–309.

Penrose, E.T. (1959): *A Theory of the Growth of the Firm*. New York, Wiley.

Perrow, C. (1986): *Complex Organizations: A Critical Essay*. Glenview, Scott-Foresman.

Peters, T.J. & Waterman, R.H. Jr. (1982): *In Search of Excellence*. New York, Harper & Row.

Pettigrew, A. (1985): *The Awakening Giant: Continuity and Change in ICI*. Oxford, Blackwell.

Pettigrew, A. (1987): Context and Action in the Transformation of the Firm. *Journal of Management Studies*, vol. 24:649–670.

Pettigrew, A. (1990): Lonigtudinal Field Research on Change: Theory and Practice. *Organization Science*, vol. 1:267–292.

Pettigrew, A., Ferlie, E. & McKee, L. (1992): *Shaping Strategic Change. Making Change in Large Organizations: The Case of the National Health Service*. London, Sage.

Pettigrew, A. & Whipp, R. (1991): *Managing Change for Competitive Success*. Oxford, Blackwell.

Pettigrew, A., Woodman, R.W. & Cameron, K.S. (2001): Studying Organizational Change and Development: Challenges for Future Research. *Academy of Management Journal*, vol. 44:697–714.

Pfeffer, J. (1981): *Power in Organizations*. Cambridge, MA, Ballinger.

Pfeffer, J. (1982): *Organizations and Organization Theory*. Cambridge, MA, Ballinger.

Pfeffer, J. (1990): Management as Symbolic Action: The Creation and Maintenance of Organizational Paradigms. In Cummings, L.L. & Staw, B.M. (Eds.), *Information and Cognition in Organizations*. Greenwich, CT, JAI Press.

Pfeffer, J. (1992): *Managing with Power: Politics and Influence in Organizations*. Boston, Harvard Business School Press.

Pfeffer, J. & Salancik, G.R. (1978): *The External Control of Organizations. A Resource Dependence Perspective*. New York, Harper & Row.

Pfeffer, J. & Sutton, R.I. (2006): *Hard Facts, Dangerous Half-Truths & Total Nonsense. Profiting from Evidence-Based Management*. Boston, Harvard Business School Press.

Pinheiro, R., Geschwind, L. & Aarrevaara, T. (2014): Nested Tensions and Interwoven Dilemmas in Higher Education: The View From the Nordic Countries. *Cambridge Journal of Regions, Economy and Society*, vol. 7(2):233–250.

Piore, M.J. & Sabel, C.F. (1984): *The Second Industrial Divide. Possibilities for Prosperity*. New York, Basic Books.

Plato (2005): *Samlede verker. Bind VII*. Oslo, Vidarforlaget.

Pollitt, C. & Bouckaert, G. (2017): *Public Management Reform: A Comparative Analysis into the Age of Austerity* (4th ed). Oxford, Oxford University Press.

Poole, M.S., Van de Ven, A.H., Dooley, K. & Holmes, M.E. (2000): *Organizational Change and Innovation Processes*. Oxford, Oxford University Press.

Porter, M.E. (1980): *Competitive Strategy: Techniques for Analyzing Industries and Competitors*. New York, The Free Press.

Porter, M.E. (2008): The Five Competitive Forces That Shape Strategy. *Harvard Business Review*, vol. 86:79–93.

Puranam, P., Alexy, O. & Reitzig, M. (2014): What's "New" About New Forms of Organizing? *Academy of Management Review*, vol. 39(2):162–180.

Quinn, J.B. (1980): *Strategies for Change: Logical Incrementalism*. Homewood, Irwin.

Quinn, J.B. (1988a): Strategic Change: "Logical Incrementalism". In Quinn, J.B., Mintzberg, H. & James, R.M. (Eds.), *The Strategy Process. Concepts, Contexts and Cases*. Englewood Cliffs, Prentice Hall.

Quinn, J.B. (1988b): Managing Strategies Incrementally. In Quinn, J.B., Mintzberg, H. & James, R.M. (Eds.), *The Strategy Process. Concepts, Contexts and Cases*. Englewood Cliffs, Prentice Hall.

Quinn, R.E. & Cameron, K.S. (1988): Paradox and Transformation. A Framework for Viewing Organization and Management. In Quinn, R.E. & Cameron, K.S. (Eds.), *Paradox and Transformation: Toward a Theory of Change in Organization and Management*. Cambridge, MA, Ballinger.

Quinn, R.E. & Rohrbaugh, J. (1983): A Spatial Model of Effectiveness Criteria: Toward a Competing Values Approach to Organizational Analysis. *Management Science*, vol. 29:363–377.

Rafferty, A.E., Jimmieson, N.L. & Armenakis, A.A. (2013): Change Readiness: A Multilevel Review. *Journal of Management*, vol. 39(1):110–135.

Raisch, S. & Birkinshaw, J. (2008): Organizational Ambidexterity: Antecedents, Outcomes, and Moderators. *Journal of Management*, vol. 34 (3):375–409.

Raisch, S., Birkinshaw, J., Probst, G. & Tushman, M.L. (2009): Organizational Ambidexterity: Balancing Exploitation and Exploration for Sustained Performance. *Organization Science*, vol. 20(4):685–695

Rajagopalan, N. & Spreitzer, G. (1997): Towards a Theory of Strategic Change: A Multi-Lens Perspective and Integrative Framework. *Academy of Management Review*, vol. 42:48–79.

Ranson, S., Hinings, B. & Greenwood, R. (1980): The Structuring of Organizational Structures. *Administrative Science Quarterly*, vol. 25:1–17.

Rasmusen, E. (1989): *Games and Information. An Introduction to Game Theory*. Cambridge, Basil Blackwell.

Ravn, J.E. (2015): Forhandling, forvaltning og forvandling – den norske samarbeidsmodellens muligheter i fremtidens arbeidsliv. In Bungum, B., Forseth, U. & Kvande, E. (Eds.), *Den norske modellen. Internasjonalisering som utfordring og vitalisering*. Bergen: Fagbokforlaget.

Reihlen, M., Albers, S. & Kewitz, T. (2009): Internationalization as Strategic Change: The Case of Deutsche Treuhand-Gesellschaft. *Management Revue*, vol. 20(2):209–233.

Rerup, C. & Feldman, M.S. (2011): Routines as a Source of Change in Organizational Schemata: The Role of Trial-And-Error Learning. *Academy of Management Journal*, vol. 54(3):577–610.

Roethlisberger, F.G. & Dickson, W.J. (1939): *Management and the Worker*. Cambridge, MA, Harvard University Press.

Rogers, E.M. & Argawala-Rogers, R. (1976): *Communication in Organizations*. New York, The Free Press.

Romanelli, E. & Tushman, M. (1994): Organization Transformation as Punctuated Equilibrium. *Academy of Management Journal*, vol. 37:1141–1166.

Roness, P.G. (1997): *Organisasjonsendringar. Teorier og strategier for studier av endringsprosessar*. Bergen, Fagbokforlaget.

Roos, G., von Krogh, G. & Roos, J. (2010): *Innføring i strategi* (5th ed). Bergen, Fagbokforlaget.

Rousseau, R.M. (1995): *Psychological Contracts in Organizations. Understanding Written and Unwritten Agreements*. London, Sage.

Russ, T.L. (2008): Communicating Change: A Review and Critical Analysis of Programmatic and Participatory Implementation Approaches. *Journal of Change Management*, vol. 8(3/4):199–211.

Røvik, K.A. (1991): *Fra teori til teknikk. Private organisasjonsutviklingsfirmaer i offentlig sektor*. Oslo, Tano.

Røvik, K.A. (1998): *Moderne organisasjoner*. Oslo, Fagbokforlaget.

Røvik, K.A. (2007): *Trender og translasjoner. Ideer som former det 21. århundrets organisasjon*. Oslo, Universitetsforlaget.

Røvik, K.A. (2016): Knowledge Transfer as Translation: Review and Elements of an Instrumental Theory. *International Journal of Management Reviews*, 18:290–310.

Sackman, S.A. (1997): Introduction. In Sackman, S.A. (Eds.), *Cultural Complexity in Organizations*. Thousand Oaks, Sage.

Sastry, M.A. (1997): Problems and Paradoxes in a Model of Punctuated Organizational Change. *Administrative Science Quarterly*, vol. 42:237–275.

Schaffer, R.H. & Thomson, H.A. (1992): Successful Change Programs Begin with Results. *Harvard Business Review*, January–February:80–89.

Schein, E.H. (1985): *Organizational Culture and Leadership*. San Francisco, Jossey-Bass.

Schein, E.H. (1987): *Process Consultation: Lessons for Managers and Consultants*. Reading, MA, Addison Wesley.

Schein, E.H. (1996): Kurt Lewin's Change Theory in the Field and in the Classroom: Notes Toward a Model of Managed Learning. *Systems Practice*, vol. 9:27–47.

Schein, E.H. (1999): *The Corporate Culture*. San Francisco, Jossey-Bass.

Schultz, M. & Hernes, T. (2013): A Temporal Perspective on Organizational Identity. *Organization Science*, vol. 24(1):1–21.

Schumpeter, J. (1942): *Capitalism, Socialism and Democracy*. New York, Harper & Brothers.

Schuster, M.H. & Weidman, S. (2006): Organizational Change in Union Settings: Labor-Management Partnerships: The Past and the Future. *Human Resource Planning*, vol. 29(1):45–51.

Scott, W.R. (1987): The Adolescence of Institutional Theory. *Administrative Science Quarterly*, vol. 32:493–511.

Scott, W.R. (1992): *Organizations. Rational, Natural and Open Systems*. Englewood Cliffs, Prentice Hall.

Scott, W.R. (2008): *Institutions and Organization* (3rd ed.). Thousand Oaks, Sage.

Scott, W.R., Ruef, M., Mendel, P.J. & Caronna, C.A. (2000): *Institutional Change and Healthcare Organizations: From Professional Dominance to Managed Care*. Chicago, University of Chicago Press.

Seidensticker, R.B. (2006): *FutureHype*. San Francisco, Berret-Koehler.

Selznick, P. (1949): *TVA and the Grass Roots: A Study in the Sociology of Formal Organizations*. Berkeley, University of California Press.

Selznick, P. (1957): *Leadership in Administration. A Sociological Interpretation*. Berkeley, University of California Press.

Senge, P. (1990): The Leader's New Work: Building Learning Organizations. *Sloan Management Review*, Fall:7–23.

Senge, P. (1991): *Den femte disiplin. Kunsten å skape den lærende organisasjon*. Oslo, Egmont Hjemmets Bokforlag.

Senge, P. (1996): Leading Learning Organizations. *Training & Development*, vol. 50:36–38.

Senge, P. (2000): The Puzzles and Paradoxes of How Living Companies Create Wealth. In Beer, M. & Nohria, N. (Eds.), *Breaking the Code of Change*. Boston, Harvard Business School.

Shapiro, D.L. & Kirkman, B.L. (1999): Employees' Reactions to the Change to Work Teams. The Influence of "Anticipatory" Injustice. *Journal of Organizational Change Management*, vol. 12:51–66.

Shook, J. (2010): How to Change a Culture: Lessons From NUMMI. *MIT Sloan Management Review*, vol. 51(2):63–68.

Simon, H.A. (1945/1976): *Administrative Behaviour*. New York, The Free Press.

Sine, W.D., Mitsihashi, H. & Kirsch, D.A. (2006): Revisiting Burns and Stalker: Formal Structure and New Venture Performance in Emerging Economic Sectors. *Academy of Management Journal*, vol. 49(1):121–132.

Singh, J.V. (1986): Performance, Slack, and Risk Taking in Organizational Decision Making. *Academy of Management Journal*, vol. 8:363–376.

Sleesman, D.J., Lennard, A.C., McNamara, G. & Conlon, D.E. (2018): Putting Escalation of Commitment in Context: A Multilevel Review and Analysis. *Academy of Management Annals*, vol. 12(1):178–207.

Smerek, R. (2011): Sensemaking and Sensegiving: An Exploratory Study of the Simultaneous "Being and Learning" of New College and University Presidents. *Journal of Leadership & Organizational Studies*, vol. 18:80–94.

Smircich, L. & Stubbart, C. (1985): Strategic Management in an Enacted World. *Academy of Management Review*, vol. 10:724–736.

Smolarczyk, K. & Hauer, G. (2014): An Investigation of the Idea of Individual Learning in Enabling Organizational Change. In Chui, C.T.B. & Rashid, W.E.W. (Eds.), *4th International Conference on Marketing and Retailing 2013*, vol. 130:247–256.

Soparnot, R. (2011): The Concept of Organizational Change Capacity. *Journal of Organizational Change Management*, vol. 24(5):640–661.

Sorge, A. & Van Witteloostuijn, A. (2004): The (Non)Sense of Organizational Change: An Essai about Universal Management Hypes, Sick Consultancy Metaphors, and Healthy Organization Theories. *Organization Studies*, vol. 25:1205–1231.

Spender, J.-C. & Grinyer, P.H. (1996): Organization Renewal. Deinstitutionalization and Loosely Coupled Systems. *International Studies of Management & Organization*, vol. 26:17–40.

Stace, D.A. & Dunphy, D.C. (1991): Beyond Traditional Paternalistic and Developmental Approaches to Organizational Change and Human Resource Strategies. *The International Journal of Human Resource Management*, vol. 2:263–283.

Staw, B.M., Sandelands, D.E. & Dutton, J.E. (1988): Threat-Rigidity Effects in Organizational Behavior: A Multilevel Analysis. In Cameron, K.S. & Whetten, D.A. (Eds.), *Readings in Organizational Decline: Frameworks, Research and Prescriptions*. Cambridge, MA, Ballinger.

Stebbins, M.W. & Shani, A.B. (1989): Organizational Design: Beyond the "Mafia" Model. *Organizational Dynamics*, vol. 17:18–31.

Steen Jensen, I. (2002): *Ona fyr*. Oslo, Dinamo Forlag.

Stensaker, I. & Falkenberg, J. (2007): Making Sense of Different Responses to Corporate Change. *Human Relations*, vol. 60(1):137–177.

Stensaker, I., Meyer, C.B., Falkenberg, J. & Haueng, A.C. (2002): Excessive Change: Coping Mechanisms and Consequences. *Organizational Dynamics*, vol. 31:296–312.

Stensaker, I. & Schei, V. (2006): Negotiations and Renegotiations in Change Processes. In Lines, R., Stensaker, I.G. & Langley, A. (Eds.), *New Perspectives on Organizational Change and Learning*. Bergen, Fagbokforlaget.

Stinchcombe, A.L. (1986): On Social Factors in Administrative Organization. In Stinchcombe, A.L., *Stratification and Organization. Selected Papers*. Cambridge, Cambridge University Press.

Strand, T. (2001): *Ledelse, organisasjon og kultur*. Bergen, Fagbokforlaget.

Strebel, P. (1994): Choosing the Right Change Path. *California Management Review*, vol. 36:29–51.

Strebel, P. (1996): *Why Do Employees Resist Change?* Harvard Business Review, May–June:86–92.

Suddaby, R. & Foster, W.M. (2016): History and Organizational Change. *Journal of Management*, vol. 43(1):19–38.

Sullivan, J.J. & Nonaka, I. (1986): The Application of Organizational Learning Theory to Japanese and American Management. *Journal of International Business Studies*, Fall:127–147.

Sun, P.Y.T. & Anderson, M.H. (2008): An Examination of the Relationship Between Absorptive Capacity and Organizational Learning, and a Proposed Integration. *International Journal of Management Reviews*, vol. 12(2):130–150.

Sydow, J., Schreyögg, G. & Koch, J. (2009): Organizational Path Dependence: Opening the Black Box. *Academy of Management Review*, vol. 34:689–709.

Teece, D.J. (2007): Explicating Dynamic Capabilities: The Nature and Microfoundations of (Sustainable) Enterprise Performance. *Strategic Management Review*, vol. 28:1319–1350.

Teece, D.J. (2009): *Dynamic Capabilities & Strategic Management. Organizing for Innovation and Growth.* Oxford, Oxford University Press.

Teece, D.J. (2018): Business Models and Dynamic Capabilities. *Long Range Planning*, vol. 51(1):40–49. doi:10.1016/j.lrp.2017.06.007.

Teece, D.J., Pisano, G. & Shuen, A. (1997): Dynamic Capabilities and Strategic Management. *Strategic Management Journal*, vol. 18:509–533.

Thomas, J., George, S. & Rose, T. (2016): Deciphering Value Discourse's Role in Explaining the Persistent Perception of Change Failure. *Journal of Change Management*, vol. 16(4):271–296.

Thompson, J.D. (1967): *Organizations in Action*. New York, McGraw Hill.

Thompson, J.D. & Tuden, A. (1959): Strategies, Structures and Processes in Organizational Design. In Thomson, J.D. (Eds.), *Comparative Studies in Administration*, Pittsburgh, University of Pittsburgh Press.

Thompson, M. (2011): Ontological Shift or Ontological Drift? Reality Claims, Epistemological Frameworks, and Theory Generation in Organization Studies. *Academy of Management Review*, vol. 36(4):754–773.

Thornbury, J. (1999): KPMG: Revitalizing Culture Through Values. *Business Strategy Review*, vol. 10(4):1–15. https://doi.org/10.1111/1467-8616.00114

Tichy, N.M. & Ulrich, D.O. (1984): The Leadership Challenge – A Call for the Transformational Leader. *Sloan Management Review*, Fall:59–68.

Tilles, S. (1968): Making Strategy Explicit. In Ansoff, I. (Eds.), *Business Strategy*. London, Penguin.

Tirole, J. (1988): *The Theory of Industrial Organization*. Cambridge, MA, MIT Press.

Tolbert, P.S. & Zucker, L.G. (1983): Institutional Sources of Change in the Formal Structure of Organizations: Diffusion of Civil Service Reform 1880–1935. *Administrative Science Quarterly*, vol. 28:22–39.

Torgersen, U. (1994): *Profesjoner og offentlig sektor*. Oslo, Tano.

Treanor, T. (2010): Amazon: Love Them? Hate Them? Let's Follow the Money. *Publishing Research Quarterly*, vol. 26(2):119–128.

Trice, H.M. & Beyer, J.M. (1986): Charisma and Its Routinization in Two Social Movement Organizations. *Research in Organizational Behavior*, vol. 8:113–164.

Trist, E.L. (1981): The Sociotechnical Perspective. In Van de Ven, A.H. & Joyce, W.F. (Eds.), *Perspectives on Organization Design and Behavior*. New York, John Wiley & Sons.

Tronsmo, P. (1998): Myten om menneskers og organisasjoners iboende motstand mot forandring. *Magma*, vol. 1:26–35.

Tushman, M.L. & Anderson, P. (1986): Technological Discontinuities and Organizational Environments. *Adminstrative Science Quarterly*, vol. 31:439–465.

Tushman, M.L. & Anderson, P. (1987): Technological Disconitinuities and Organization Environments. In Pettigrew, A. (Eds.), *The Management of Strategic Change*. Oxford, Basil Blackwell.

Tushman, M.L. & Murman, J.P. (1998): Dominant Designs, Technology Cycles and Organizational Outcomes. *Research in Organizational Behavior*, vol. 20:213–266.

Tushman, M.L. & O'Reilley, C.A. III (1996): Ambidextrous Organizations: Managing Evolutionary and Revolutionary Change. *California Management Review*, vol. 34:8–30.

Tushman, M.L. & O'Reilley, C.A. III (2002): *Winning through Innovation. A Practical Guide to Leading Organizational Change and Renewal*. Boston, Harvard Business School Press.

Tushman, M.L. & Romanelli, E. (1985): Organizational Evolution: A Metamorphosis Model of Convergence and Reorientation. *Research in Organizational Behavior*, vol. 7:171–222.

Tushman, M.L. & Rosenkopf, L. (1992): Organizational Determinants of Technological Change: Toward a Sociology of Technological Evolution. *Research in Organizational Behavior*, vol. 14:311–347.

Tushman, M.L., Smith, W.K. & Binns, A. (2011): The Ambidextrous CEO. *Harvard Business Review*, vol. 89(6):74–80.

Tushman, M.L., Smith, W.K., Wood, R.C., Westerman, G. & O'Reilley, C. (2010): Organizational Designs and Innovation Streams. *Industrial and Corporate Change*, vol. 19(5):1331–1366.

Underdal, A. (1997): Mellom akademi og bedrift. In Christensen, T. & Midgaard, K. (Eds.), *Universitetet som beslutningsarena*. Bergen, Fagbokforlaget.

Valikangas, L. & Okumura, A. (1997): Why Do People Follow Leaders? A Study of a U.S. and a Japanese Change Program. *Leadership Quarterly*, vol. 8:1–26.

Van de Ven, A.H. & Poole, M.S. (1988): Paradoxical Requirements for a Theory of Organizational Change. In Quinn, R.H. & Cameron, K. (Eds.), *Paradox and Transformation: Toward a Theory of Change in Organizations*. New York, Harper-Collins.

Van de Ven, A.H. & Poole, M.S. (1995): Explaining Development and Change in Organizations. *Academy of Management Review*, vol. 20:510–540.

Van Knippenberg, D. & Sitkin, S.B. (2013): A Critical Assessment of CharismaticTransformational Leadership Research: Back to the Drawing Board? *Academy of Management Annals*, vol. 7(1):1–60.

Van Maanen, J. (1992): Drinking Our Troubles Away: Managing Conflict in a British Police Agency. In Kolb, D.M. & Bartunek, J.M. (Eds.), *Hidden Conflict in Organizations*. Newbury Park, Sage.

Van Maanen, J. & Schein, E.H. (1979): Toward a Theory of Organizational Socialization. In Staw, B. (Eds.), *Research in Organizational Behavior. Vol. 1*. Greenwich, JAI Press.

Van Meter, D.S. & Van Horn, C.E. (1975): The Policy Implementation Process: A Conceptual Framework. *Administration & Society*, vol. 4:43–103.

Veiga, J.F., Floyd, S. & Dechant, K. (2001): Towards Modelling the Effects of National Culture on IT Implementation and Acceptance. *Journal of Information Technology*, vol. 16:145–158.

Virany, B., Tushman, M.L. & Romanelli, E. (1992): Executive Succession and Organization Outcomes in Turbulent Environments: An Organization Learning Approach. *Organization Science*, vol. 3:72–91.

Vroom, V.H. (1964): *Management and Motivation*. New York, John Wiley.

Vroom, V.H. & Yetton, P.W. (1973): *Leadership and Decision-Making*. Pittsburgh: University of Pittsburgh Press

Wang, C.L., Senaratne, C. & Rafiq, M. (2015): Success Traps, Dynamic Capabilities and Firm Performance. *British Journal of Management*, vol. 26(1):26–44.

Ware, M. & Mabe, M. (2015): *The STM report. An Overview of Scientific and Scoholarly Journal Publishing*. The Hague, NL, International Association of Scientific, Technical and Medical Publishers. Retrieved from: https://www.stm-assoc.org/2015_02_20_STM_Report_2015.pdf

Warren, D.I. (1968): Power, Visibility and Conformity in Formal Organizations. *American Sociological Review*, vol. 33:951–970.

Watzlawick, P., Weakland, J.H. & Fisch, R. (1974): *Change: Principles of Problem Formation and Problem Resolution*. New York, Norton.

Weber, M. (1971): *Makt og byråkrati*. Oslo, Gyldendal.

Weick, K.E. (1979): *The Social Psychology of Organizations*. Reading, MA, Addison Wesley.

Weick, K.E. (1995): *Sensemaking in Organizations*. Thousand Oaks, Sage.

Weick, K.E. (2000): Emergent Change as a Universal in Organizations. In Beer, M. & Nohria, N. (Eds.), *Breaking the Code of Change*. Boston, Harvard Business School.

Weick, K.E. (2011): Reflections: Change Agents As Change Poets – On Reconnecting Flux and Hunches. *Journal of Change Management*, vol. 11(1):7–20.

Weick, K.E. & Quinn, R.E. (1999): Organizational Change and Development. *Annual Review of Psychology*, vol. 50:361–386.

Weick, K.E., Sutcliffe, K.M. & Obstfeld, D. (2005) Organizing and the process of sensemaking. *Organization Science* 16(4):409–421.

Weick, K.E. & Westley, F. (1996): Organizational Learning: Affirming an Oxymoron. In Clegg, S.R., Hardy, C. & Nord, W.R. (Eds.), *Handbook of Organization Studies*. London, Sage.

Werr, A., Stjernberg, T. & Docherty, P. (1997): The Functions of Methods of Change in Management Consulting. *Journal of Organizational Change Management*, vol. 10:288–307.

Whelan-Berry, K.S. & Somerville, K.A. (2010): Linking Change Drivers and the Organizational Change Process: A Review and Synthesis. *Journal of Change Management*, vol. 10(2):175–193.

Whittington, R. (1988): Environmental Structure and Theories of Strategic Choice. *Journal of Management Studies*, vol. 25:521–536.

Whittington, R. & Pettigrew, A. (1999): Change and Complementarities in the New Competitive Landscape: A European Panel Study 1992–1996. *Organization Science*, vol. 10:183–195.

Williamson, O.E. (1975): *Markets and Hierarchies: Analysis and Antitrust Implications*. New York, The Free Press.

Williamson, O.E. (1990): The Firm as a Nexus of Treaties. In Aoki, M., Gustafsson, B. & Williamson, O.E. (Eds.), *The Firm as a Nexus of Treaties*. London, Sage.

Wilson, J.Q. (1989): *Bureaucracy. What Government Agencies Do and Why They Do It*. New York, Basic Books.

Wood, R. & Bandura, A. (1989): Social Cognitive Theory of Organizational Management. *Academy of Management Review*, vol. 14(3):361–384.

Yukl, G. (2006): *Leadership in Organizations* (6th ed.). Upper Saddle River, NJ, Prentice Hall.

Yukl, G. & Falbe, C.M. (1990): Influence Tactics and Objectives in Upward, Downward and Lateral Influence Attempts. *Journal of Applied Psychology*, vol. 75:132–140.

Yukl, G., Falbe, C.M. & Youn, J.Y. (1996): Patterns of Influence Behaviors for Managers. *Group and Organization Management*, vol. 18:5–28.

Zeira, Y. & Avedisian, J. (1989): Organizational Planned Change: Assessing the Chances for Success. *Organizational Dynamics*, vol. 17:31–45.

Østerud, Ø. (1979): *Det planlagte samfunn*. Oslo, Universitetsforlaget.

Østhus, S. (2011): *Downsizing and Health in Norway*. Ph.D. dissertation, Sosiologisk institutt, Universitetet in Oslo, Oslo.

Notes

1 Clegg & Hardy 1996.

2 This increase is significantly larger than the yearly increase in scientific journal articles, estimated at approximately 2.5% per year (Ware & Mabe 2015).

3 The following discussion should be read in relation to views forwarded by Hernes et al. 2015 and Hernes 2014.

4 March 1991.

5 https://hbr.org/2012/10/this-is-your-brain-on-organizational-change (accessed 17 February 2018).

6 Burnes 2011; Meaney & Pung 2008; Whittington & Pettigrew 1999.

7 Hughes 2011; Thomas et al. 2016.

8 Du Gay & Vikkelsø 2012.

9 Van de Ven & Poole 1995:512.

10 Hernes 1976.

11 Bakken & Hernes 2006; Thompson 2011; Weick 1979.

12 Plato 2005:138.

13 Op.cit.:186.

14 Graham 1997; see also Fajoun 2010 for such a duality view.

15 Poole et al. 2000.

16 See, for instance, Liker & Kranz 2011.

17 See Lincoln & Guba 1985 for such a discussion.

18 Røvik 2007.

19 Scott 2008; Thompson 1967; Weber 1971.

20 March 1991.

21 Dacin et al. 2002; Van de Ven & Poole 1988.

22 Weick & Westley 1996.

23 This point of view was first described by Pettigrew 1987, and refined further in Pettigrew, Woodman & Cameron 2001.

24 March 1981:564.

25 See Greenwood & Hinings 1996; Tushman & Romanelli 1985 for helpful reviews.

26 See Coleman 1986; Giddens 1979 & 1985; Ranson et al. 1980 for helpful reviews of this classic debate in the social sciences.

27 Pettigrew 1990:268.

28 This is thus more like a process theory than a variance theory, where the latter approach is more interested in defining which elements create which type(s) of change; see Roness 1997:49–60.

29 Van de Ven & Poole 1988:25–28.

30 See Crozier 1964 for a classic example of unintended consequences.

31 Van de Ven 2005.

32 See, for instance, Armenakis et al. 1999; Berg 1995, French & Bell 1995; Galpin 1996; Golembiewski 1972, Judson 1991; Kotter 1995; Lyngdal 1992; Levin & Klev 2002.

33 Todnem By 2007a.

34 Pettigrew 1990.

35 Gersick 1991; Suddaby & Foster 2016.

36 Van de Ven & Poole 1995:511.

37 The four perspectives are similar to Suddaby & Fosters' (2016) four perspectives on the role of history in organizational change.

38 See Borum 1995; Huy 2001.

39 See Simon 1945/1976.

40 Monnot 2017.

41 This model was inspired by Cummings & Worley 2001:28 and Nadler 1987:361.

42 The SWOT (Strengths, Weaknesses, Opportunities, Threats) analysis is probably the most common form of strategic analysis. See Andrews 1965 for the original, or Roos et al. 2010 for an introduction and overview.

43 Oliver, C. 1992.

44 Crozier & Friedberg 1977.

45 O'Reilley & Tushman 2008.

46 Van de Ven & Poole 1995:515.

47 See Ivanova & Persson 2017 for a variation on this topic.

48 Whittington 1988.

49 Groth 1999; Jacques 1990.

50 Van de Ven & Poole 1988.

51 Greenwood & Hinings 1988.

52 Hannan & Freeman 1989.

53 Scott 2001.

54 Lee & Pennings 2002.

55 http://time.com/4865957/death-and-life-shopping-mall/ (accessed 28 February 2018).

56 Selznick 1949.

57 Scott 2001.

58 Borum 1999.

59 Døving & Nordhaug 2006; Espedal 2006; Jacobsen 2001a, 2001b; Miner 1990.

60 Feldman & Pentland 2003.

61 March & Olsen 1989.

62 This is a point also made by Hannan & Freeman (1989), who make a distinction between "selection theories", where human agency is toned dramatically down, and "adaption theories", which opens for the possibility that organizations adapt to environmental change through strategic choice.

63 Meyer & Zucker 1989; Puranam et al. 2014.
64 Pfeffer 1981.
65 Pfeffer & Salancik 1978.
66 Pfeffer 1981.
67 Rasmusen 1989.
68 Blair & Haynes 2011; Pfeffer & Salacik 1977; Thompson 1967.
69 The authors discsuss the garbage can model as a theory that does not apply any of the four "motors"; see Van de Ven & Poole 1995:528.
70 March 1988 167.
71 Cohen, March & Olsen 1972.
72 March & Olsen 1976.
73 Røvik 1998.
74 Langley & Denis 2006; Rerup & Feldman 2011.
75 Døving & Nordhaug 2006.
76 Miner 1987, 1990; Miner & Akinsanmi 2016.
77 Pfeffer 1982
78 Antonsen & Beck Jørgensen 2000a:5 (my translation).
79 Busch 2011.
80 Beck Jørgensen 2000.
81 Groth 1999.
82 Anderson & Tushman 1990.
83 See Berger & Luckman 1967; Burrell & Morgan 1985; Jacobsen 2006.
84 See March 1988; Simon 1947; Schott 1991.
85 Smircich & Stubbart 1985.
86 Dunphy & Stace 1990:135.
87 Thompson & Tuden 1959.
88 This is Lewin's main point (1951), and is even more central to Weick (1979, 1995) who places the concept of equivocality at the centre of his theory of sensemaking. See also Eisenberg 2006.
89 See Røvik 1998 for a discussion of these concepts.
90 Amankwah-Amoah et al. 2017; Carlzon 1985.
91 The philosopher Husserl is central in this way of thinking; see Jacobsen 2006 for a simple introduction.
92 This is elaborated by Kotter 2008.
93 The following argument is inspired by the discussion about what distinguishes public and private organizations. See Allison 1983; Bozeman 1987; Jacobsen 2017; Peters 1998; Wilson 1989.
94 Pollitt & Bouckaert 2000.
95 Jacobsen 1995.
96 Hall 1972; Jacobsen & Thorsvik 2013; Mintzberg 1979; Scott 1992; see Johannessen 2003 for a critique.
97 Roos, von Krogh & Roos 2002.
98 Mintzberg 1979.
99 Schein 1985.
100 Pfeffer 1981.

101 Brusoni et al. 2001.

102 Authors like Brunsson 1989; March & Olsen 1976; Orton & Weick 1990 are critical to such an approach.

103 Scott 1992.

104 Meyer & Scott 1992.

105 Modified from Jacobsen & Thorsvik 2013.

106 Kotter 1995:59.

107 This is Kurt Lewin's main argument in his classic theory from 1951.

108 Jensen 2001.

109 Autor 2015; Piore & Sabel 1984.

110 Norris 2000.

111 Kee-Young & Hyunchul 2010.

112 Beer 1987:51.

113 Cullen et al. 2014.

114 Cartwright & Schoenberg 2006; Kuvaas 2008; Østhus 2011.

115 Based on Mintzberg 1979.

116 See, for instance, Williamson 1975.

117 Miles & Snow 1978; Mintzberg et al. 1988.

118 Schein 1985.

119 See Argyris & Schon 1974 for a discussion. The definition used in this book is consistent with the one used by Hinings & Greenwood 1988b.

120 The following is inspired by Greenwood & Hinings 1987, 1988, 1993.

121 https://no.linkedin.com/pulse/bank-eller-teknologibedrift-rune-bjerke (accessed 8 March 2018).

122 Kikulis et al. 1995.

123 Kikulis et al. 1995:75–78.

124 Chatman & O'Reilly 2016; Chatman et al. 2014.

125 Underdal 1997.

126 Pinheiro et al. 2014.

127 Scott 1987, 2001.

128 Greenwood & Hinings 1988, 1993; Hinings & Greenwood 1988a, 1988b. The quotation is from Greenwood & Hinings 1993:1055. The concept of archetype was originally Greek and can be translated as "pattern." See Tushman & Romanelli 1985 for a somewhat different approach to the concept.

129 See interviews with several Norwegian entrepreneurs in connection with the Gaselleprisen 2011 (http://www.dn.no/gasellene/article2251648.ece).

130 There are striking similarities with the culture described here and what has been known as "the Toyota Way"; see Shook 2010.

131 See Brock et al. 1999 for more examples.

132 This is why Mintzberg (1979) claims that this configuration will be ridden with "Balkanization".

133 See Steen Jensen 2002 for a Norwegian example.

134 Greenwood & Hinings 1988.

135 Kanter 1983.

136 See Pfeffer & Sutton 2006.
137 Jacobsen 1995; Johnsen 2007.
138 Argyris & Schon 1974.
139 Argyris 1982, 1990.
140 Perrow 1986.
141 Argyris 2000; Galbraith 2000.
142 A strong Swedish influence is present her; see, for instance, Brunsson 1989, 2003; Brunsson et al. 1989; Löfström 2003.
143 Orton & Weick 1990.
144 Brunsson 2007, 2009; Mintzberg 1994; Røvik 1998, 2007; Weick 1995.
145 Brunsson 1989; Heese et al. 2016; Meyer & Rowan 1977; Reihlen et al. 2009; Røvik 1998; Stensaker & Falkenberg 2007.
146 Huy 2001.
147 Brunsson 1989.
148 Brunsson 1989.
149 Carlos & Lewis 2018.
150 The following was inspired by Levinson 1986.
151 Gersick 1991.
152 Gersick 1991; Tushman & Romanelli 1985; Tushman & O'Reilley 1996; Tushman & Murman 1998.
153 Barton 1993.
154 Tushman & Anderson 1987.
155 March 1991.
156 Nadler & Tushman 1990.
157 Pettigrew, Woodman & Cameron 2001.
158 Van de Ven & Poole 1995.
159 Greenwood & Hinings 1987.
160 Battilana & Cascario 2012; Kikulus et al. 1995.
161 Watzlawick et al.1974
162 See Grant 2010.
163 Stortingsmelding 7 (2008–2009).
164 Treanor 2010.
165 Tushman & Romanelli 1985; Tushman & O'Reilley 2002.
166 Tushman & Rosenkopf 1992.
167 Tushman & Anderson 1986:442.
168 March 1991.
169 Bostrom 2014.
170 https://www.ft.com/content/cefc066c-fd4e-11e7-9b32-d7d59aace167 (accessed 9 March 2018).
171 Hammer 1990.
172 Greenwood & Hinings 1988.
173 See Groth 1999.
174 Hofsteede 2001.
175 Chin & Benne 1994.

176 This way of viewing change was inspired by different modes of cognitive learning: cumulative, assimilative, and accomodative. See Busch 1990 for an introduction.
177 Nadler & Tushman 1990.
178 Gersick 1991:13–16.
179 Greenwood & Hinings 1993:1063.
180 Op.cit.:1073.
181 Hannan & Freeman 1989; Whittington & Pettigrew 1999.
182 See, for examplc, French & Bell 1995.
183 Tushman & O'Reilley 1996:24.
184 Benner & Tushman 2003, 2013; Greenwood & Hinings 1988.
185 Hannan & Freeman 1989; Nadler & Tushman 1990; Whittington & Pettigrew 1999.
186 Abernathy 1978; Christensen 1998; Levinthal & March 1993; March 1991; Tushman & O'Reilley 1996.
187 Christensen 1998 introduced the concept of "disruptive technology", but the concept should not be limited to technology as it also refers to changes in the product/service and the business model. See Christensen 2002, 2006.
188 Abernathy 1978:173.
189 March 1991.
190 March 1991.
191 Benner & Tushman 2003.
192 The concept originates from Schumpeter 1942
193 Benner & Tushman 2003, 2013; March 1991.
194 Lavie et al. 2010.
195 Beer & Nohria 2000b; Whittington & Pettigrew 1999.
196 Pettigrew & Whipp 1991.
197 Greenwood & Hining 1988
198 Rajagopalan & Spreitzer 1997.
199 Cohen & Levinthal 1990; Meyer & Stensaker 2011.
200 Levinthal & March 1993.
201 Burns & Stalker 1961; Galbraith 1977; Hannan & Freeman 1989; Mintzberg 1979.
202 Burns & Stalker 1961; Galbraith 1977; Hannan & Freeman 1989; Mintzberg 1979.
203 Johns 2006, 2017; Pettigrew 1987.
204 Thanks to Erik Døving for drawing my attention to this concept; see also Lewin 1997.
205 Jansen 1996:286.
206 Mintzberg 1979; Greenwood & Hinings 1996.
207 This is a main point in the writings of Hannan & Freeman 1989 when they claim that organizations are characterized more by inertia than by a willingness to change.
208 See Tirole 1988:307–308.
209 Hannan & Freeman 1989:67.
210 Dixit & Pyndick 1994; Colombo & Delmastro 2002.
211 Williamson 1975, 1990.
212 The example is lifted from Braddon 2000.
213 Ghosal 2003; Miles & Snow 1978; Porter 2008.
214 Leitner & Guldenberg 2010; Parnell & Hershey 2005.

215 Leitner & Guldenberg 2010; Parnell & Hershey 2005.
216 March 1991.
217 Blau & Scott 1963.
218 Crozier 1964.
219 Quinn & Rohrbaugh 1983.
220 Ghemawat & Costa 1993.
221 Mintzberg 1979.
222 This is also a main point for those working within a configurational perspective; see Miller & Friesen 1984; Greenwood & Hinings 1988.
223 Colombo & Delmaestro 2002.
224 See Orton & Weick 1990 for an overview; Weick 1979.
225 Galbraith 1977.
226 Daneels 2003.
227 See Thompson 1967 for an early discussion of internal coupling which he calls "technologies".
228 Weick 1979.
229 This is also the main point in the argument connected to "the strength of weak ties", Granovetter 1973.
230 Bartlett & Ghosal 1993; Williamson 1975.
231 This is one of Granovetter's (1973) main points.
232 Spender & Grinyer 1996.
233 Weick & Quinn 1999:375.
234 Dunphy & Stace 1988.
235 Arguments about both size and age are taken from Barnett & Freeman 2001; Hannan & Freeman 1989; Josefy et al. 2015.
236 Donaldson 2001.
237 Josefy et al. 2015; Kanter 1983.
238 Bowman & Hurry 1993; Hannan & Freeman 1989; Josefy et al. 2015.
239 Kraatz & Zajak 2001.
240 Meyer & Zucker 1989.
241 Barnett & Freeman 2001:544.
242 Hinings & Greenwood 1988; Pettigrew et al. 2001; Scott et al. 2000.
243 Ghemawat 1991.
244 Tushman & O'Reilley 1996.
245 Levinthal & March 1993.
246 See Lant et al. 1992 for an overview.
247 Schaffer & Thompson 1992.
248 Gordon et al. 2000:916.
249 Meyer & Zucker 1989.
250 Weick 1979.
251 Kiesler & Sproull 1982; Milliken & Lant 1991; Ocasio 1995.
252 Staw et al. 1988.
253 Gordon et al. 2000:935.
254 Amburgey et al. 1993.
255 Beck et al. 2008.

256 Cyert & March 1963; Galbraith 1977.
257 Kraatz & Zajac 2001.
258 Donaldson 2000; Singh 1986.
259 Kraatz & Zajac 2001:634.
260 Levitt & March 1988.
261 Grobman 2005.
262 The argument of "the liability of newness" is central in Hannan & Freeman 1989.
263 Penrose 1959.
264 Hannan & Freeman 1989; Nelson & Winter 1982.
265 Chatman et al. 2014; Tushman & O'Reilley 1996.
266 Martin 1992.
267 Deal & Kennedy 1982, 1999; Kotter & Heskett 1992.
268 Collins 2001; Collins & Porras 1994; Pettigrew 1985; Tushman & O'Reilley 1996.
269 O'Reilley & Chatman 1996.
270 Janis 1982.
271 Meyerson & Martin 1987.
272 Tushman & O'Reilley 1996:23.
273 Cohen & Levinthal 1990; Kotter & Heskett 1990; Meyerson & Martin 1987.
274 Axson 2010:52.
275 Chatman et al. 2014.
276 Cummings & Worley 2001:505.
277 Jacobsen et al. 2018.
278 Brandi et al. 2001; Mintzberg 1983; Nordström & Ridderstråle 1999; Pfeffer 1981; Pfeffer & Salancik 1978.
279 I am not taking into account Stephen Lukes' point (1972) that agreement may be the result of someone having exerted power to affect meanings through socialization.
280 Borum 1999; Heldal 2015; Mintzberg 1979.
281 Torgersen 1994.
282 Abel 1989:131, quoted from Greenwood et al. 2002:62.
283 Brandi et al. 2001.
284 For a lively description, see Steen Jensen 2002.
285 Hambrick et al. 1993; Hambrick et al. 1996.
286 Barker & Duhaime 1997; Gordon et al. 2000; Virany et al. 1992.
287 See Thompson 1967 and Benson 1975 for a definition of the domain concept, and Hannan & Freeman 1989 for a discussion of the field concept.
288 Hofsteede 1997.
289 D'Aunno et al. 1991 & 2000; Scott 1995.
290 The following is heavily based on Porter's (2008) branch analysis.
291 Hannan & Freeman 1989.
292 D'Aveni & Gunther 1994.
293 Jacobsen 1995.
294 Meyer & Zucker 1989.
295 This triad is based on Scott 2008.
296 Dacin et al. 2002; Hannan & Freeman 1989; Oliver 1992.

297 Tolbert & Zucker 1983.
298 Greenwood et al. 2002:62.
299 Poole 2001; Morris et al. 1992.
300 Craft 1991:393.
301 Koch 2000; Lincoln & Kalleberg 1990; Morris et al. 1992.
302 Bryson et al. 2013; Morris et al. 1992; Schuster & Weidman 2006.
303 Hofstede et al. 1990.
304 Meyer & Rowan 1977.
305 Hofstede 1983, 1991. "Masculinity" has been proven difficult to operationalize and thus to scrutinize empirically (see Veiga et al. 2001), but is still retained. Hofstede & Bond (1988) included time orientation in a later work, while hedonism was first introduced by Hofstede et al. 2010.
306 Olsen & Peters 1996.
307 Olsen 1996.
308 Hofstede 1997:26.
309 Gustavsen 1990.
310 Although not addressed directly at this point, Golembiewski 1991 provides plenty of thoughts about it.
311 Lau & Ngo 2001.
312 Martinsons 1996.
313 Røvik 1998, 2007; Scott 2008.
314 Gratton 2011.
315 Campbell 2007.
316 See Soparnot 2011 for a general discussion, and Meyer and Stensaker 2011 for a definition connected to an organization's ability to handle many parallel changes.
317 Ford et al. 2008.
318 Dawson 2014; Huy 2001; Pettigrew et al. 2001.
319 Bluedorn & Denhardt 1988.
320 Pettigrew et al. 2001:703.
321 Huy 2001; Mintzberg & Westley 1992.
322 Hatch 1993.
323 Chin & Benne 1994.
324 Hofstede 2001; Schein 1999.
325 Kotter 1995; 1996, 2008.
326 Carroll & Hatakenata 2001.
327 See Pfeffer & Sutton 2006.
328 See Anderson & Tushman 1990 for such a perspective.
329 Mintzberg 1994; Østerud 1979.
330 Doz & Pralahad 1987.
331 Dunphy & Stace 1988.
332 Hannan & Freeman 1989.
333 See Fry & Killing 1989, chapter 12 for a discussion on urgency.
334 Mahoney 2000; Nelson & Winter 1987; North 1990.
335 Kieser 1994.

336 Greenwood & Hinings 1988; Strebel 1994.
337 Schein 1985.
338 Gersick 1991:14–16.
339 Burke 2002; French & Bell 1995.
340 Sydow et al. 2009.
341 Lindblom 1959; Masuch 1985; Quinn 1980.
342 Sleesman et al. 2018.
343 Crozier 1964.
344 Janis 1982.
345 Quinn 1980; Lindblom 1968.
346 This is also the main point in the influential book by Quinn (1980).
347 Meyer & Stensaker 2009.
348 Meyer & Stensaker 2011; Røvik 1998.
349 Stensaker et al. 2002.
350 Sastry 1997.
351 https://www.wsj.com/articles/scandinavian-airline-sas-to-cut-costs-as-losses-widen-1403089343 (accessed 13 March 2018).
352 https://e24.no/boers-og-finans/sas/sas-sjefen-kutter-egen-loenn/20298584 (accessed 13 March 2018).
353 Oreg et al. 2018.
354 Herscovitch & Meyer 2002.
355 Amenakis et al. 1993.
356 See also Coch & French 1948; Davidson 2002.
357 Argyris & Schön 1974.
358 Op.cit.:79–80.
359 See Herscovitch & Meyer 2002; Meyer et al. 2007.
360 Coetsee 1999:207–208.
361 Dunsing & Matejka 1994:40–42.
362 See Hirschman 1970 for a more detailed description of this type of resistance.
363 See Oreg et al. 2018:69.
364 Foster 2010; Oreg et al. 2018.
365 Brunsson & Olsen 1997:6–7.
366 Kotter 2008.
367 Diamond 1986; Nadler 1987; Tichy & Ulrich 1984.
368 McHugh 1997.
369 Nadler 1982:43.
370 Dykman & Davis 2012; Helliwell & Fowler 1994.
371 Davidsson 2002.
372 Miron et al. 2015.
373 Herscovitch & Meyer 2002; Iversen 1996.
374 Stinchcombe 1986.
375 Pollitt & Bouckaert 2017.
376 Jacobsen 2004.
377 Lawler 1987.

378 Meyer et al. 2007.
379 There are clear parallels to findings in the research on motivation where intrinsic and extrinsic incentives seem to have different mechanisms; see Kuvaas 2008.
380 Bolman & Deal 1991:390–391.
381 McHugh 1997.
382 Olsen & Stensaker 2014.
383 Huber 1996.
384 Jaques 1951.
385 Jaques 1951.
386 Rousseau 1995; Strebel 1996 calls it "personal compact".
387 Egeberg 1984; Mintzberg 1983.
388 Pfeffer 1981.
389 Rogers & Argawala-Rogers 1976.
390 Clegg 1989.
391 Daft 1983; Gagliardi 1990.
392 Jacobsen 1989.
393 Stinchcombe 1986:223.
394 Oliver 1986.
395 Ford 2010; Ford et al. 2008.
396 Pfeffer 1992:19.
397 Gustavsen 1990.
398 See Jacobsen 1992 for a description of such a process.
399 Crozier & Friedberg 1977.
400 Trist 1981:31.
401 Burke & Litwin 1992:523.
402 The following arguments are drawn from Pettigrew, Woodman & Cameron 2001.
403 See Kotter 1995, 1996; Stace & Dunphy 1991; Whittington & Pettigrew 1999.
404 Laine & Kuoppakangas 2015:337.
405 Pennings 1992.
406 See Røvik 1991 who describes how consultancy firms often operate with standardized "recipes". For an example of this type of "recipe literature", see Leigh 1988, or, in Norwegian, Langslet 1999, 2002.
407 Beer & Nohria 2000a:3.
408 Beer & Nohria 2000a:3.
409 Bourgeois & Brodwin 1984.
410 Stace & Dunphy 1991.
411 Roos, von Krogh & Roos 2002; Van Meter & Van Horn 1975.
412 Inspired by Simon 1945.
413 Thanks to Kåre Slåtten for this clarification.
414 Quinn & Weick 1999.
415 Donaldson 1999.
416 See Mueller 1989 for a discussion on the vote-maximizing politician.
417 Byrkjeflot 2011; Jacobsen 1995.
418 Schaffer & Thomson 1992.

419 Op.cit.:82–83.
420 Jensen 2000:40.
421 House 1996.
422 Mintzberg 1973.
423 See Jacobsen & Thorsvik 2013, chapter 3, for an overview.
424 Cyert & March 1963/1992.
425 Conger 2000:104.
426 Nadler 1987.
427 Lewicki & Litterer 1985.
428 Mintzberg 1973.
429 Pfeffer 1992.
430 Just a small selection: Burnes 1992; Cummings & Worley 2001; French & Bell 1995; Levin & Klev 2002; Lyngdal 1992.
431 See, for instance, Barnard 1938 (1968); Roethlisberger & Dickson 1939.
432 Beatty & Ulrich 1991; Kotter 1996; Miles 1997.
433 Galbraith 2000.
434 Egeberg 1984, 2012; Galbraith 1977; Mintzberg 1979.
435 Groth 1999.
436 Cyert & March 1963/1992; Ocasio et al. 2018.
437 Allison 1971; Ocasio et al. 2018.
438 Meyer & Rowan 1977; Pfeffer 1981.
439 Abrahamson 1996; Røvik 1998.
440 Brunsson 1989.
441 The following is based on Roos, von Krogh & Roos 2010.
442 Tilles 1968.
443 This is very similar to traditional project planning; see Jacobsen 2016.
444 Ghosal & Bartlett 2000.
445 Kuvaas 2008; Lawler 1987.
446 Vroom 1964; Nadler & Lawler 1995.
447 Kotter 1996.
448 Hagedorn-Rasmussen 2003; Werr et al. 1997.
449 Røvik 1991, 1992; Schein 1987.
450 Stebbins & Shani 1989:19.
451 The following arguments are drawn from Schein 1987; Neill & Mindrum 2000.
452 Ginsberg & Abrahamson 1991.
453 Peters & Waterman 1982.
454 Harrison 1991.
455 French & Bell 1995:85-86.
456 Quinn 1988a, 1988b.
457 Dunphy & Stace 1988.
458 Cummings & Worley 2001; French & Bell 1995; Lyngdal 1992; Gustavsen 1990; Levin & Klev 2002.
459 March & Olsen 1976.
460 Beck et al. 2008; Senge 2001.

461 Senge 2006:14.
462 Argyris 1990.
463 Argyris & Schon 1974:84.
464 Argyris 2000:421.
465 Argyris 1990.
466 Senge 2006.
467 Nonaka et al. 2014 & 2016.
468 These points are a synthesis of Sullivan & Nonaka 1986; Nonaka 1994; Nonaka, Takeuchi & Umemoto 1996, Nonaka et al. 2014, 2016.
469 Nonaka et al. 1996:835.
470 Bennis 2000:117.
471 See for instance Hersey & Blanchard 1988 for an overview of different leadership styles.
472 Weick 1979.
473 Gustavsen 1990.
474 Lee et al. 2017; Shapiro & Kirkman 1999.
475 Bies & Tyler 1993:355.
476 Dunphy 2000:132.
477 French & Bell 1995:261.
478 Bennis 1969:15.
479 French & Bell 1995; Huy 2001.
480 Argyris 1962, 1964; see Crosby 2013 for an updated version.
481 See French & Bell 1995, chapter 9, for an overview.
482 Levin & Klev 2002.
483 Senge 1991:315.
484 See Deal & Kennedy 1982, 1999; Hernes et al. 2015.
485 van Maanen & Schein 1979.
486 See Jacobsen & Thorsvik 2013 for an overview.
487 Røvik 1998.
488 Argyris 1973.
489 Borum 1980, 1993.
490 Quinn 1988b:676.
491 Lindblom 1968:27.
492 Quinn 1988a.
493 Senge 1991; Weick 2000.
494 Compare Hamel & Pralahad 1989, who in this article introduce the concept "strategic intent".
495 Quinn 1988a:103.
496 Kouzes & Posner 1987.
497 Weick 2000:227.
498 Herzberg 1968/2003.
499 Meyer & Herscovitch 2002.
500 Ledford & Heneman 2000:317–320; see also Kuvaas 2008.
501 Zeira & Avedisan 1989.
502 Bartunek et al. 2011; Cunningham 2006; Jacobsen 2010; Jaros 2010; Meyer & Herscovitch 2002; Meyer & Stensaker 2009.

503 Kotter & Heskett 1992.
504 Deal & Kennedy 1982.
505 Van Maanen 1992.
506 Ledford & Heneman 2000.
507 Schein 1987.
508 Lyngdal 1992:136 (my translation).
509 Lyngdal 1992:149.
510 French & Bell 1995.
511 See Gustavsen 1990 for a brilliant overview.
512 French & Bell 1995.
513 For a discussion of the implicit assumptions on power, see for instance Cobb 1986; Bouwen 1995; Boonstra & Gravenhorst 1998.
514 Tronsmo 1998.
515 Argyris 1973.
516 March 1988:261.
517 French & Bell 1995:45–46.
518 Stace & Dunphy 1991:268 (Note that this is based on an intensive study of only 13 firms.)
519 Beer & Nohria 2000b.
520 Boonstra & Vink 1996.
521 Ginsberg & Abrahamson 1991.
522 Huy 2001.
523 See Strand 2001 for a discussion.
524 Jermier & Kerr 1997.
525 See Jacobsen & Thorsvik 2013 for an overview.
526 This distinction overlaps the distinction between steering and leadership; see Ladegård & Vabo 2010.
527 Lewin 1948, 1951, reprinted in Lewin 1997. See also the special issue on Kurt Lewin in Journal of Change Management, vol. 17 (2); Burns & Bargal 2017.
528 Lewin 1997:330. Although a sketch occupying just a few pages, the impact of this model has been enormous; see Elrod & Tippet 2002.
529 See Armenakis et al. 1999 who use the phases "readiness", "adoption", and "institutionalization"; see also Bakari et al. 2017.
530 Armenakis et al. 1993:681.
531 Beer 1987; Burke 2002; Kotter 1995, 2012; Oreg et al. 2011; Rafferty et al. 2013.
532 Kotter 2008 argues that this is the change agent's most important job in any change process.
533 Armenakis et al. 1999, Holt et al. 2007.
534 This triad was inspired by Schein 1980:291–293 and Armenakis et al. 1993.
535 Kotter 2008 is central to this argument.
536 Pfeffer & Sutton 2006:179.
537 Maitlis & Morance 2007; Weick et al. 2005.
538 Røvik 2007; Weick 1995.
539 Jacobsen 2016.
540 Lines et al. 2011.
541 Inspired by Kraft et al. 2015:310.

542 See Maitlis & Christianson 2015 for an overview of the empirical research.

543 See Brown et al. 2009.

544 Maitlis 2005.

545 Suddaby & Foster 2016.

546 Smircich & Stubbart 1985.

547 The following is based on Burke & Trahant 2000; Gioia & Chittipeddi 1991; Hirschhorn 2002; Kotter 1995, 2008; Maitlis 2005; Maitlis & Morance 2007; Smerek 2010; Suddaby & Foster 2016; Weick 1995, 2011.

548 Schultz & Hernes 2013.

549 Kotter 2008, chapter 4

550 Conferring *ethos*, a concept in rhetoric linked to the legitimacy of the sender.

551 See Kotter 1995, 2008; Pfeffer & Sutton 2006.

552 Meyer & Stensaker 2011:121–123; see also Gilbert 2005.

553 Amundsen & Kongsvik 2008.

554 Nielsen & Riiskjær 2013.

555 Clemente & Roulet 2015; Oliver 1992.

556 Meyer & Stensaker 2011.

557 The distinction between fear and want as driving forces for change was developed by Fiol et al. 1999:458.

558 Bass 1990b.

559 O'Toole 1999:303.

560 Bass 1990b.

561 Burke 2002:256.

562 See Fiol et al. 1990 who study the wording used by American presidents.

563 Beyer 1999.

564 Nonaka et al. 2000:18.

565 Senge 1996:9, where he builds on Fritz' 1990 work on creativity.

566 Se Yukl 2006:218–223 for an overview of path-goal theory; see also Wood & Bandura 1989.

567 McClellan 2014.

568 Russ 2008.

569 Røvik 2007, 2016.

570 Higgs & Rowland 2010.

571 Dailey & Browning 2014.

572 Kotter 1995a, 1996, 2008; Whelan-Berry & Somerville 2010.

573 Daft & Lengel 1986.

574 Ekman 2004.

575 Nonaka 1994.

576 This point is regarded as important not only to theoreticians like Nadler 1987; Burke 2002; Gardner 1995; but also to Nonaka 1994. See also Dailey & Browning 2014 about the repetition of narratives.

577 Amundsen & Kongsvik 2008.

578 Weick & Quinn 1999:380.

579 Pfeffer 1992; Pfeffer & Sutton 2006.

580 Schein 1985; many of Scheins' ideas are followed up by Bolman & Deal 1991; Collins & Porras 1994; Deal & Kennedy 1982, 1999; see also Weick 1995.
581 Grugulis & Wilkinson 2002.
582 Alvesson 1992; Grugulis & Wilkinson 2002.
583 Bass 1990a, 1999; Beyer 1999; Bryman 1992; Trice & Beyer 1986.
584 Antonakis et al. 2011; Bryman 1992.
585 Armenakis & Harris 2009; By 2007.
586 The figure in Meyer & Stensaker 2011:71, for example, can be interpreted in this way.
587 Yukl 2006, chapter 8; Miner 2005.
588 Bourgeois & Brodwin 1984.
589 Inspired by Hirschorn 2002; Cobb 1986.
590 This is also emphasized by researchers not easily associated with leadership style E; see, for instance, French & Bell 1995; Greiner & Schein 1988; Kotter 2008; Nadler 1987. Others see this as an integral part of any organization, and thus of organizational change; see Pfeffer 1981, 1992, Mintzberg 1983.
591 Cobb 1986.
592 Pfeffer 1992.
593 This is also French & Raven's (1959) main point.
594 See Nadler 1987 as an example.
595 Hernes 1975.
596 Pfeffer & Salancik 1978.
597 Meyer & Stensaker 2009.
598 Pfeffer 1992.
599 The following is taken from Nadler 1987:362–363.
600 Nadler 1987.
601 Meyer & Stensaker 2009.
602 Lehman et al. 2011.
603 Burke 2002:247.
604 March & Olsen 1976.
605 See Egeberg 1984.
606 Thornbury 1999.
607 Stensaker & Schei 2006.
608 Burke 2011:288.
609 Kotter 1995a.
610 This the fascinating argument set forward by Pascale et al. 2000.
611 Hirschorn 2002:104
612 Based on a classic piece of work by Warren 1968, as well as more recent contributions by Falbe & Yukl 1992.
613 Much is based on Kelman 1961 and Etzioni 1982; see also Valikangas & Okumura 1997.
614 Emans et al. 2003:38.
615 Yukl & Falbe 1990.
616 Mintzberg 1983.
617 Lawler 1986.

618 The following is based on writings about transformative leadership; see Bass & Avolio 1993; Miner 2005; Yukl 2006.

619 Bass 1985.

620 Miner 2005.

621 Brown et al. 2009.

622 Laudal et al. 2017.

623 Locke & Latham 2002.

624 Bass 1985; Burns 1978.

625 See Gjerde 2003 for a solid Norwegian introduction to the field.

626 The following rests heavily on Nonaka 1994; see also Nonaka et al. 1996; Nonaka et al. 2000; Sullivan & Nonaka 1986.

627 Senge 1990

628 Senge 1996

629 Johnson 1998.

630 Lowe et al. 1996:387.

631 Bass 1985.

632 Bass 1998, 1999; Lowe et al. 1996; van Knippenberg & Sitkin 2013.

633 The classic Norwegian books on organizational development (OD) (see Lyngdal 1992; Gustavsen 1990; Levin & Klev 2002) are grounded in such an approach.

634 Langley & Denis 2006; Meyer & Stensaker 2011; By et al. 2016.

635 See Lines et al. 2006; Coleman et al. 2011 for good examples from Norwegian firms.

636 Ford & Ford 2012.

637 See Greenwood & Hinings 1988, 1996; Burke & Litwin 1992; Peetigrew, Woodman & Cameron 2001.

638 Donaldson 1996; Pennings 1992.

639 By this I mean attempts to elaborate "laws" in the relationship between elements like age, size, structural complexity, and the like (see for example Hall 1972).

640 Galbraith 1977:28.

641 Porter 1980.

642 Quinn 1980; Weick & Quinn 1999.

643 Dunphy & Stace 1990; French & Bell 1995.

644 Cole & Scott 2000; Nonaka et al. 2000.

645 Mintzberg 1979; Pfeffer & Sutton 2006.

646 Langley & Denis 2006; Pfeffer & Sutton 2006; Stace & Dunphy 1991.

647 The following arguments are derived from Gersick 1991; Miller & Friesen 1994; Romanelli & Tushman 1994.

648 Gersick 1991:13–16.

649 The idea of punctuated equilibria in organization theory is elaborated by Gersick 1991; Anderson & Tushman 1990; Tushman & Anderson 1986.

650 Lawler & Worley 2005; Tushman & O'Reilley 1996.

651 Denis et al. 2001:834.

652 This is one of the most common critiques against the classic OD approach to organizational change; see Cobb 1986; French & Bell 1995; Levin & Klev 2002.

653 Leitko & Szczerbacki 1987:53.

654 Nadler 1987.
655 Cobb 1986.
656 Cohen, March & Olsen 1972.
657 Cobb 1986; French & Bell 1995; Boonstra & Gravenhorst 1998.
658 Jermier & Kerr 1997; Mintzberg 1983.
659 Jespersen 1999:162 (own translation).
660 Espedal 2009.
661 Hofstede 1983; Hofstede et al. 1990.
662 Clugston et al. 2000:9.
663 Gustavsen 1990.
664 This viewpoint is clearly inspired by Fiedler's (1967) concept of contingency theory.
665 Bourgeois & Brodwin 1984.
666 Dunphy & Stace 1988; Stace & Dunphy 1991.
667 Buono & Kerber 2010.
668 The concept is homemade, but inspired by Meyer & Stensaker 2011; Bourgeois & Brodwins "Change model" (1984).
669 Kotter 1995a, 1996.
670 Buono & Kerber 2010; Krause et al. 2007; also inspired by the decision-making model of Vroom & Yetton (1973).
671 Borum 1976; Hargrave & Van de Ven 2006; the model was also inspired by political decision models; see Jacobsen & Thorsvik 2013 for an overview.
672 See Ravn 2015 for Norwegian examples.
673 Stace & Dunphy 1991.
674 Herrero 2008.
675 Hardy et al. 2005; Lyngdal 1992; Vroom & Yetton's (1973) theory of decision models is also central in this argument.
676 Cummings & Worley 2001; Smolarczyk & Hauer 2014.
677 Such "schizophrenia" can also be detected in the writing of proponents of a soft approach; see Beer 1987.
678 Burrell & Morgan 1979.
679 Amundsen & Kongsvik 2008; Jacobsen 2010. For more classic examples, see Lyngdal 1992; Klev & Levin 2002.
680 Huy 2001.
681 NOU 2016:1.
682 Baron & Hannan 2002; Håkansson & Waluszewski 2002; Sydow et al. 2009.
683 Huy 2001.
684 Shapiro & Kirkman 1999.
685 Amundsen & Kongsvik 2008.
686 Jacobsen 2010; Meyer & Stensaker 2011.
687 Brunnsson 1989.
688 Boeker 1997; see also Huy 2001 (appendix B) for good examples.
689 Mintzberg 1973 was one of the first to discuss this; see also Pfeffer & Salancik 1978; Pfeffer 1992; Strand 2001.
690 Sydow et al. 2009; Greiner 1988; Mintzberg 2007; March 1991.

691 This is based on the 3rd edition, reprinted in 2001.

692 Op.cit.:83.

693 Op.cit.:121–122.

694 Mintzberg 1979.

695 Damanpour 1991; Sine et al. 2006.

696 Cohen & Levinthal 1990.

697 Teece 1997, 2009, 2018; Wang et al. 2015.

698 Senge 1991, see also Sun & Anderson 2008.

699 Lawler & Worley 2006:xv.

700 Quinn & Cameron 1988.

701 Teece et al. 1997.

702 From the Latin: ambi = both sides, dexteritas = ability.

703 Henderson & Clark 1990.

704 O'Reilly & Tushman 2013:324.

705 See Tushman et al. 2011 for a discussion of the leader team's role.

706 Andriopolous & Lewis 2009; Benner & Tushman 2003; O'Reilly & Tushman 2013; Raisch & Birkinshaw 2008; Raisch et al. 2009; Tushman et al. 2010.

707 O'Reilly & Tushman 2013.

708 Berends and Van Witteloostuijn 2001; cited in Arendt & Van Witteloostuijn 2004:1219.

709 Mintzberg 1996.

710 See Seidensticker 2006 for (a not always reliable) critique of the "hype of technological change"; see also Sorge & Van Witteloostuijn 2004.

711 Hagedorn-Rasmussen 2003.

712 McKendall 1993.

Index